William Stephens Blacket

Researches Into the Lost Histories of America

Or, the zodiac shown to be an old terrestrial map in which the Atlantic isle is

delineated; so that light can be thrown upon the obscure histories of the

earthworks and ruined cities of America

William Stephens Blacket

Researches Into the Lost Histories of America
Or, the zodiac shown to be an old terrestrial map in which the Atlantic isle is delineated; so that light can be thrown upon the obscure histories of the earthworks and ruined cities of America

ISBN/EAN: 9783337272197

Printed in Europe, USA, Canada, Australia, Japan

Cover: Foto ©ninafisch / pixelio.de

More available books at **www.hansebooks.com**

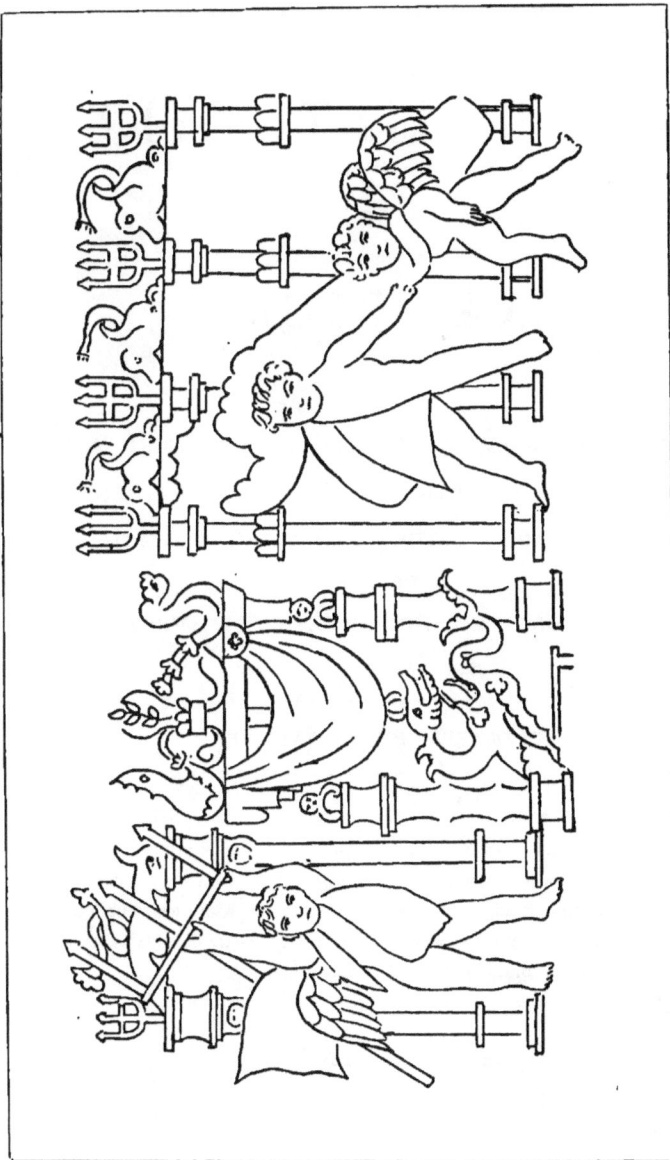

THE THRONE OF NEPTUNE OR POSEIDON

TO WHOM THE CENTRE OF THE ATLANTIC ISLE WAS CONSECRATED.

RESEARCHES INTO THE

LOST HISTORIES

OF

AMERICA;

OR

The Zodiac shown to be an Old Terrestrial Map
in which the Atlantic Isle is delineated;
so that Light can be Thrown upon the Obscure Histories
of the
Earthworks and Ruined Cities of America.

ILLUSTRATED BY 77 ENGRAVINGS.

"The Athenians had not wit enough to find out the true reason why
two natures were ascribed to Peteos; for every man knows that
he was called half a man and half a beast, and the true ground
was, because he was a member of two several commonwealths—a
Grecian and a Barbarian."—Diodorus Siculus.

BY W. S. BLACKET.

———◆———

LONDON : TRÜBNER & CO., LUDGATE HILL.
PHILADELPHIA : J. B. LIPPINCOTT & CO.
MDCCCLXXXIV.

THIS VOLUME

IS RESPECTFULLY DEDICATED

TO

THE INTERNATIONAL AMERICANISTS

WHO HAVE LATELY HELD

THEIR FIFTH BIENNIAL CONGRESS

AT COPENHAGEN,

AS CONTAINING MATERIALS FOR THE STUDY & DEVELOPMENT

OF THE

MYSTERIOUS HISTORIES OF PRE-COLUMBIAN AMERICA,—

IN THE ASSURANCE THAT

THEIR DISCOVERY WOULD RECTIFY THOSE OF

EUROPE AND THE WORLD.

CONTENTS.

PICTURES, MAPS, & DIAGRAMS.

CHAPTER I.

The American Question.

AMERICA is a great country. The banner of the Stars and Stripes waves over a land, which, for resources and extent, is second to none in the known world. Occupied in chief by a race famous in the annals of history as migrating into distant portions of the globe, and there laying the base of future nationalities and empires,—admired by all the great and small nations of the old continent, and envied by none,—it stands out, prominently, as one of the greatest and mightiest portions of the Earth's surface. Justly proud of its enormous advantages in natural features, and confident in the skill and enterprise of its population, America looks forward in the great future, near and distant, to histories that must materially affect the peace and happiness of the whole world.

Yet, this great country, in the literature of the world, is destitute of history. In the historical antiquities of the human race, it is a blank—an absolute blank. Its annals, in the books and universities of all European nations, are supposed to date from what is called the discovery of America, by Columbus. No obscure and insignificant island in the vast Ocean of Polynesia is more completely hidden in the remote annals of the vast past of the world's being, than the great double continent of America. In books on ancient history America has no chapter;—in the discussions of Archæologists concerning the ruined cities of the world, America is not mentioned. In any estimate of the mysterious movements recorded in the Bible concerning the great dispersion, America and its people have no place. Ancient America is a nonentity—an hiatus—a vast terra incognita, in the Geography of the Old World.

The only thing which acts as a sort of shadow of a shade, in history, touching this great question, relates to some obscure tradition, given by some old author, of a supposed Island of great extent, which sunk in the waters of the wide Atlantic.

B

But that obscure tradition has been allowed, like the Island itself, to sink. It has long since been wiped out of remembrance, as a ridiculous story too insignificant to notice. All sensible authors have treated the sunken island as real. Any allusion to it, as having con' ction with the vast continent of America, would expose a wr'   · contempt. Yet, that tradition is all that appears in t'   .amon and received literature of Europe, relating, in a..y way, to what is now called the New Hemisphere.

It is not difficult to account for the obliteration of Ancient America, from the annals of the Earth. The poet says, that "the noblest study of mankind is man." But, for some unaccountable reason, the study of human antiquities has been lost sight of. Antiquarianism has busied itself with tombs, ruins, and sculptures, and no money has been spared for the retention and display of stones, implements, and Gods. But somehow or other, ancient Ethnology and the movements of races of men in times of high antiquity have been neglected. There is no Society of learned men to foster research into the remote antiquities of the human race.

Even if there had been a strong desire to penetrate the darkness of high antiquity, the ancients have contrived to hand down their histories in a form so uncertain, as to throw men off their guard in the pursuit of such studies. The Geography of the old world, lying hid in what, curiously enough, is called Poetical Astronomy, has led the enquirer to the heavenly bodies, rather than to the surface of the Globe. The historical documents, which supply the materials for the investigation of the oldest antiquities, have come down from the Bards and Muses of the earliest times, dressed in a garb of mystery, such as to baffle the pursuit of every body, except the keen witted book-worm, who has perseverance enough to stick to his books till age and blindness supervene.

Yet it is exceedingly unreasonable to suppose, that the vast region of America could be destitute of histories earlier than Columbus. Is it likely, that one-third of the Globe should have been unknown to the inhabitants of the other two-thirds? On the score of probability, it must be concluded, that so great a country as North and South America, must have been a component part of the known world, at all periods of the residence of man upon the Earth. In the North, the continents are nearly united. In the South, the distance between the mouth of the Amazon and Africa, is not greater than the length of the Mediterranean Sea.

Besides that, when Strabo, a geographer of reliable character, is found stating that 6000 years before his time, there was an Arsenal at Cadiz and ships celebrated for voyages at sea : and when Plato, as will afterwards be seen, described great warlike eruptions from beyond the Pillars of Hercules, it becomes too plain for contradiction, that there must have been extensive intercourse between the two hemispheres in times of high antiquity.

It is equally unreasonable to suppose, that the earliest writers of Italy, Greece, and India, should have left no written records of the geography and history of so large a portion of the Globe as America. That land exhibits ocular evidences of the presence of former races in possession of building capacity, who have forsaken their homes. The ruined cities of Mexico and Central America, and the earthworks of the United States, show that some race or races, have left their homes and migrated into other lands. If so, they must have gone to the old continent. There is nowhere else to go to. The descendants of those races must have been in possession of the traditions of their forefathers. Those people were themselves addicted to writing, or they lived among others who were so; so that those traditions must still be extant, among the records of the people that wrote them. Every now and then, there appears a work written by some unknown author, who wants to prove, it may be, that the Trojan War never took place where it is generally supposed; or, that the travels of Ulysses must have been somewhere else than the Egean Sea, and so on. Such surprising works excite a laugh; but they serve to show that the minds of thoughtful students cannot be satisfied with the ordinary interpretation and allocation of Classic Geography. There is something wrong somewhere,—some mistake, that baffles the critical acumen of enquiring minds.

But the stickler for Orthodoxy in history, who adheres closely to received opinions, is himself often puzzled to account for a great many things, with which he is familiar. How Oceanus and Tethys, the parents of 3000 rivers, and of all the Gods besides, should be the stemparents of the Greek people—how the banner of Corinth should be a flying horse, that sprang from the blood of the Medusa,—how the first King of Italy should have been a Faune, dressed in all the toggery of a Goat-man, and so on. It is quite time that some one should try to explain the mystery that underlies such improbable circumstances, and discover the secret that would give to acknowledged history the element of veracity.

The American question has been long upon the tables of the learned, and numerous books of great value have been published, bearing upon different phases of the subject: as for instance Prescott's "Mexico" and "Peru": Aglio's "Mexican Antiquities," Stephen's "Travels," Brinton's "Myths of the Red Men," and others too numerous to specify. Most of these works relate to the histories of modern times, and to the ruins scattered through the length and breadth of the hemisphere. Perhaps the work of Brasseur de Bourbourg tends more than any other, to bring the mystery of the land into view, but even that valuable contribution to the American question, fails to throw the needed light upon the obscurity; its details, however, supply invaluable materials for the development of the true question at issue.

The subject has been recently revived, and that under Royal auspices. Fresh discoveries of ruins in Yucatan have attracted the attention of Americanists to the matter, and a conference has been held at Madrid, and adjourned for two years, to meet again at Copenhagen; while the German government has shown its interest in the question, by securing for itself some remains from the Province of Guatemala. In these fresh discoveries, Uxmal in Yucatan attracts to itself the most attention, as being the Pompeii of America.

But it is not in the power of ruins and stones to remove the great veil of mystery which shrouds the antique histories of America, even should these fresh discoveries and labours bring to light the reading of the Hieroglyphics that adorn the remains. They may serve to disclose the names of the builders and chiefs by whom they were erected, but it would be of exceedingly small use to find out that the Great Red Fox, or the flying dragon, or some person of unpronounceable name, was the grandee that laid the basis of Uxmal's grandeur. It is greatly to be hoped, that the present explorations will be pushed to their utmost limits, and that the land may be made to disclose more of those subterraneous cities, which not only America but the whole earth may reasonably be supposed to possess beneath its crust.

The true and only way, in which the origin and histories of the earthworks and ruins of America can be discovered, is to search into the writings of the ancient European and Asiatic authors. Those writings are in themselves mysterious; but their incomprehensibility arises from the circumstance that a very large part of them belong, not to the Old Continent, but to America. America is the underground world of the Ancients. There is no lack of materials for the development of the Geography and history of Antediluvian America; but they lie scattered in the fragmentary traditions and obscure cosmogonies of other lands. If ever the secrets of the great mounds and pyramidal erections are brought to light, it will be by that means. The lapse of ages and the lack of alphabetical writing in the vast past of the world's being, have disarranged and thrown into confusion the records of its career. In the disentanglement, classification, and correction of the known writings of the Classic ages, lies the only possible hope of reading off the Secrets of American Antiquities.

It is not to be denied, that the task proposed in this observation, is one of great difficulty, and its execution must be effected amidst conflicting opinions, and in all probability, under some laughter, if not ridicule. So effectually have the ancients shrouded their national histories by the veil of mystification, that it requires some courage to propound a natural interpretation of their funny stories. One has to get off his stilts, become a babe that he may be wise,—throw away the prejudices of scholastic education, and bend some close attention to the subject, in undertaking the task. But the game is worth the candle. The discovery of the esoteric meaning of ancient mysteries, is one of the noblest achievements of the human mind. To decipher an hieroglyphic, and to evolve from that decipherment the secrets of the Nile valley—to interpret a solitary cuneiform word, and to form upon that interpretation, a system that would read off the mysterious gravings of the colossal Men Bulls of Assyria, are feats of the intellect, which are worthy of the choicest minds.

But the mysteries of America are deeper mysteries than those of the Nile valley and the subterranean palaces of the Euphrates. One-third of the great histories of the world undiscovered! Where are they and what? This is the great historical problem to be solved in this work.

As a suitable frontispiece to the present work, the celebrated picture of the throne of Neptune or Poseidon has been selected. Its beauty and its adaptability to the subject recommend it to the reader's attention, as highly illustrative of the enquiry into which he is about to enter. The scene is highly significant in all its details. It is to be recollected that all ancient pictures speak. Before the discovery of letters, pictures had to do the duty of the modern press. But the present scene is more than usually instructive. It is vocal with meaning.

The God of navigation is supposed to occupy the throne. The emblems which the ancients have used to delineate the water God, abound. They form the enrichments of the palace. Dolphins and tridents decorate the throne and enrich its accompaniments. The Captain, or one who may be considered as invested with the functions of that modern officer, stands at the side of the throne, carrying a fine trident. The Sailors are Cupids, or more correctly the bird-men,—the Harpies of antiquity. They are employed in furling or unfurling the sails,— they bend under the weight. Beneath the throne is a splendid dragon, in a form truly graphic. The God himself is concealed. He is behind the veil.

But what is the meaning of all this imagery? The picture when interpreted, tells its own tale. Poseidon is the Ocean God, to whom the Atlantic Isle was assigned. The scene must relate to that subject, because the dragon belongs to that hemisphere. It is Neptune on his dragon-throne. The God is concealed, to intimate that the mysterious region over .which he reigned, is concealed. America is concealed, and its histories are behind the curtain. This beautiful picture teaches to the eye, what the present work is intended to teach to the understanding. The reader is invited to approach the throne,—to draw aside the veil of concealment, which hides the histories of the dragon land—to get a peep behind the curtain, and to see the Ocean God.

CHAPTER II.

AMERICA IS DISTINCTLY DELINEATED IN ONE OF THE OLDEST MAPS EXTANT.

The art of map construction, in any form worthy of the name, is quite modern. The Atlases of the present day, elongated at the Poles,—in a spherical form,—composed from actual measurement, and furnished with latitude and longitude, afford no idea, whatever, of the conceptions of the ancients. The maps which go by the name of Herodotus, Strabo, and others, convey the probable idea of the form of the Earth, in old systems of Geography. Such maps have no America. The maps used in Schools and called ancient, but constructed upon the modern scientific form, are all limited to the old continent. The earliest English map, attributed to the 10th century, is too confused for accurate discrimination: but it is equally free from America.

The Japanese have maps. They are constructed in the most simple and unscientific manner,—without spaces for oceans, and with rivers unnaturally large: but they are not so badly drawn, as to make the identification of countries impossible. These maps are remarkable, as exhibiting the coast line of the land, now known to exist, at the ant-arctic pole. In fact, they have that coast well defined, all across the Southern Ocean; as if the Japanese navigators had penetrated further than modern British sailors. These maps have America as largely and as well delineated, as the lands of Asia and Europe.

It is to India one has to look, for the earliest maps. The intelligent and keen witted sages of India are in possession of a very extensive and minute system of Geography, in their Puranas. Unfortunately, it is too mystical for use, and the nomenclature of countries differs so largely from ancient European geography, as to create for it a good deal of incredulity, which may or may not be unreasonable. But the Sages have maps, many of which have been published in the Asiatic Researches. One of these maps is of singular importance in any enquiry into the Geography of the ancient world. A copy of it is here given for examination.

OLD HINDOO MAP OF THE WORLD.

The form of the map proves the Hindoos to have had the most imperfect idea of the art of map construction; but the contents of it, equally show that they must have had a very extensive knowledge of the whole Globe. The antiquity of the map is proved by the nomenclature of the countries. The Hindoos are in possession, of great geographical knowledge, and their books are replete with ancient histories, in a mythic form, similar to those of Greece. By these books it is shown that the names of countries into which the old continent is divided, in the present map, are the sons of Agnidhra, who himself is the son of Adima and Iva. In this map, Asia and Europe are drawn in the unnatural form of an oval encircled by the Ocean.

The observant reader will not fail to notice that in this map, America is distinctly delineated. The ocean is made to surround the old continent. Although there may be inaccuracy in the form in which it is drawn, yet the fact is plain. The ocean, here represented, comprises the Atlantic in the West, and the Pacific in the East. Africa is here mentioned by name, and must be comprised in the oval; so that the Geography is not incorrect.

Beyond the ocean there is another land, which surrounds the ocean; of course, that is America. In a map formed upon the construction of a dish, which is the form in which the maps of Herodotus and others are drawn, the geography is perfectly correct. This encompassing land has a chasm in the west. The chasm does really exist. It is the Caribbean Sea and the gulf of Mexico, which divide the two great insular continents of North and South America, and which serve as an inlet of approach to both.

But the actual identity of this land with America is seen by the name which is given to it and the character said to inhabit it. It is Suvarna Bhumi or the land of Gold. In the geography of India, Suvarna is joined to Swetam dwipa. They are said to be two parts of one whole. This Swetam dwipa is a very important place in the Indian history and antiquities, as will afterwards appear. Now Vishnu is said to preside over Swetam dwipa, so that Swetam dwipa must be a part of America. In the Asiatic Researches, Swetam dwipa is always called the White Island in the west. Under these circumstances, it is plain, that Swetam dwipa and Suvarna are Hindoo names for North and South America.

c

Then, the reader will notice, that this land is called the land of darkness, and that it is full of waters, and the abode of the Great Spirit Vishnu. In this epithet, appears the exact name which the North American Indians invariably give to their God. In a later part of this work, it will be shown, that the blue and water God, Vishnu, is an impersonation of America. On the whole, the teaching of the map is too plain to be misunderstood. America is distinctly delineated in the oldest Hindoo map.

Let it not be judged, that the inaccurate form of the map deprives it of value, or spoils its teaching. All old maps are wrongly drawn, and the present will bear comparison with those of Europe. Perhaps it ought to be admitted that the Hindoo map is in advance of those of western lands. It will be noticed that the land now detected as America, is also termed Mountains of Localoca. The Orientals appear to have supposed, that the earth was surrounded by mountains which are impassable. On the old hypothesis of a flat world, it seems necessary to fancy it so; or the inhabitants would be exposed to accident at the remote extremities. Yet, as a matter of fact, those mountains do really exist. The Rocky Mountains in North America, and the Andes in the South, may have given rise to the supposition. That long line of mountains answers not badly to the Hindoo idea of Localoca. Let the traveller go west, and the mountains hem him in. Let him go east, and he finds himself stopped in the same manner.

Let not the map be rejected because it is not European. It is true that it belongs to a class of literature, not hitherto employed in the development of history: but it is not the less valuable on that account. It is a great pity that Oriental and Indian writings should have been so long unused, not to say neglected, in the literature of western lands. It is the absence of Asiatic writings that has to be credited with a large part of the intellectual darkness, which pervades both profane and sacred literature.

In the present work, the Hindoo mythology and other writings will be used, simultaneously with Greek and Latin works. The Hindoos are a branch of the Indo-European family. It will be found, on a comparison of myths and traditions, that the two branches of the family are in possession of the same histories and in the same names. So closely do they resemble each other, that it may be a fair hypothesis that the Sanscrit writers must, originally, have been Europeans who had migrated into the plains of India. If so, the traditions they carried with them must necessarily have been identical with those of Europe.

However that may be, it only requires a reasonable amount of study and research into the Sanscrit writings, to discover that they may be considered equal or even superior to those of Greece, in the elucidation of the mysteries of high antiquity. Especially is this the case in reference to the immediate subject of the present enquiry. There can be no elucidation of the mysteries that enshroud the hemisphere of America, without the aid of the Sanscrit literature. On this account, it will be used in the following pages, *pari passu* with that of Greece and Scandinavia.

CHAPTER III.

THE ZODIACS ARE TERRESTRIAL MAPS OF THE MYTHIC AGES, BY WHICH IT IS SEEN, THAT AMERICA FORMED A PART OF THE KNOWN WORLD, AT THAT TIME, AND THAT IT WAS SET IN THE STARS.

It will readily be admitted, that the map now described, affords but a very poor idea of America. Its features are far too imperfect, and its names far too few, for the elucidation of the great mystery that hangs over the land. One has to look about for something better than Hindoo Geography for the present enquiry.

And yet, a map must be found. if any successful attempt is to be made to solve the present problem. It is difficult to tell which is worse, geography without history, or history without geography. The first is a picture only, which conveys no instruction. The last is a story only, the facts of which cannot be located. What would a tourist do in any excursion without a map! However excellent his descriptive Guide might be, it would be misleading and useless without an accurate and complete map. In the present case, the great *terra incognita* of Ancient America must remain for ever, like the sealed roll of Scripture which no man could open,—an enigma, beyond the reach of the human understanding.

If any clever individual whose mind is full of Homer and the Poets and who is an enthusiastic student of the Classics, would sit down and construct a map from his own knowledge of mythic characters, it might be supposed that it would facilitate the study of antiquity: but that is a mistake. However clever the man might be and however learned, the map would amount to no more than a mere speculation. It might, or it might not, be right. If right, it would be suspected of error, and if wrong, it might be supposed correct. Speculation is not sufficient. Mythology, at best, is an inexact science, and an inexact science, illustrated by an uncertain map, would remind people of the text about "the blind leading the blind."

But the case would be very different, if a map could be discovered, which was constructed by the ancients themselves, from their own knowledge, with the real names of nations fairly written on it, and where each country occupies the position which it actually possessed, in relation to surrounding nations. Such a map, if it could be discovered, would be entitled to every consideration which the most scrupulous geographer might demand, and the most critical historian need, in the compilation of his work. It would, in fact, set at rest all questions, as to the localization of mythic characters, and serve as a key for the elucidation of all myths.

This imagined map is in existence. It lies upon everybody's table and forms a part of the furniture of every school. Like a great many other very common things, it is so easily seen, as to escape observation. It is the Zodiac,

The Zodiac, on the most searching examination, will be found to be a terrestrial map of the mythic ages, used in later times for the purposes of astronomy. It does not bear the name of map, but that makes no difference;—names do not alter things. Its construction is very unlike a modern School map; but that makes no difference—fashions vary. It is true that the countries are all thrown into Zoomorphic or Anthromorphic forms, but that makes no difference, as they have names upon them. It is a map, and the exact map wanted; and no other map would fulfil the conditions requisite to make it an indubitable guide in mythic studies.

It would ill become a modern map maker to vaunt his superior maps, and to laugh at the ancients for drawing countries as birds, beasts and fishes. Modern maps are singularly deficient in natural and characteristic features. Of course, sixpence more will buy one coloured, so that the countries look pretty in blue, red and green. To make geography ridiculous, maps are divided into two sorts, ancient and modern; as if the world never had more than two names to each country, one at the present day and one about the time of Julius Cæsar. Undoubtedly, modern maps are superior in point of accuracy; with latitude and longitude, in a spherical form, and with countries measured and surveyed: but, on the other hand, the Zodiacal map maker had a great advantage, by constructing his map in a pictorial form, in which the national heraldry of countries stands as the delineation of their localities, the Eagle for Italy, the Lyre for England, and the Bear for Russia.

The theory that the Zodiac was originally a terrestrial map, is open to contradiction, and the subject, therefore, requires some argumentation. The history of the Zodiac is unwritten or lost. Its origin is involved in darkness, and its progress to completion is hardly less obscure than its origin. Real history being silent about it, the matter must be determined by secondary and internal evidence. As Hesiod and Homer both refer to it, it must belong to the oldest mythic period. There is an excellent work by J. Landseer, entitled Sabean Researches, enriched by beautiful engravings. At page 52, the author expresses an opinion, that the Heavens were constellated before the time of Job, and that many of its asterisms were the same, then, as now.

In the absence of real evidence, it may be observed that it is exceedingly unlikely that the early astronomers should have constructed the Ptolemaic constellations for the allocation of Stars. Astronomy is an exact science, founded on nice calculations and great precision. It therefore passes belief, to suppose that they would have selected mythic figures for their purpose. What would be thought of a scientific Society, abhorring, as it must, the slightest deviation from nature, adopting for its heraldic crest a Sagitarius or a giant grasping a snake, or a bloody head? The telescope and the other scientific instruments would have suited the astronomers very well, but they are modern.

On the other hand, it is exceedingly reasonable and natural to suppose, that the early astronomers found, in existence, a pictorial map of the earth, planned and delineated according to the peculiar natural history and crest of each country, with real names attached, and that they adopted it, as a convenient basis of Sidereal allocation. However that may be, no one will deny that if they did mark out the heavens into its present constellations, they must have had very funny ideas of the sparkling groups, forming themselves into Lions, Bears, Fishes, and Giants. A man may stand in an observatory and stare at the Stars till his neck aches, before he can, by any stretch of fancy, construct out of them any real figure whatever, except a triangle.

It is a common expression, in myths, that a person "was set in the stars"; but this act is not once ascribed to an Astronomer. It is always attributed to a God. It belongs not to the period of science, but to the period of mythic history. Take Callisto, for instance: "Jupiter, apprehensive of her being hurt by the huntsmen, made her a constellation of heaven, under the name of a Bear." If this were astronomical, the name of the astronomer would be given and not Jupiter. It is Bootes that holds the hunting dogs in leash, that are referred to. From this, it is manifest, that the act of turning Callisto into a Bear is a piece of history. It belongs to things terrestrial, not celestial. It is part of a map. Now, what is said of Callisto, applies to all the constellations. They belong to the histories of the mythic ages; consequently they must be geographical in origin.

To understand this subject, one is obliged to throw away modern notions and to catch hold of the ridiculous conceptions of people, who thought that the earth was flat and in the shape of a dish, with another dish or shelf underneath, as an underground world, and a third dish above the others, of the same size and shape, for the heavens. This is seen in the Vishnu Purana, where it is said, that the heavens and the earth had the same diameter and circumference. Let it be supposed, that the terrestrial map were stretched out, and that the heavens above it were a vast mass of wax. Then let the earth, like a great seal, be lifted up and pressed against the wax, and it would produce an exact *fac simile* of itself. In this case, the countries of the earth would be impressed upon the heavens and the saying would be fulfilled "they are set in the Stars." Of course, this is all very silly: but to understand mythology, "one must become a fool to be wise." At any rate, a map of the earth, thus used, would serve the purposes of the astronomers and the allocation of the stars to perfection. In process of time, Zodiacs lose their original use, and maps are substituted for them: but, in the study of antiquity, they may still be treated as maps of the earliest ages.

It is fair to argue that these reasonings are insufficient, and that it requires some distinct proof from the writings of the ancients themselves, to establish the theory. This proof is at hand, both in a negative and a positive form. Landseer gives a quotation from Sextus Empericus, that shews that the Zodiac was employed in Chaldea, for astrological purposes. It is as follows, "The way in which the Chasdim, from the very beginning, observed the horoscope was this: A Chaldean, in the night time, sat in his lofty observatory, contemplating the stars. Another sat by the woman in travail. When the woman was delivered, he informed the Chaldean in the Observatory, who then observed the sign rising for the horoscope. In the day time he observed the ascendants and the sun's motions." This was for the purpose of giving the

child a name; that is to say, a Sidereal sygnet. The sygnet
became the child's heraldic crest. The Babylonian cylinders
exemplify this custom. Now, unless astronomy preceded
astrology, the astronomers could not have invented the Zodiac.
It must have been in existence for other purposes, before
they used it. This is the negative proof.

The positive proof is taken from Aratus, who was a Greek
poet of Cilicia, about the 124th Olympiad. It is important
to notice that Aratus was a Cilician, because Cilix was one
of the Phœnicians, who, according to Cæsius, were the first
who put the constellations into classes. Aratus wrote a work
on Astronomy, which Cicero, when young, translated into
Latin verse. Aratus says that the great effusion of water, in
the Celestial Sphere, was the Nile. Now, in what conceivable
sense could the constellation Eridan be the Nile, if it were
a parcelling out of a cluster of Stars? Aratus calls it a great
effusion of water: but what water is there in the Stars?
Such language is intelligible only, upon the principle, that
the Zodiacal sign was part of a terrestrial map. It was the
Egyptian river. The statement of Aratus concerning Eridan
must be taken to apply to all the other signs: because it
would be absolutely impossible, that one sign should be a
part of a terrestrial map, and the others, Celestial. Cetus
the whale, for instance has his paws upon Eridan. Cetus
therefore and all the others must be terrestrial.

In the Sixth Volume of the Asiatic Researches there is an
article on the Zodiac of Burmah, accompanied by a pictorial
representation of the asterisms of that country, with their
names. Unfortunately they are not in position, like the Ptolemaic and Coptic Zodiacs, and therefore they cannot be used
in this work; but in the article mentioned, the theory now
advocated is fully sustained. The constellations all represent
countries and even towns. No. 8 for instance is a duck and
stands for Shan or Siam. No. 10 is a horse, standing for
Europe. No. 23 is a Brahman called Kaleingareet, representing India. No. 51 is Tarouttara, the Burmese name for
China. This Burmese Zodiac may be fairly taken as indicative
of the original nature of Zodiacs, in general. Western nations
must, in course of time, have restricted their use to astro-

nomical purposes: but this Asiatic people, less changeful than Europeans, have retained their old form and geographical character.

It is now time to complete this argument, by shewing that the Zodiacal map is, in point of fact, a good delineation of the countries of the ancient world. The signs adapt themselves to the countries that lie beneath them, as a seal to the map before mentioned. This must be proved, or the argument fails. There ought to be an universal agreement between the constellations and the nations that lie beneath them. They ought to agree, in name, nature and place. If the sign is a human being, he ought to be the proper person to educe the histories of the country. If it is an animal, it ought to be some animal peculiar to the country, making allowance for artistic mistakes, and the animal ought to have the name of the nation he represents. If the sign is a fish, the sign ought to overhang some sea or to lie along some sea coast. In all cases, the position of the sign must correspond with the relative position of surrounding countries.

This triple proof is a very strong test of accuracy. It is rather too strong. The Zodiac is a very rough and complicated picture, and ancient maps exhibit very erroneous conceptions of the construction of the earth. A good deal of latitude is required, in the adaptation of the Zodiac to a map. It will be found that there are some constellations that, at first sight, do not appear to tally at all with the countries beneath them, as for instance, Cepheus, the moor king situated in the arctic circle. But it will be found that those incongruous matches always relate to some terra incognita, or some country about which there is very scanty or doubtful knowledge. In point of truth, the uses of the present treatise apply prominently to such cases, inasmuch as it will always be found, that those discordant matches cover some blunder in history, which the Zodiac alone can correct.

There are two sorts of proof, a primâ facie proof and a proof in detail. An extended proof in this chapter is unnecessary. The present volume is cast into a form, by which all the countries of America are thrown under the light of

D

mythology. It is a comprehensive attempt to pry into the antiquities of the land, by giving considerate attention to the mysterious writings of the ancients. Each sign will be taken separately, so that the adaptation of the constellation to the locality will be examined, and in most cases, it will form the basis of the study.

The primâ facie proof is as follows: Aratus says, that the great efflux of water in the celestial sphere is the Nile. This removes all doubt as to the exact position in which the Zodiac is to be placed, in making this experiment. Let the Eridan be placed upon the Nile. It then acts as a pivot, by which the rest of the constellations find their own localization. It will be seen, that this throws Bootes, the old man of the gods, on the great bend of the Hoang Ho. This tallies exactly, because, in ancient maps, say for instance, the Harrow School Atlas, the Hoang Ho is called Bautes fluvium, or river. It will then be noticed, that the Great Bear is thrown into the Russian Empire. The two Leos cover the two Loos, Pe-loo and Nan-loo. Orion is thrown over Iran. Perseus falls into Persia. Andromeda fixes itself over the country of the Selucidœ, whose banner was the Andromeda. Taurus covers Assyria (Oriental Tsour) the land of the man bull.

Let the Zodiac then be shifted to Europe and Africa. Here the Lyre hangs over Britain, its emblem, with the Welsh name Lloegr. Taurus minor covers Spain, the ancient Terra-connensis and the land of Bulls. The Eagle adjusts itself to Rome, and Greece gets two constellations, the dolphin over Delphi, and Pegasus over the bay of Pegasus. Here it may be noticed, that these two figures form the banner of Corinth. Capricorn takes its place at the entrance of the Mediterranean, for Africa. Aquarius lies along the North of Africa. Grus falls into the land of the Negro, and Piscis Australis, the southern fish, lies on the coast of Guinea. Africa has no names in the Zodiac. In this, it agrees with the the description of Africa, by Diod: Siculus, who identifies African nations, by what they ate, not by what they were called.

It must be confessed, that it is not very easy to make

the experiment just described, especially if it be done for the first time: but if any observant and critical reader will take the trouble to test the fairness and accuracy with which the adjustment has now been made, he is almost sure to demur to it as incorrect. He will readily admit that Asia adapts itself to the Zodiac with surprising exactness. As to Europe and Africa, he will most likely perceive a great deal that is convincing, but which requires study and thought. But his attention is sure to be arrested by what looks like a glaring defect. A large slice of the map from North to South is left out altogether. The signs have no localization at all. It is quite plain that Bootes and Virgo define the eastern limits of Asia. It is just as plain that the Lyre and Taurus Minor define the western limits of Europe. What then is to be done with the large number of constellations, between the west of Europe and the east of Asia? There is Hercules and Ophiuchus, the Serpent and the Crown, Sagitarius and Cerberus, Scorpio and Libra, the Wolf and the Centaur, with others. What can they belong to? There can be but one answer to that question. They represent America. America must have been known to the Ancients. The countries belonging to it, named and described, with equal distinctness to those of the old continent, are delineated in their maps. It must have been a constituent part of their known world. America is "Set in the Stars."

Fortunately for the present enquiry, the Ptolemaic Zodiac is not the only one that the Egyptians have handed down to posterity, drawn in the form of a terrestrial map. There is another. Kircher, in his great work, called Œdipus Egyptiochus, has published a Coptic Zodiac. This is not the Dendera Zodiac. The signs of that Zodiac are not in position. Kircher wrote in Rome, but he had the good sense to employ a Coptic amanuensis, who gave him the Zodiac. This Coptic Zodiac is a most valuable exponent of the most ancient geography, inasmuch as it answers to the Ptolemaic Zodiac and serves to elucidate it. It must have been Egyptian, because the human figures are drawn in the Egyptian style, and some of them have Coptic names. Some of the signs are the same as the Ptolemaic, so that their position is certain.

The great utility it has, when treated as a map, appears
in the Latin descriptions which are added to the Signs. In
this Zodiac, America is pourtrayed, just as it is in the
Ptolemaic, and called for the most part Regio Typhonis and
Demonium Statio. This valuable Zodiac is used throughout
the present work, and admitted as an exponent of Geographical
nomenclature at the earliest possible period of history.

The Hindoo Sages have a Zodiac, but it is not in position.
It is also limited to the constellations that mark the Sun's
course. This Zodiac shews much less antiquity than the
Ptolemaic, and has evident marks of the Indo European
relationship. Many of the signs are the same as those of
the Grœco-Egyptian, but with different names. While this
Zodiac cannot be used for the purposes of allocation, it is
useful in the present enquiry, because its nomenclature defines
some uncertain signs in the Greek list.

An interesting question arises out of the preceding argument. Who were the people that first constructed Zodiacs?
Three quotations from ancient authors are called for to answer
this question. Landseer gives a passage from Lucianus, a
celebrated writer in the reign of Trajan, who says, that
"Astronomy came originally from Ethiopia." He tells a story,
where Philosophy declares to Jupiter, that "from the Brachmans she repaired straight to Ethiopia and thence to Egypt,
whose Poets and Prophets she instructed and then betook
herself to Babylon, to instruct the Chaldeans." Diodorus
Siculus says, that it was Atlas Egyptius or Phœnix, king of
Mauritania and brother of Prometheus, who first constructed
the sphere of heaven." The learned Bryant has a quotation
from the Paschale Chronicle. "At the time when the tower
of Babel (Purgopoiias) was erected—a certain person made
his appearance in the world, who was (Indus) an Indian
and said to have been of the race of Arphaxad. He was
famed for wisdom and astronomy. His name was Andoubarios.
He first delineated schemes of the heavens and instructed
the Indi in that science."

According to received opinions, relating to ancient Ethnology,
these three quotations are irreconcileable. Josephus makes

the Arphaxadites to be the Chaldeans: so that in these extracts, there are no less than five races, and they spreading from Mauritania to India, to whom is ascribed Astronomy and the Zodiacs ;—Brachmans of India, Ethiopians of Africa, Chaldeans of Babylonia, Phœnicians of Mauritania, and Atlantides. But, in the light of the present work, where mythology is allowed to correct misconceptions of antiquity, the quotations agree. These five races are all Atlantides. They acquire their distinctive names, in the countries to which they migrate.

But who are the Atlantides? They are the children of Atlas, king of the Atlantic Isle. The Atlantides are also called Oceanides, that is to say, they are people living in the Atlantic Ocean. It is true, that Diod: Siculus makes Atlas Egyptius, king of Mauritania, but Mauritania is not an Island, and it can, by no forced construction, be called the Atlantic Isle, and Mauritania offers no evidences of having been the abode of astronomers. To find Atlas, as an astronomer, one must look beyond the Atlantic Ocean. In other words, one must look to America for the Atlantides who "knew all the soundings of the deep and had obelisks, on which were drawn the system of heaven and earth," that is to say, Zodiacal maps, descriptive at once both of heaven and earth.

Now, at the present day, it requires very little research to find Atlas, the astronomer, in America. The Spaniards, in their discovery of America, found Atlas himself, still engaged, at the lapse of thousands of years, on his astronomical studies. In Mexico, it is the Aztlans that were astronomers. Here is Atlas himself in his old name. He is King of the Atlantic Isle. That the Aztlans were astronomers is manifest, from the accounts given of them by the Spaniards, and that they are the same as the Atlas Egyptius, of whom Diod: Sic: speaks, is plain, from the resemblance observable between the Aztlan astronomy and that of Egypt. The following extracts from Prescott's "Conquest of Mexico" will prove that fact. "The Epoch they reckoned from, was 1091, the time of the reform of their calendar, a little after their migration from Aztlan. Their calculation of the year was more exact than ours. The Cycle of 52 years is encompassed by a Serpent-Symbol of an age, both by Persians and Egyptians." At

p. 106, he says, "their astrological year was divided into months of 13 days. It is a curious fact, that the number of lunar months of 13 days, with the intercalation, should correspond precisely with the number of years in the great Sothic period of the Egyptians, viz., 1491, a period in which the seasons and festivals come round to the same place in the year again."

This reasoning is convincing, yet it is most likely that the reader will require confirmation of it, especially in regard to the point that the Aztlans were astronomers before the Egyptians, and that they were their teachers. It is too early in this treatise to introduce mythic pedigrees. Let the question be confined, at present, to a pictorial argument. In the great work of Lord Kingsborough on Mexican Antiquities, there is the picture of Atlas himself, of which the present is a copy. A Greek Atlas is given with it for comparison.

MEXICAN ATLAS.

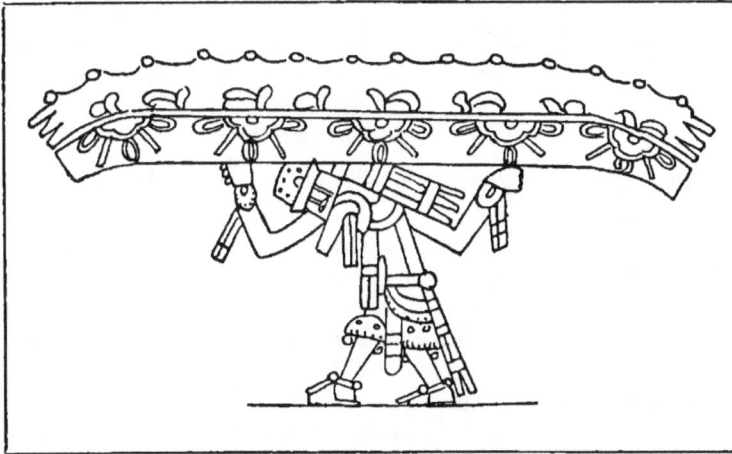

In the study of comparative mythological pictures, which are, in point of fact, a substitute for letterpress, when the identification is satisfactory, the grand point to be decided for the purpose of deducing historical conclusions, is to ask the question, which is the type and which the antitype:

GREEK ATLAS.

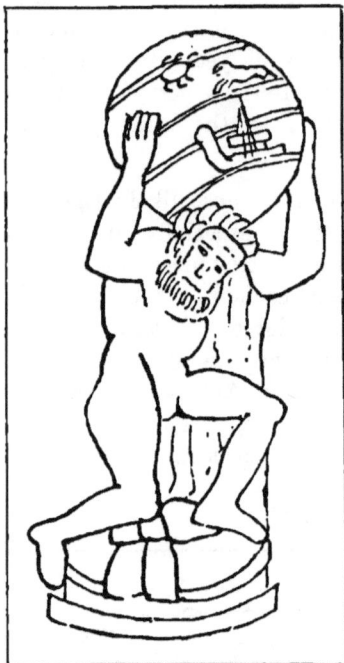

which is the original and which is the copy. The rule that must decide the question, is that the simple is father to the complex. The natural picture is sure to be the oldest. In this case it is manifest, that the Mexican is the oldest, because the Greek figure exhibits a much later and more advanced stage of astronomical knowledge. The Mexican Atlas carries the simple vault of heaven. The Greek Atlas shews that the spherical form of the earth has been discovered. The Zodiacal signs have been placed in position: it is altogether later: so that the conclusion is inevitable, that the American Atlas is parent of the Greek.

This pictorial argument is strongly confirmed by two other pictures found in the Mexican Antiquities. It has been already shown, that among the constellations that adjust themselves to America, are the Serpent and the Serpentarius. The Serpent overhangs Mexico itself, and the Serpentarius or Ophiuchus delineates the Southern States of North America, as will be seen presently. These two pictures are now exhibited on the next page. The Serpent is found in the Dresden Collection, and the lower figure—that of the Ophiuchus, is in Laud's collection.

It is, certainly, very curious to find two Ptolemaic constellations among the Mexican antiquities. How could they have got there? If the ancients were unacquainted with Mexico, they could not have been copied from the Grœco-Egyptian Zodiac. But a little careful study of the lower figure shews,

MEXICAN SERPENT AND SERPENTARIUS.

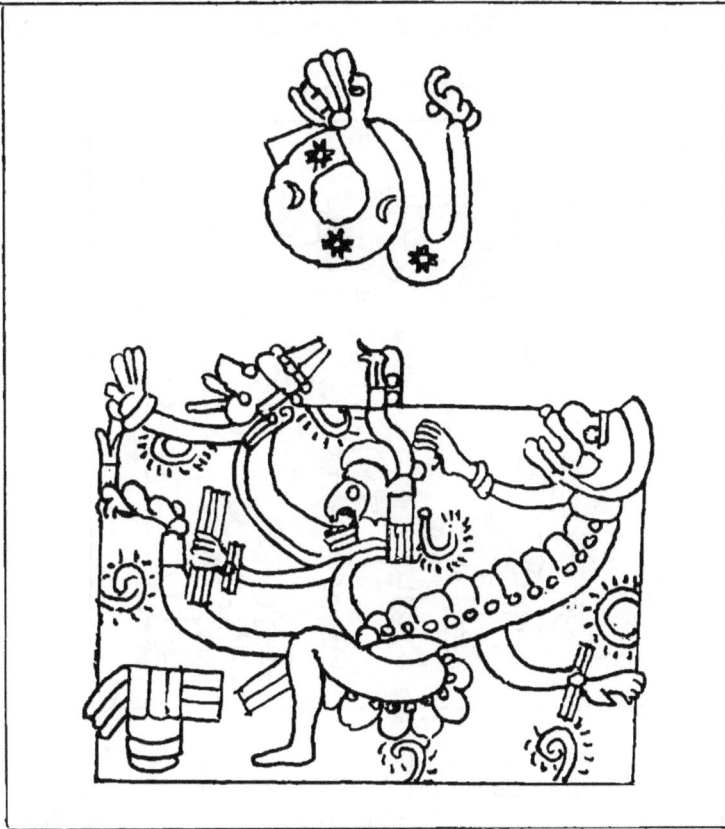

that the Ptolemaic Ophiuchus and the Mexican figure are
one and the same. Not only do the human figures both hold
the Snake or Snakes, but the posture of both is the same.
In point of execution, the Mexican figure is much the most
natural, and consequently it is entitled to be considered the
earliest design. These two figures certainly lead to the inference, that the Atlantides, in crossing the Atlantic Ocean
and settling in Europe and Egypt, must have brought with
them that part of the Ptolemaic and Coptic Zodiacs which
belongs to America, even if they were not themselves, the
original inventors of the Zodiac.

But this is not all. In this magnificent collection, among the larger specimens, there is a picture, which, on examination, proves to be the identical sphere or Zodiac with which

MEXICAN DIAGRAM.

Diodorus Siculus credits Atlas. It is here given. It is necessary to notice that this is not the Cycle, which is commonly published in works on Mexico, and which seems to have been used for fixing the occurrence of historical events.

On comparison of this Zodiac with the Egyptian, it will be seen, that it has the same claims for prior antiquity, as were found in the figures of Atlas. The Ptolemaic Zodiac is vastly more advanced in scientific structure. This is a simple attempt to delineate the heavens, and is quite rude. A man in the Sun occupies the centre. The constellations, such as are seen in the Mexican Cycle, surround the sun. At each corner stands a man surmounted with wings, to represent the four winds of heaven. The whole is surmounted by a Colossal head, an object found so often in Mexican pictures, as to

E

suggest the idea, that it must have been an Heraldic device.
A fancy border completes the Zodiac.

In a quotation already given from Lucianus, the Brachmans
are credited with early philosophy. This suggests an examination of Hindoo pictures, to find if the Hindoo Sages have
any pictorial evidence of an acquaintance with Aztlan as-

HINDOO PRAN.

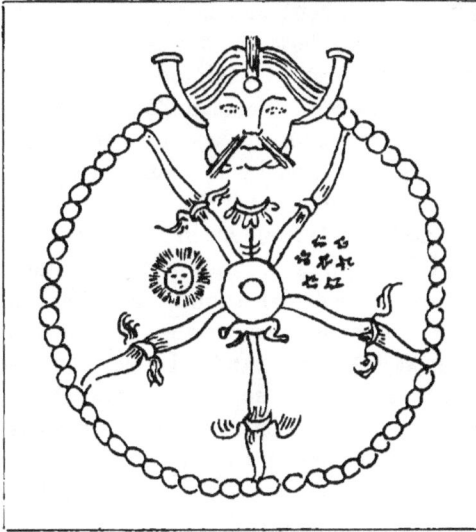

tronomy. This results in the discovery of a picture, which
must actually have been copied from the identical Mexican
Zodiac just presented. It is found in a valuable work by
Niklas Mueller, entitled "Glauben, Wissen und Kunst, der
Alten Hindus." The author says that it was taken from a
Vignette, on a copy of a Veda. There is another slightly
different. It is called Pran.

It scarcely requires an expert to compare the two pictures:
a little thought is sufficient. The Colossal head surmounts
the diagram, as in the Mexican Zodiac: but the Indian Artist
has thrown it into a different position, and has mistaken
the ribbons of the Mexican head dress for an unmeaning
horn. This circumstance proves that the Mexican picture is

the original and the Hindoo a copy, on the rule that decides such questions, namely, that the natural is father of the unnatural. In the same way, the border is drawn in a slovenly manner and the square has got rounded. The four men in the Mexican Zodiac, representing the four winds, are reproduced by winged scrolls. The sun is a little out of the centre, in this specimen, but it is not so in another. The moon and stars stand for the asterisms.

One starts in astonishment at the sight of these two pictures, and asks the question, how it is possible that the ancient Hindoos could have been acquainted with Mexico, and be in possession of an ancient Mexican Zodiac. It seems beyond belief. But the question is no sooner put, than it gets an answer perfectly satisfactory, by a quotation from the Vishnu Purana, where it is said, that "the ancient sage Garga, one of the oldest writers on Astronomy in India, having propitiated Sesha, acquired from him a knowledge of Astronomy and Astrology." Now, it will be shown, in other parts of this work, that the Sesha here mentioned is the seven headed Serpent of Central America and Mexico, the very country of the Aztlans themselves: so that this ancient sage must actually have been to America to learn Astronomy, and have brought with him, on return to India, the identical Mexican Zodiac just given, of which the metaphysical Pran is an imperfect copy.

These facts and reasonings are now held to be sufficient to justify the use of the two Zodiacs—the Ptolemaic as a Græco-Egyptian, and the Coptic as a native Egyptian delineation of the world. To test this hypothesis to the full, the principle should, certainly, be applied to what is called the Old Continent; but it is held, that the reference already made to it, is enough to prove that the principle is just. Yet it is not to be supposed that the study of the old continent would disprove the principle; for it has been subjected in the most careful way, to the same process of reasoning as will be used in the present work. America is not the only terra incognita of the world. There are many other extensive lands, in the other quarters of the world, equally mysterious and unknown.

Upon a comprehensive and searching investigation of the subject, it has been found, that the adaptation of the Zodiacs to the countries of Europe, Asia, and Africa, is complete. There is hardly a solitary pictorial sign which does not serve to educe histories more or less obscure. Should the public take an interest in the matter, that work can be produced. In the meantime, the reader is invited to study the maps in relation to the Oceanic hemisphere. It is of no use to enter upon an enquiry into the obscurities of the Old Continent, until those of America are examined. So intimately are the antiquities of the two hemispheres linked together, and so largely have the American races mingled with those of what are called the older countries, that until the great blunder has been corrected, which shuts out America from a participation in the world's ancient affairs, no useful progress can be made, in the rectification of those of the other quarters of the Globe.

This enquiry into the nature and origin of the Zodiac has many important bearings upon the objects of the present volume, in their relation to the discovery of the lost histories of America.

The vast collection of pictures which form the contents of Lord Kingsborough's great work on the Mexican Antiquities, constitutes the best part of the native materials for the compilation of the history of the hemisphere. It cannot be supposed, for a moment, that the Mexican pictures appertain solely to that province. Their subject matter makes it manifest that they comprise the pictorial history of all America. Witness the well-known scene which has been published in many works, and which depicts the travels and migrations of the Aztlan race.

These pictures have never hitherto been utilized for the purposes of history; but the series of pictures, just studied, presents a lively idea of the service they are calculated to afford in the unravelling of the mysterious traditions concerning the land, in pre-historic times. It may be advantageous to collate the inferences deducible from these pictures.

If the common Greek figure of Atlas is a copy of a Mexican picture, the mythological traditions of the Titan race, of which race Atlas is the most distinguished member, must belong to

America and not to the old continent. These traditions form a very large part of the Classical Lexicon. If the constellations of Egypt and Greece have any sort of identity with those of America, there must have been intercourse between the two hemispheres across the Atlantic Ocean. If the Hindoos were in possession of a Mexican Zodiac, and if they sent a sage to that land to study Astronomy, there must have been intercourse between India and Mexico, thousands of years before the present time.

But the chief inference arising from these pictures relates to the Zodiac. If the Zodiac were an ancient map of the world, and if the signs which delineate the American lands are pourtrayed—placed in geographical position and named,— there is a sound basis laid for the allocation of a very large part of the mythological personages that are mentioned in the literature of the old world. In that case, it only requires research, diligence and judgment, to recover and arrange the lost histories of America.

Undoubtedly such teachings require ample and conclusive confirmation. That is the subject of the next chapter.

CHAPTER IV.

EVIDENCE THAT AMERICA WAS KNOWN TO THE ANCIENTS IN ALL PARTS OF THE WORLD.

From what has been advanced in the two last chapters, it is evident, that the ancients must, at some time or other, have been acquainted with America. If it is drawn in their old maps, it must have formed a part of their known world. If Egypt and India received astronomical knowledge from Central America, there must have been maritime intercourse between the two hemispheres. But the theory is a breach of received opinions, and it requires more evidence to establish it. There ought to be found in the writings of acknowledged authors, at least in the earliest stages of real history, some mention of the continent and its affairs.

The first extract will be taken from the writings of Plato, in his work, entitled Critias. Plato was a celebrated Athenian philosopher, who died about 384 years before the Christian era. Only the opening passages of this work will be given here. More of it will be transcribed in the Chapter on Central America. "First of all, let us recollect, that it is about 9000 years, since war was proclaimed between those dwelling outside the Pillars of Hercules and all those within them. Of the latter party, then, this city was the leader. Of the former, the kings of the Atlantic Island. To the Gods was once locally allotted, the whole Earth:—different Gods having received, by lot, different regions, proceeded to cultivate them. But Hephæstus and Athena, having a common nature, from having the same father, arranged the order of government."

This calls for comment. Plato puts this great warlike eruption, at 9000 years before his time. Yet he speaks of it, as a common well-known fact. There are certainly no writings transmitted by the Greeks, that can be referred to that age. They must either have been lost, or he must draw his knowledge from the mythic traditions, which form quite a large volume in the Greek literature. That certainly justifies the use of those traditions, in the construction of the present work. It stamps them with an historical value, which is not ordinarily assigned to them. Again, Plato refers to this warlike attack on Europe as great. It could not have been the arrival of a few canoes or small vessels. There must have been big ships and national troops, for Plato speaks of the Kings of the Atlantic Isle. If so, not only must America have been known to the ancients, but its power must have been felt. Not only so: for the language employed by Plato, leads to the unavoidable conclusion, that the early history of Europe must have been affected by this hostile attack. On the other hand, the histories of the Atlantic Island, must have undergone some great change by the loss of people and kings.

The next quotation is from the same author, and is found in Timœus. There is a conversation with an Egyptian priest. The priest says to the Greek, "Our sacred writings relate, what a prodigious force your city once overcame, when a mighty warlike power, rushing from the Atlantic Sea, spread itself with hostile fury, over all Europe and Asia. That sea was, indeed, then navigable, and had an Island fronting that mouth, which you, in your tongue, call the Pillars of Hercules, and this Island was larger than Libya and Asia put together, and there was a passage hence for travellers of that day to the rest of the Islands, as well as from those Islands, to the whole opposite continent, that surrounds that, the real sea. In this Atlantic Island, then, was formed a powerful league of kings, who subdued the entire Island, together with many others and parts also, of the continent; besides which they subjected to their rule the inland parts of Libya, as far as Egypt and Europe also as far as Tyrrhenia. Subsequently, through violent earthquakes and deluges which brought destruction in a single day and night, the whole of your warlike race was merged under the earth, and the Atlantic Island itself was plunged beneath the sea and entirely disappeared; whence even now, that sea is neither navigable, nor to be traced out, being blocked up by the great depth of mud, which the subsiding Island produced."

This quotation proves that the Egyptians knew America as the Atlantic Isle. Plato says that the Atlantic Sea was navigable 9000 years before his time : so that there must have been navigation across the Atlantic Ocean, in the mythic ages. The features of the passage are exceedingly clear. The Island was larger than Libya and Asia put together. That may be put roughly at 8000 miles across. It was reached by travellers, who first landed on Islands, before they arrived at the main land. That is plain enough. They, like Columbus reached the West India Islands first. The cause of the destruction mentioned was Earthquakes. This points to the Volcanic regions of Central America and the Andes, where such disasters have occurred in modern times, with melancholy frequency. The invasion of Africa and Europe, referred to, constitutes a very large portion of the mythology of all nations, and in later chapters, it will be worked out, in detail, throwing light on all the obscurities of history.   This is the comment.   Now, a little argumentation is necessary.

Learned men, generally, have adopted the theory, that this Atlantic Isle must be some Island between the two hemispheres that has actually sunk; but the theory will not admit of the slightest examination.   In the first place, it is absolutely contrary to the nature of things and therefore impossible. What is an Island?   An Island has no independent existence. It is simply an outlying part of a continent, so depressed at its sides, that water flows round it.   England, for instance, is part of the continent of Europe, with a shallow channel. But England is just as much a part of America, as it is of France.   The waters of the Atlantic are comparatively speaking, a small quantity of water, lying in a depression of the vast crust of the Earth.   To talk, therefore, of an island sinking, is to talk of an island sinking, not into water, but into the crust of the Earth, that is to say, into itself, which is absurd. But in the second place, if an island could sink at all, this Atlantic Isle could not possibly sink in the Atlantic Ocean. Learned men, who believe in the Sunken Island, could never have measured distances.   They must have jumped to con-clusions without thought.   Let the Atlantic Ocean be computed at 4000 miles across.   The quotation makes the Island some 8000.   How, therefore, in the name of footrules and yard-sticks, could an Island 8000 miles wide exist at all, in an Ocean only 4000,—to say nothing of sinking!   The theory may be dispatched as a joke, or as an illustration of the trick of putting a shilling into a sixpenny piece.   Yet upon this extraordinary blunder, the histories of the human race are written!   While the histories of America are veiled, or supposed to have been lost, those of Africa, Europe, and Asia have been overloaded with what does not belong to them.

The next quotation is a fragment by Marcellus.   It is pub-lished in Cory's fragments.   "That such and so great an Island, formerly existed, is recorded by some of the historians who have treated of the concerns of the outward sea.   For they say that, in their times, there were seven islands situated in that sea, which were sacred to Persephone, and three others, of an immense magnitude, one of which was consecrated to Pluto, another to Ammon, and that which was situated between them, to Poseidon. The size of this last was no less than 1000 stadia. The inhabitants of this island preserved a tradition, handed down from their ancestors concerning the existence of the Atlantic Island, of a prodigious magnitude, which had really existed in those seas, and which, during a long period of time, governed all the Islands in the Atlantic Ocean. Such is the relation of Marcellus in his Ethiopian History."

This fragment is of singular value, in the present argument. The writer refers to historians generally, who had written on western Oceanic matters; so that in the geography of those times, the Atlantic Island was well recognised. No attempt will here be made to identify the Island or Islands with America. Of course there is imperfection in the description of the Island, but not more than has existed concerning many parts of the earth in modern times. The value of the present fragment consists in the light thrown upon the subject, by the names mentioned. The names are not unknown to European literature: so that a clue is acquired for further research. But, in fact, it will be found, as this work proceeds, that the names specified are exactly the same as will be found in the following pages.

The next quotation, in proof that America was known to the ancients, is the well-known verse in Homer, where the poet says—

"The utmost bounds of Earth far off I see,
" Where Tethys and Ocean boast to be,
"The Parents of the Gods."

That the Macedonians had intercourse with South America is evident from a passage in the preface of Brasseur de Bourbourg's work, entitled "Histoire des Nations Mexiques:"

"At a village of Dolores, near Montevideo, in Brazil, a planter discovered a stone with Greek characters. Beneath the stone was a cave with two old swords, a cask, and a vase. There was on it the following inscription " Alexander, son of Philip, king of Macedonia, 63 Olym."

F

The next evidence is taken from Kœmpfer's great work on Japan, Vol. ii. p. 13.

THE HISTORY OF PEIROUN.

"Maurigasima was an Island in the Pacific Ocean, near Formosa, or Tyroraan, famous for porcelain vessels. The inhabitants were rich and luxurious, and had a contempt for religion. The king was named Peiroun. He himself was religious. He had a dream of a coming flood. It was to happen, when the two faces of the Idols in the temple turned red. These two idols were named In‐fo‐ni‐woo and Awun— gods of generation and destruction. They were naked with a loin cloth. Some one, seemingly to play the king a trick, one night painted the faces of the idols. The king, hearing of it, lost no time in going on board a ship. Then the Island sunk, and all was swallowed up. The king got safe to China. At the present time, particularly in the southern provinces, they row about in boats, as if to flee away, crying out—Peiroun. Over the spot to this day they dive for the porcelain vessels, which, when found, are disfigured by shells. They have short narrow necks."

This tradition is the Asiatic counterpart of that which the Egyptian priest narrated to the Greek. The Japanese have preserved a tradition of a sunken Island in the Pacific Ocean, not unlike that of the European nations, concerning the Atlantic Isle. There must have been a deteriorated navigation, in times comparatively modern, on both sides of the old continent. But the Japanese have kept alive a remembrance of the Island, supposed to have sunk, by a service of ceremonies, to this day. It need not be said, that no evidence of ancient events is so strong, as festivals and ceremonies, to preserve their remembrance.

The next proof is in Homer's Odyssey, and is supplied by the travels of Ulysses. The following quotations will comprise a succinct epitome of those celebrated movements. "O Muse, sing to me of the man full of resources, who wandered very much, after he had destroyed the sacred city of Troy, and saw the cities of many men and learned their manners. Many griefs, also, in his mind did he suffer on the sea, although seeking to preserve his own life and the return of his companions; but not even thus, although anxious, did he extricate his companions: for they perished by their own infatuation, fools! who devoured the oxen of the sun, who journeys on high; but he deprived them of their return. O Goddess, daughter of Jove, relate to us, also, some of these things. Now all the others, as many as had escaped from utter destruction, were at home, having escaped both the war and the sea. But him alone, anxious for a return home and for his wife, the venerable nymph Calypso, a divine one of the Goddesses, detained in her father's grot, desiring him to be her husband." In the 11th Book, Ulysses relates his voyage, "But when we were come down in the ship and the sea, we first of all, drew the ship into the divine sea, and we placed a mast and sails in the black ship, and taking the sheep we put them on board, and we ourselves, also embarked, grieving, shedding the warm tear. And fair haired Circe, an awful goddess, possessing human speech, sent behind our dark blue prowed ship a moist wind, that filled the sails, an excellent companion. And we sat down making use of each of the instruments of the ship, and the wind and the pilot directed it. And the sails of it, passing over the sea, were stretched out the whole day and the sun set, and all the ways were overshadowed, and it reached the boundaries of the deep flowing ocean, where are the people and city of the Cimmerians, covered with shadow and vapour, nor does the shining sun behold them with his beams."

Then Tiresias speaks and has the following remark, "I know that going hence from the house of Pluto, thou wilt move thy well wrought ship at the Island of Æœa." On reaching his destination, he says, that "the women came, for the illustrious Proserpine excited them, as many as were the wives and daughters of chiefs." Then he says, "There then I saw Tyro first, born of a noble father, who said that she was the offspring of the blameless Salmaneus." "After her, I beheld noble Antiope, the daughter of Asopus." "After her, I beheld Alcmene, the wife of Amphitryon, who, mingled in the arms of great Jove, brought forth bold lion hearted Hercules, and I beheld the mother of Œdipus, and I saw the very beautiful

Chloris, whom Neleus once married, on account of her beauty, when he had given her countless dowries, the youngest daughter of Amphion, son of Jasus,—and she bore to him noble children, Nestor and Chromius and proud Periclymenus, and besides these she brought forth strong Pero, a marvel to mortals, whom all the neighbouring inhabitants wooed; nor did Neleus at all offer to any one, who could not drive away from Phylace, the crumpled horned oxen of mighty Iphicles. And I beheld Leda, the wife of Tyndareus, who brought forth two noble minded sons Castor and Pollux. After her, I beheld Iphimedia, wife of Alœus, who said that she had been united to Neptune and bare two sons: but they were short lived god-like Otus and far-famed Ephialtes, whom the fruitful earth nourished the tallest and far the most beautiful, at least after illustrious Orion; for at 9 years old, they were also 9 cubits in width, but in height, they were 9 fathoms; who then threatened the immortals, that they would set up a strife of impetuous war, in Olympus. They attempted to place Ossa upon Olympus, and upon Ossa leafy Pelion, that heaven might be accessible. And I beheld Phædra and fair Ariadne, the daughter of wise Minos. And I beheld Mæra and Clymene and hateful Eriphyle."

This requires some comment. It is transcribed rather fully, because of its singular interest in itself. The author being Homer, it may be accepted as veracious. When read in the light of common sense and divested of imaginary divinity, it is a simple story of a warrior, who after the Trojan war, went to sea. But where did he go to? In the present volume, this question has to be answered by the localization of the dramatis personæ. Ulysses first visits Circe. Circe has her location in Italy. She was a daughter of a King of Colchis, who was expelled from the country and carried to the coast of Italy.

Ulysses remains with Circe for the space of a year, and then at the advice of Circe, he descends to what is called Æœa. He then takes ship and sails, with his companions, to what is then designated "the land of darkness." Where the land of darkness was, may be seen from an examination of the old Hindoo map, which has been introduced in the Second Chapter, on account of its geography of high antiquity. It is America. Not only do the Hindoos call America the land of darkness, but the classic writers do so likewise. The Odyssey opens with an account of the arrival of Ulysses in that land. He is found in company with "the venerable Nymph" Calypso. But who is she? She is a Nymph, that is to say, she is an inhabitant of the Atlantic Isle. In the myth of Calypso, she is called "an Oceanide, or one of the daughters of Atlas," already seen to have been located in Central America. Ulysses is detained in "her hollow grot," and after "revolving years, he returns to Ithaca."

Ulysses then gives an account of the people he saw, during his residence in his Oceanic domicile. When the names are subjected to the process of localization, as far as ancient literature affects them, they are all found to be American. This work has not yet sufficiently advanced, to identify the names; but Homer seems to have availed himself of "the licence of antiquity" as Josephus calls it, or of poetry, his own vocation; for the list comprises a very fair and comprehensive enumeration of the mythic or historical personages, whom a critical enquiry must put in America.

Had it not been for the strange hallucination which appears to have pervaded the minds of men, in relation to the old traditionary stories of the Bards and Muses of history, the story of Ulysses would read as nothing more nor less than a good poetical account of a temporary residence of a Greek warrior, in the land of America. Under these circumstances, the narrative is a strong evidence, that the Ancients were acquainted with America.

The following passage from Ahmed de Tous, a Persian Author, in the 12th century, will shew, that the Chinese had communication with the American continent. "The Narsik and Mensik are Gog and Magog. They are Turks. Another people are the Baris and Maris. They ravage the world. When the sea of China is agitated, it casts the Gog and Magog one by one upon the banks. There they multiply in the forests, having a human figure but feet of stags and skins of sheep, devouring all they see. They are of the race of Japhet. Another Chinese people, the Sandjli, are of the race of Gog. They live on the borders of China. They have short feet and come from the bottom of the sea. They come up at night in boats."

The following wild Irish story is fairly entitled to a place in this category. It is taken from the transactions of the Ossianic Society, Vol. I., Battle of the Gabhra. "In a Fenian Poem, St. Patrick asks Oisin, how he outlived his Fenian friends, 300 years. Oisin replied—They were cut off at the battle of Gabhra. He was afterwards hunting at Lake Lene (Killarney). A golden haired lady appeared. She said, she was Niamh-cinn-oirs, daughter of Cailac, king of Tir-n-og, who came to marry Oisin, who was to take her to Tir-na-r-og, and he should never die. Oisin took her over a boundless ocean to a great city of a giant, who had previously carried away a daughter of the king to Tir-ra-m-bea, another Paradise of the Pagan Irish. Oisin killed the giant and having reached Tir-na-r-og, married her. He remained there 300 years. After that, he revisited his friends, but the raths and duns of the Fenians were all demolished, and they were all dead and gone. On reaching Stearn, his foot touched the ground, and he became withered and old."

The following extract from Herbelot's valuable dictionary of Oriental matters, will shew that the Oriental nations were acquainted with America under the name of Mount Caf. " Caf, a mountain, that Mahommedans, ignorant of Geography, as the Alcoranists and people attached to fables, due to the false prophet, believe to go round all the globe of the earth and water, and to bound the hemisphere on all sides. On this supposition, they say, that the sun at its rising, appears upon the summit of this mountain, and that it sets behind the other, which is opposite to it: so that you often find, in their ancient books, such as the Caherman Nameh and others, to express the rising of the sun, this sort of speech. " As soon as this star appears on the mount Caf, the world was lighted." So to understand the whole extent of the earth and water, they say, "from Caf to Caf," that is to say—from one extremity to the other. At the same time, they make mention in their ancient books of a country which they call " the dry island," which is a continent separated from ours, a word borrowed from Jabaschah of the Hebrews, which the

Vulgate has interpreted Arida, *i.e.* dry, to signify the continent
of the earth. They say that this island is situated beyond
Mount Caf, in which it appears, that this ancient tradition
of the Orientals, is taken from the Isle Atlantic of Plato,
which is no other thing than the continent of America. The
same Orientals call it, " Agiash al Makh loucat," *i.e.* the marvel
of nature, and Jeni Dunia, which signifies in Turkish, the
new world. The Tarikh Tabari in the Persian language, reports
in the first part of it, following the same fabulous traditions,
that " the Almighty God, after having created the Earth, surrounded it by a girdle of mountains, that the Arabs call Caf.
It is in this mountain that the Divs and the Giants have
been confined, after having been defeated and subjugated by
the first heroes or the posterity of Adam, and where the Peri
and the Fees make their ordinary abode."

It is not difficult to see how America became lost to the
Ancients. Isolated in its position, and with immense oceans
on each side, it must necessarily have been dependent wholly
on navigation, to keep it known to the nations of the old
continent. On the supposition of a lost navigation, America
itself is lost. Either with a navigation deteriorated, or with
ships of a smaller tonnage and sailors of less nautical courage,
it would be cut off from the rest of the world. With timid
navigators, it was easier to conclude that the land had sunk,
than to push forward till it was reached.

CHAPTER V.

In the Greek Mythic Traditionary Histories, America
appears as Oceanus: and it is peopled by Gods, Giants,
Nereids, Furies, Gorgons, Faunes, and Demons.

Plato puts the irruption of warlike races from the Atlantic
Isle at 9000 years before his time. Then, where are the
histories of that long period? Are they lost? No: they
are comprised in the mythic stories of Greece, India, and

Scandinavia. Those stories are the only histories of the world, as sung and recited by the Bards and Muses of the ancients They have come down to modern times somewhat altered and overlaid by the mistaken conceptions of the learned men of old, and they have become painfully confused by additions made to them by learned men in modern times, who have taken no pains to arrange chronologically, the incidents comprised in them.

Still they are histories, and they can, by study and research, be classified and reduced to order, in a sufficient degree, as to contribute to the elucidation, expansion and correction of history. It is true, that they have never been used in that way. They are, in truth, of no use without localization. But with the assistance of a map, that desirable end can be gained. Now that the Ptolemaic and Coptic Zodiacs have been shown to be pictorial maps, named and in position, there is no reason at all why they should not be utilized in the present enquiry into the mysterious and concealed histories of ancient America.

Under these circumstances, it is desirable to lay down a few rules for the use of these traditionary tales. The first rule is one of great importance. They should not be made use of at all, unless they are distinct, and unless they have a good claim to confidence, in regard to pedigrees and geography. Another rule is, that the localization of a mythic personage should be decided, not by reasoning, nor by the apparent suitability of the movement, but by the map. Every kind of evidence is admissible, and literature may be ransacked for knowledge; but the decision must be by map, even if it seem wrong. Again, the legends must be taken with all faults. One must make the best he can of them. As when a Jury is required to give an united verdict upon complicated and dubious testimony, the Jurymen do the best they can; so in the interpretation of myths, one must discover their meaning and localization by the exercise of sharp witted judgment. Again, when a mythic personage is not in either of the pictorial maps, his proper location may be found by combination. His relationships and symbolism may serve the same purpose.

In the classic literature, America can be detected in the person of Oceanus, the father of the Oceanides, an important race of people who are discoverable in all parts of the old continent. Diodorus Siculus even puts them in India.

There is some difference between the Greek and the Latin cosmogonies, in relation to Oceanus. The Greek list makes him to be one of the Titans. The Latin list makes him to be a brother of Saturn, Hyperion and Titan. This difference is quite immaterial, when it is seen, that the characters mentioned, are not individual men; but that they embody what may be called ancient Ethnology and Geography. It is certainly very curious to find the great Gods of antiquity to be impersonations of countries and stemfathers of races; but it cannot be helped. It is a part of the system of concealment, by which the muses of history have handed down their knowledge.

Oceanus is not in the maps, so that he must be localized by combination. Homer makes the localization of Oceanus quite plain, when he puts Tethys and Ocean "far off," at the bounds of the earth. The Hindoo map and the Oriental description of Mount Caf shew what the ancients mean by "the bounds of the earth." It is the land which surrounds the great Ocean, which flows round the old continent. It is America. It may be objected, that the expression "far off at the bounds of the earth" must mean the extremity of Western Europe: but what claim has Gaul or Britain to be the parent of 3000 rivers? It may be said, that it is the Ocean that is the parent of the rivers. But, in that case, how can Oceanus have a wife and 3000 nymphs for children? No: Oceanus is an impersonation of America. But let his myth be read. "Oceanus was a powerful deity of the Sea, son of Cælus and Terra. He married Tethys, by whom he had the most principal rivers, such as the Alpheus, Peneus, Strymon, &c., with a number of daughters, who are called from him Oceanides. According to Homer, Oceanus was the father of all the Gods, and on that account he received frequent visits from the rest of the deities. He is generally represented as an old man with a long beard and sitting upon the waves of the sea. He often holds a pike in his hand, while ships

G

under sail appear at a distance, or a sea monster stands near him. Oceanus presided over every part of the sea, and even the rivers were subjected to his power." Add to this the myth of his wife. "Tethys, the greatest of the Sea deities, was wife of Oceanus and daughter of Uranus and Terra. She was mother of the chiefest rivers of the universe, such as the Nile, the Alpheus, the Mœander, Simois, Peneus, Evenus, Scamander, &c., and about 3000 daughters called Oceanides. Tethys is confounded by some mythologists with her grand-daughter Thetis, the wife of Peleus and the mother of Achilles."

A few comments on these myths are needed. One sees here, how the Greeks have forgotten the nature of their own myths, and to what silly mistakes their misconceptions have led them. Oceanus and Tethys are the parents of the greatest rivers in the universe; yet, Alpheus and Peneus, their own little streams, are made to represent them. Again, when Homer makes Oceanus the father of all the Gods, that expression must be limited to the Oceanic hemisphere. A careful collation and classification of myths reveal the fact, that the great ancient deities of antiquity belong to the vast empires of Asia, not to America. The Oceanic Gods are but reproductions of the Colossi.

This allocation of Oceanus as the America of the old world, is one of the grandest conceptions discoverable in the highly poetical and figurative writings of the Muses. The Ocean of the terrestrial globe is the vast extent of water, which stretches from Great Britain to Japan. It occupies a very large part of the world. Oceanus, as the great sea deity, reclines on his watery couch, right in its very centre. He is the father of the greatest rivers of the earth, such as the Mississippi, the Ohio, the Missouri, the Amazon, and the Orinoco. He is the father of 3000 nymphs, who, in their own spacious prairies and woods, have given rise to races, which have peopled their own great land, and by migrations into other parts of the habitable globe, have become the mothers of mighty nations. But he is not a solitary God, sitting in his own domain, Lord of the mighty Ocean. He receives frequent visits from the rest of the deities. Then, to crown the magnificent description of the watery king, he is the father of all the Gods—

source of divinities to Europe, Asia, and Africa. Such is the poetical imagery and Bardic conception of ancient America! The following is the pedigree of Oceanus—

OURANUS AND GÆA
||
OCEANUS AND TETHYS
||
INACHUS, PROTEUS, CLYMENE, CLYTIA, CALLIRHOE,
NEREUS AND DORIS.

To this must be added the names of some of the 3000 Oceanides or Sea nymphs, mentioned in the tradition. Apollodorus gives the following: Asia, Styx, Electra, Donis, Eurynome, Amphitrite, and Metis. Hesiod, 944 years before Christ, mentions 41: Pitho, Admete, Prymno, Ianthe, Rhodia, Hippo, Callirhoe, Urania, Clymene, Idyia, Pasithoe, Clythia, Zeuco, Galuxaure, Plexaure, Perseis, Pluto, Thoe, Polydora, Melobosis, Dione, Cerceis, Xanthe, Acasta, Janiva, Telestho, Europa, Menestho, Petrea, Eudora, Calypso, Tyche, Ocyroe, Crisia, Amphiro, with those mentioned by Apollodorus except Amphitrite.

Oceanus, in this pedigree, has a wife who must also have been his sister. This character comes under the first rule just given for the allocation of mythic characters. There is a great temptation to consider her as representative of South America; but it is better to avoid dubious identifications.

The children of this marriage are very numerous. The names of all of them might be given; but in all probability, the reader would be inclined to "take them as read." Yet, really, one looks at them with a thoughtful if not a philosophical mind. If the present theory be correct, the long list of mysterious names, must represent the geography and ethnology of prehistoric America. One despairs of any attempt to fix the location of all these Oceanides. A great many of them are utterly beyond the reach of research. Yet, some of them arrest attention and create some astonishment. Here is Styx, Electra the wife of Atlas, Eurynome God of the under world, Pluto the husband of Proserpine and Europa, who gives name to Europe. One thing is certain, that the names call for study.

One of the sons of Oceanus and Tethys here enumerated, is Inachus. His legend is as follows: "Inachus, a son of Oceanus and Tethys, who founded the kingdom of Argos, about 1980 years before the Christian Era. He was succeeded by his son Phoroneus, and gave his name to a river of Argos, of which he became the tutelar deity. He reigned 60 years."

This requires the legend of Phoroneus. "The God of a river of Peloponnesus, of the same name. He was son of the river Inachus, by Melissa, and he was the second king of Argos. He married a nymph called Cerdo, or Laodice, by whom he had Apis, from whom Argolis was called Apia, and Niobe, the first woman of whom Jupiter became enamoured. Phoroneus taught his subjects the utility of laws and advantages of a social life and of friendly intercourse, whence the inhabitants of Argolis are often called Phoronæi. He received divine honours after death."

It is certainly very remarkable to find these two characters in America! Their myths have to be scanned with a little thought. At first sight, it looks as if they explode the present mode of tracing history. But, upon second thoughts, that criticism disappears. These two personages, when looked at carefully, change into rivers and gods. It is true, that they give name to two races in Greece, the Inachi and the Phoronæi; but that fact is suggestive of the idea, that they must have been strangers, who, on arrival and settlement on a certain river, become river Gods. If so, that is not a bad illustration of the myth of Oceanus, when it is said, that "he was the father of all the Gods." The myths are clearly suggestive of a very high antiquity, and taken as they stand, they lead to the conclusion, that there must have been a very early intercourse between America and the Mediterranean nations.

Another son of Oceanus is Proteus. He is a slippery sort of personage, that changes a little too often, for accurate localization. He is not beyond research; but he is better studied, in connection with Cetus, the whale, a figure that belongs to Africa and Egypt. He swims across the Atlantic. Let him pass.

Clymene comes next. "A daughter of Oceanus and Tethys, who married Japetus, by whom she had Atlas, Prometheus,

Menoetius, and Epimetheus." This is a short legend, but of
the highest possible importance to the present enquiry. She
heads the Titan race, and in future pages of this work, her
husband and her children will be found to embody some of
the most important histories of Mexico and Central America.

Clythia is uncertain.

Nereus and Doris come next. They separately are children
of Oceanus. "Nereus was generally represented as an old
man, with a long flowing beard and hair of an azure colour.
The chief place of his residence was in the Œgean Sea,
where he was surrounded by his daughters, who often danced
in choruses round him. He had the gift of prophecy and
informed those that consulted him, with the different fates
that attended them, &c." Nereus and Doris are the parents
of the Nereids, the mermaids of antiquity, of whom 50 are
mentioned. It is not necessary to transcribe the names.

As the names of the Nereids are to a great extent the same
as those of the Oceanides, it must be inferred that there is
little difference between Nereus and Oceanus, as impersonations
of the Oceanic hemisphere. If there is any difference, that
of the father seems to be descriptive of geography and that
of Nereus of personality, according to the fine verse of Hesiod:

"The Sea with Earth embracing, Nereus rose,
"Eldest of all his race; pure from deceit,
"And true with filial veneration named,
"Ancient of years: for mild and blameless he,
"Remembering still the right: still merciful
"As just in counsels."

In a future chapter of this work, the Nereids will be met
with again, as wives of the Dragon or Serpent. It is that
circumstance, which brings out to view the real character
and position of Nereus, in relation to the present enquiry.
The Serpent gives portraiture to Mexico: so that Nereus
must be located on the west coast of North America, in the
lands where are found the great temples and pyramids that
indicate the former residence of a race devoted to religion, or,
what stands for it, in the minds of semi-civilized people.

Another member of this extraordinary family is Callirhoe.
Her legend is short, but significant. "Callirhoe, daughter of

Oceanus and Tethys, mother of Echidna, of Orthos and Cerberus, by Chrysaor."

This calls for the myth of Echidna. "A celebrated monster sprung from the union of Chrysaor with Callirhoe, the daughter of Oceanus. She is represented as a beautiful woman, in the upper parts of the body, but as a Serpent, below the waist. She was mother of Typhon, Orthos, Cerberus the Hydra, &c, According to Herodotus, Hercules had three children by her, Agathyrsus, Gelonus, and Scytha."

It is most likely, that the reader who has had patience enough, to read through the description now given of this family, has been smiling at the simplicity of a writer, who could suppose that these personages have any thing to do with the great secret histories of pre-historic America. They look like the natural biography of certain individuals, who lived in the Archipelago surrounding the shores of Greece. But the moment the myth of Echidna is introduced, the spell is broken and the truth starts up. So completely have the Hierophantic writers of the old world succeeded in casting the veil of concealment over the histories and ethnology of the vast past, that it takes an extraordinary amount of penetration and self-reliance, to detect the real facts which underlie such writings.

There is a beautiful description of Echidna in Hesiod :

"Another monster Ceto bore, anon,
"In the deep-hollowed cavern of a rock,
"Stupendous, nor in shape resembling aught
"Of human, nor of heavenly: the divine
"Echidna, the untameable of soul,
"Above, a Nymph, with beauty-blooming cheeks,
"And eyes of jetty lustre : but below,
"A speckled Serpent, horrible and huge
"Bloody-devouring, monstrous, hid in caves
"Of sacred earth. There, in the uttermost depth,
"Her cavern is, within a vaulted rock,
"Alike from mortals and immortals deep
"Remote : the gods have there her place assigned,
"In mansions known to fame."

The wonderful monster thus so graphically described, appears to be the creation of the Greek poets and mythologists, as a sort of general embodiment of the motherhood of the half caste races of pre-historic, or it may be said, antediluvian America; for such it really is. Not that they had any clear idea of what they described, and the mysterious histories comprised in the person of Echidna. The true facts must have been lost, in the lapse of ages and the misconceptions inevitable to a system of allegorical traditions.

Echidna is the sea monster of antiquity. It is this sea monster, on which Oceanus himself reposes. In the picture of the God, which is given in the commencement of the next chapter, it will be seen that the sea monster is present, in the scene. The existence of this sea monster seems to have pervaded the minds of men, as a sort of frightful apparition, afar off, upon the uncertain ocean. Even down to the present day, the sea serpent is an object of wonder to the seafaring world, and many a tale of the sea has been woven out of its supposed appearance to the astonished sailors. It is one of those traditions, which, arising out of the uncertain histories of a past world, cannot be forgotten.

Echidna, in the present myth, has the widest possible motherhood. She is the mother of Typhon. It will be found, as the work proceeds, that Typhon, in the Coptic Zodiac, is a general character, used to delineate the whole of America, North and South. The Cerberus will be met with in its proper place, at the Eastern and Southern entrance to North America. The Hydra is one of the numerous names which are employed to characterise the Serpent of the Ptolemaic Zodiac, overhanging the land of Mexico. The marriage of Hercules with Echidna, to which reference will be made in the chapter on the mound cities of North America, puts Echidna in that region. Thus, Echidna stands for a generic motherhood of races which for untold ages, must have occupied the fair lands of the Oceanic hemisphere.

From the writings of classic authors, it appears, that the ideas entertained of the people beyond the pillars of Hercules and in the transmarine regions of the Atlantic Isle, were most extraordinary. Their imagination seems to have dressed them in all sorts of outlandish and supernatural forms. It may be well to enumerate them before entering upon the specific his-

tories, which will bring them out to view in the several
locations assigned to them.

First, there are the Gods. This has already been brought out,
by the legend of Oceanus, who is the father of all the Gods.
Judging of the word God, by the light of Asiatic mythology, the
race or races that have the name, ought to have been Japanese,
for Japan is the land of Gods and Celestial Spirits. In all
probability the term has been used for the people of Asia
generally, who have mingled their blood and fortune with the
aborigines of the land. In the course of the present work, it
will be brought out to view, that these Gods have, in the
course of their residence in the mound cities of the red men,
given rise to a new order of Gods, which has linked itself on
to European life.

In the imagination of the ancients, America must also have
been peopled by Giants. This is not only the case in the
classics, but it seems to have been the notion entertained by
the Scandinavians. "The Gigantes were the sons of Cælus and
Terra." According to Hesiod, they sprang from the blood of the
wound which Cælus received from his son Saturn. Hyginus
calls them sons of Tartarus and Terra. They are represented
as men of uncommon stature, with strength proportioned to
their gigantic size. Some of them, as Cottus, Briareus, and
Gyges, had each 50 heads and 100 arms, and serpents instead
of legs. They were of a terrible aspect: their hair hung loose
about their shoulders, and their beard was suffered to grow
unmolested."

But Oceánus and his race are by the mythologists treated
as Giants. "Titanes, a name given to the sons of Cælus and
Terra. They were 45 in number, according to the Egyptians.
Apollodorus mentions 13, Hyginus 6, and Hesiod 20. The
most known of the Titans are Saturn, Hyperion, Oceanus,
Japetus, &c. They were all of a gigantic stature and with
proportionable strength."

Among these extraordinary characters, Typhœus or Typhon
is reckoned. "He was a famous giant, son of Tartarus and
Terra, who had 100 heads like those of a serpent or a dragon.
Flames of devouring fire were darted from his mouth and from
his eyes, and he uttered horrid yells like the different shrieks

of different animals. He was no sooner born, than to avenge the death of his brothers, the giants, he made war against heaven, and so frightened were the gods, that they fled away and assumed different shapes."

Another strange and wonderful notion which the ancients appear to have entertained concerning the inhabitants of pre-historic America, is contained in the story of the Gorgons. It is worth transcription. "The Gorgons were three celebrated sisters, daughters of Phorcys and Ceto. Their names are Stheno, Euryale, and Medusa. They were all immortal, except Medusa. According to the mythologists, their hairs were intertwined with serpents, their hands were brass, their body was covered with impenetrable scales, and their teeth were as long as the tusks of a wild boar, and they turned to stone all those on whom they fixed their eyes. Medusa, alone, had serpents in her hair, according to Ovid, and this proceeded from the resentment of Minerva, in whose temple Medusa had gratified the passions of Neptune, who was enamoured of her, on account of the beauty of her locks, which the Goddess changed into serpents.—The residence of the Gorgons was beyond the Ocean in the west."

The last sentence in this tradition proves that the Gorgons were Americans. They must have been so if they resided beyond the Ocean in the west. They are children of Phorcys and Ceto, and grandchildren of Pontus, who coalesces with Oceanus. The Medusa is easily located by her serpentine attributes. She must be put in the Serpent land,—that is to say,—Mexico and the surrounding region. Euryale is a daughter of Minos, who, in later chapters, will be found in Peru; so that she must stand for a settlement on the west shores of South America. Stheno will be located, ultimately, as representative of the Earth-works, scattered over the woods and prairies of North America.

It may be objected that, while Hesiod places the Gorgons beyond the Ocean in the West, Œschylus puts them in Eastern Scythia, and Ovid in the Eastern parts of Libya; but that is not inconsistent with the present localization. The Gorgons are the forefathers of the savage races, known as Gog and Magog in the old continent, in the historic

H

period of the world. They were found, where these writers place them, both in Eastern Scythia and in western Africa. It will be remembered, that a Persian author has recorded that Gog and Magog came across the sea of China, so that they came into Eastern Scythia. On the other hand, the African branch of the Gorgon race is a part of that invasion from the Atlantic Isle spoken of by the Egyptian priest.

Another class of wondrous creatures, whom the Classic Authors have put in the Oceanic hemisphere, is that of the Nereids, referred to in an earlier part of the present chapter, as the children of Nereus and Doris. They have been located in Mexico, or thereabouts; but it is not to be supposed, that all the fifty mermaids harboured in that spot. One of them will be found in the Lake of Titicaca, when the story reaches that part of America. These curious Ladies have served, in all ages, for nursery tales and fancy stories. Perhaps the sea monster himself has not excited more astonishment in the minds of the youthful members of society. They must be put among the wonderful inhabitants of the lost and sunken Island.

Then there are the Harpies, the Stygian birds of school books. They also are among the inhabitants of antediluvian America. In some mythological lexicons, the Harpies are the children of Atlas. In India, Atri, who coalesces with Atlas, is their father. They will be met with again in a later chapter. Perhaps there are no characters among the wondrous creations, mentioned in old books and delineated in the monuments of the dark ages, that have played a rôle so important in the histories of the world as the men birds. Some of them have been already presented to the notice of the reader in the frontispiece of this volume, and they will reappear. These Harpies are especially American, inasmuch as, in the splendid pictures found in Aglio, the bird man occupies a special place. He not only is found in many separate instances in a highly graphic form, but he serves for decoration to all the palaces of the Mexican Kings.

The next race which can be detected as belonging to America, in the mythic period, is that of the Faunes. The

Faunes locate themselves by their name as Pawnees. This well-known tribe of red men, seems to have retained its name, to the present day, or at least, till the discovery of America, when it was spread over the region west of the Mississippi. The following is the legend of the Faunes, "Fauni, certain deities of the country represented as having the legs, feet, and ears of goats, and the rest of the body human. They were called Satyrs by the Greeks. The peasants offered them a lamb or kid with great solemnity." "The Satyrs were demi-gods of the country, whose origin was unknown."

This makes it necessary to introduce Pan. In his tradition, he is called the God of Shepherds and huntsmen. "Pan was a monster in appearance. He had two small horns on his head. His complexion was ruddy. His nose was flat, and his legs, thighs, tail and feet were those of a goat. Pan, according to some, is the same as Faunus, and he is the chief of all the Satyrs."

As Pan is a very important God, and will be met with again, more than once, in the following pages, it is necessary to study the character a little. "The Orphic cosmogony confounds him with the universe, and the fire that animates it. Hours and seasons are placed around his throne. He is master of the world and spreads the light. He holds seven circles in his right hand, and he has wings on his shoulders. He is the first that comes out of the egg of the world."

Much the best idea of this subject is derived from a description of the Lupercalia, which was "a yearly festival observed at Rome, on the 15th February, in honour of Pan. It was usual, first, to sacrifice two goats and a dog, and to touch, with a bloody knife, the forehead of two illustrious youths, who always were obliged to smile while they were touched. The blood was wiped away with soft wool dipped in milk. After this, the skins of the victims were cut into thongs with which whips were made for the youths. With these whips the youths ran about the streets all naked, except the middle: and whipped freely all those they met. Women, in particular, were fond of receiving the lashes, as they superstitiously believed that they removed barrenness and eased the pains of childbirth. This excursion in the streets of Rome was per-

formed by naked youths, because Pan is always represented
naked, and a goat was sacrificed, because that deity was
supposed to have the feet of goats."

In view of these myths and practices there cannot be the
least doubt that Pan and the Faunes are representatives of
the red Indians of North America. Pan is a savage—a naked
savage with a loin cloth. A bloody knife must bring blood
to the youths, and while suffering the gash they must smile.
Pan is ruddy or red, and he is God of the woods and the
chase. Here is a North American Indian to the letter. It
reads like a description in Cooper's novels of guides captured
and tied to a tree and cut with the tomahawk. Or one sees
a Pawnee Indian caught or tortured, or a young man initiated
into the religious observances of the tribe, as described by
Mr. Catlin; while suffering the most excruciating agony, he
must not move a muscle or flinch the least. Then whips are
used and flagellations all round. The identity is complete.

Perhaps the most remarkable mythic description of the
North American Indians, which is given in the mythological
lexicon, is that of the Furies, the very name of which is
graphically expressive of the people whom the first settlers
in America, in modern times, found to be the inhabitants of
the great forests. The tradition which gives a full account of
the Furies, is as follows:—

"Eumenides, a name given to the Furies by the Ancients.
They sprang from the blood of the wound which Cœlus
received from his son Saturn. According to others, they were
the daughters of the Earth, and conceived from the blood of
Saturn. Some make them daughters of Acheron and Night,
or Pluto and Proserpine. According to the more received
opinions they were three in number, Tisiphone, Megara, and
Alecto, to whom some add, Nemesis. Plutarch mentions only
one—Adrasta, daughter of Jupiter and Necessity. They were
supposed to be the ministers of the vengeance of the Gods.
They were stern and inexorable, and were always employed
in punishing the guilty, upon earth, as well as in the infernal regions. They inflicted their vengeance upon Earth by
wars, pestilences and dissensions, and by the secret stings of
conscience, and in hell they punished the guilty by continual

flagellation and torments. They were also called Furies and Erinnys. Their worship was almost universal, and people dared not mention their names, or fix their eyes upon their temples. They were honoured by sacrifices and libations, and in Achaia they had a temple, which, when entered by any one guilty of crime, suddenly rendered him furious, and deprived him of the use of his reason. In the sacrifices the votaries used branches of cedar and of alder, hawthorn, saffron, and juniper, and the victims generally were turtle doves and sheep, and libations of wine and honey. They were generally represented with a grim and frightful aspect, with a black and bloody garment, and serpents wreathing round their head, instead of hair. They held a burning torch in one hand, and a whip of scorpions in the other, and were always attended by terror, paleness, and death. In hell, they were seated round Pluto's throne, as the ministers of his vengeance."

If this is not a description of the Red Indians of North America, it ought to be. Of whom else can it be a picture? A crowd of reflections spring up in the mind on the perusal of this tradition.

"They sprang from the wound that Cœlus received from Saturn." "They were daughters of Jupiter." But these are the great Gods of Europe! What conceivable histories could be connected with North America,—supposed to have been unknown to the Ancients, that the European Gods could spring from North American Indians? This is a clue for enquiry, and the reader must be prepared to find that there was not only intercourse between the two hemispheres in ancient times; but that there was also consanguinity between the red and white races! Then "they surrounded the throne of Pluto and were ministers of his vengeance." What has Pluto to do with North America and the red men of the woods? Can it be possible that Pluto is to be found in America? If so, here is a further fact by which to open up the concealed histories of this great terra incognita; for there are remarkable traditions concerning Pluto which must have some relation to America.

But what is to be thought of the extraordinary statement, that the Furies had a temple in Achaia? Did the red Indians have a temple in Achaia? "Their worship was almost universal." Then they must have crossed the Atlantic Ocean in vast numbers, and they must have entered into the religious systems of all nations,—Greece not excepted. If this is to be relied upon, all history must be topsy turvy, and the Gods and stemfathers of European races must be sought for in the forests of North America!

America appears also, according to the conceptions of the Ancients, to have been the land of demons. It will be shown, in after pages, that the Poetical Astronomers and the pictorial map makers have treated the west coast of South America as especially demoniacal. The mention of Pluto, in the myth of the Eumenides, supplies the same idea. It is however chiefly in Demonology that this dark subject receives its full development. The Demons of the Sabbat, and the pictures which pourtray them, must be taken to belong to this category.

Take it altogether, it must be admitted that ancient literature has drawn a very pretty picture of the inhabitants of the Oceanic hemisphere. Just take a look at them again, in their assembled attitude. They suit very well in the transformation scene! Gods! well, a specimen of them is given in the next chapter, in the person of Oceanus himself, a fine noble looking character, against whose physical well-being no exception can be taken. Then there are the Giants—giants of the Spitfire denomination, with serpents for legs, and giants of overgrown dimensions and rapid growth. A specimen of that kind of gentry is seen in the person of Typhon, in the Coptic Zodiac. Then, there are the Gorgons—lovely Ladies with one eye among three, and one without a head. Specimens of them are seen further on. Take the Mermaids next—half women, half-fish. Just by way of diversity, Echidna herself may be mentioned. Some of this class of characters can be found in a future chapter. The Harpies must not escape observation. Specimens of them appear in the frontispiece and elsewhere. Then come the Faunes, with Pan at their head. He will make his appearance, in propriâ personâ, when Central America is reached. The Furies cannot well be hidden. They have played too large a part in human history. One will show himself shortly on the Egg of the world. Fill up the picture with the Demons.

Yet, it must not be supposed, for a moment, that this wonderful collection of people and races of men, should ever have been seen in the fair plains and spacious forests of beautiful America. It is all a matter of dress and heraldry. It is the intense love of nature which has given rise to these fanciful forms of humanity. It is personal attire which has supplied the muses of antiquity with their notions of trans-marine people. There is a wonderful difference between the customs of the ancients and the moderns in dress. At the present day, the acme of perfection in costume is made to consist in plainness. It was not so in olden times. Fashions vary.

FASHIONS OF PRE-HISTORIC AMERICA.

What the fashions were in America, can be seen in the great collection of pictures, which was published under the name of Aglio, and which must be consulted, to a large extent, as illustrations of the present work. Those pictures supply quite a picture gallery of pre-historic American costume. As they exhibit the antiquities of the country, they must be taken, as showing the habits and customs of American life before the

flood. Two or three specimens are given to exhibit the
fashions of the period. There can be no wonder that the
Gods, who made frequent visits to the great Oceanus, should,
on their return home, have described the inhabitants of the
land as giants, monsters and demons.

One sees in the account given of these races, the origin of
Heraldry. There can be no great wonder that people, living
in the great woods and daily occupied in hunting wild beasts,
should have been Zoomorphic in their notions. Mr. Catlin
gives a picture of a chief, dressed as a Bear, like Hercules, in
the Zodiac. Nothing could be more natural, than to call their
chiefs and tribes by the names of the animals which abounded
among them. Hence one is a Serpent, another an Eagle,
another a Beaver, and so on. The principle of totem is incipient
Heraldry. There is but one difference between the ancient
Indian and the modern Nobleman. The Indian put his crest
upon his back, and the Nobleman upon his escutcheon.

There is one of the Oceanides, by means of whom the
geography and river system of ancient America can be traced.
It is Styx. "Styx is the name of a principal river in the
under world, around which it flows nine times." *Homer.* As
a river, it is a branch of Oceanus flowing from its tenth source.
The river Cocytus is a branch. The myth is as follows:—
"Styx, daughter of Oceanus and Tethys, or, of Erebus and
Styx. A nymph who dwelt at the entrance of Hades, a woman
in black, with an Urn, in a lofty grotto, supported by silver
columns." *Hesiod.* By Pallas the Titan, she became mother
of Zelus, Nice, Bia and Cratos. She was first of the immortals,
who took her children to Zeus to assist him against the
Titans: and in return her children were allowed for ever to
live with Zeus. Styx herself became the divinity, by whom
most solemn oaths were sworn. In an oath, Iris fetched a
cup of water from Styx, and the God poured out the water.
Zeus, by Styx, became father of Persephone, and Peiras the
father of Echidna." *Pauly.*

To locate this highly mythical personage, recourse must
be had to the Poetical Astronomers. Poetical Astronomy is,
in fact, the mythic Geography of the Ancients. Firmicus says,
that "the ancient astrologers fixed the 8th degree of the

Balance for the place of Styx." The Balance is rather an
equivocal sign, but it may be placed in the North-West of
South America. The myth says, that Styx lived at the entrance of Hades. As Cerberus is at the entrance of Hades,
and he is constellated over the Caribean Sea, which carries
his name to this day, Styx ought to represent the gulf of
Texas. This curiously brings Styx to a gulf that bears her
name, the circuitous form of which answers well to the idea
of Homer, as flowing round the under world nine times, or
in nine bays. In this case, it is a branch of the Ocean, or
a son of Oceanus.

Closely connected with Styx, and a figure equally mythical,
is the impersonated river, called Acheron. Pauly gives it thus;
"Acheron, a mythic river—a river of Hades into which the
Pyriphlegoton and Cocytus flow. Virgil makes it the chief
river of Tartarus, and from which Styx and Cocytus spring.
Acheron is called the son of Helios and Gaa, or Demeter
changed to a river of hell, because he had refreshed the Titans
with drink, in their contest with Zeus. Esculapius was the
son of Acheron and Orphne, or Gorgra. The Etruscans were
acquainted with it."

Now it will be remembered that in the tradition of the
Eumenides, it is said, "they were the children of Acheron."
Let the case of these rivers be put into a small compass.
It runs thus: If Styx is the gulf of Texas—if Acheron flows
into it,—and if Acheron is the biggest river of Tartary, the
Acheron must be the Mississippi, and if the Phlegethon and
Cocytus flow into Acheron, they must be the Missouri and
the Ohio, and the Eumenides, being the children of Acheron,
they must have been the ancient inhabitants of the great
valley of the Mississippi. This conclusion is proved to be
correct, by the circumstance, that Professor Rafinesque, in his
enumeration of the Red races, gives the native name of
the Missourian Indians as Oman or Œman.

The present identification of Oceanus, as a mythic impersonation of America, ought to be proved in every respect.
It ought to be shown that the Greeks have used the word,
with that signification. It is so. *Homer* has the following
lines—

I

" When down the smooth Oceanus impelled,
" By prosperous gales, my galley once again,
" Cleaving the billows of the spacious deep,
" Had reached the Ocean Isle."

In this verse, the Poet makes the galley cross the Ocean to the Ocean Isle. By the word Ocean he evidently means Ocean. The letter c has got softened into a diphthong. The same thing is observable in the word Œgean, as the Sea in which Nereus and the Nereids reside. In this case Ocean softens into Œgean. It is natural to look for the Nereids in the Grecian Sea: but Pauly, the German lexicographer, has Aegä as a golden wave palace in the depth of the sea, where dwelt Poseidon and the Tritons. By no stretch of language can the Grecian Sea be called the depth of the sea. It implies great distance from Greece. By comparison of terms, this Aegä is seen to be the Ocean isle of Homer.

There can be no doubt that the word has been a perplexity both to ethnologists and mythologists, and to all enquirers into ancient things. The learned Bryant labours to shew the extensive use of it in classical works, for some great race that has spread itself abroad as the Ionim. In the Phœnician cosmogony it stands at the head of the Phœnicians as Œon.

The Gnostics have the word as Eon, as expressive of their powers and intelligences. It forms the name of the woman-fish, which instructs the Babylonians and Egyptians as Oannes. The name is also found in one of the Gods of Gaul at Claremont and Montmorilon, and with the same fish attributes and forms as Onuava. In China, it is at the top of the Chinese Sovereigns, as the three Hoangs, authors of letters, gold and precious stones.

But not only so: Mr. Schoolcraft gives a tradition of the Iroquois Indians, where the word is used for the native name of America itself. "The shell of the tortoise expanded till it became a continent, and it was named Aoneo." The same word can be detected in the common but mysterious Americanism, Yankee Doodle. Teotl is God in Mexico, so that Yankee Doodle is the God Oceanus or the Ocean God.

It is necessary here to note, that the myths in this work, are taken from Lempriere's Classical Dictionary, unless otherwise stated.

CHAPTER VI.

VISHNU, THE WATER GOD OF THE HINDOOS, CORRESPONDS
IN NAME, NATURE, AND PLACE, WITH THE OCEANUS OF EUROPE.

It has been seen that the Greeks, in their mythic system
of ancient Geography, have impersonated America as the
marine God, Oceanus. It is just the same with the Hindoos,
in India. The sages have the same symbolism exactly. The
names themselves are the same. Vishnu is Oceanus, written
in Sanscrit—Oceanu. Then they have the same attribute of
water, as Vishnu is the Water God of India, and Oceanus
reposes on the water. Then, again, they both recline upon
the sea serpent. The pictures, on page 60, are given for
comparison, and they shew that the two branches of the
Indo-European family have had the same ideal conception.
They have both turned America into a divinity, and have represented him in a like posture, and with the same Serpentine
accompaniment. It will be observed, however, that the Hindoo
picture is much better drawn, and is itself much more significant than that of Greece.

Both Gods, according to the principle of the present work,
locate in America by the presence of the Serpent. In the
Ptolemaic Zodiac, the Snake abounds all over what may be
considered North America. The Draco—the Serpent and the
Serpentarius taken together, surround the region, creating a
suspicion, that this is what is meant by the symbolism of the
serpent surrounding the whole earth. In the other picture,
Vishnu is on the seven headed Sesha Serpent, a figure of
great significance in Hindoo mythology and antiquities. The
picture, now under notice, is to be taken as a pictorial history.
Such was the nature of all old mythic drawings. Such were
the picture writings of the North American Indians. Three
personages appear in the scene besides the serpent, which
stands for the land itself.

Vishnu is the blue and water God of India. He rides the
man bird Garuda. Sometimes he is identified with Ganesa,
who is said to have had a paradise in Swetam dwipa. Again,
he is one of the twelve Adityas, or rays of the Sun. As to

OCEANUS ON THE SEA MONSTER.

VISHNU ON THE SESHA SERPENT.

what relates to him in America, he is said to have been born between the Cumuda and Anjana 'Mountains, among waters and in a land of darkness. He was born of a virgin in the house of a shepherd. He resides on the north shore of the Swetam dwipa or White sea. He rescued the Earth from sinking into hell. He had conflicts with the Giants after his marriage with Lacksmi. Then he was born in India and assumed the shape of a tortoise.

Lacksmi is the consort of Vishnu, and called Ada Mya, mother of the world. She is also called Rhemba and Sri.

Brahma is the Red God of India. He has a wife, Saraswati, and his Vahan is the Goose. The sun is his image. He had his birth on a lotus, from the navel of Vishnu. He has five heads, each of which is crowned, and one of which was cut off. He formed Saturupa out of one half of his body. Swayambhuva sprang from his body. He fashioned the Earth after it had sunk into hell.

It takes a little, or not a little, study and thought to understand the present mystic picture and the histories which belong to it. But, if any one will take the trouble, he will find that the three characters, now described, represent Asiatic races, which, at some period of high antiquity, have colonized America. Vishnu stands for the Chinese. Lacksmi is the Hindoo Venus, who in the Greek system, is turned into a Serpent, instead of sitting upon it. Brahma is a form of the primæval Brahma. There is hardly any difference between the Sanscrit and Greek systems. Vishnu is Oceanus by name and nature. In the Greek pedigree, Oceanus is the son of Uranus. Urania is the name of Venus. In the European system, Uranus is the first king of the Atlantic Isle, and his histories will be traced in future chapters. In the Hindoo system, those histories hang on to Brahma. He spreads out into five races, corresponding with his heads. In the Asiatic researches he is glossed by Cronus. The histories which will be traced in later chapters, under the name of Cronus, belong equally to Brahma.

What little difference there is between the two systems, is reconciled when Varuna is taken into account. Varuna is the God of the Ocean in the West. He rides upon a fish and is called the Lord of punishments. It is true, that this makes Varuna, in which the name of Uranus is found, a sort of competitor with Vishnu for the honour of marine deity. But there is exactly the same thing in the European system. Although Uranus is its first king, Poseidon is said to have had the Atlantic Isle allotted to him.

The Hindoos have a long series of traditions which must belong to America. They are the Avataras or incarnations of Vishnu. If Vishnu himself is a representative of the hemisphere, or any part of it, those Avataras must be parts of American history. In the myth of Vishnu, it is said, that "he resided on the Northern Shores of the White Sea." The Serpent, on which he reclines, must be located by the Serpent of the Zodiac. This puts Vishnu himself in the country north of modern Mexico, and it is there that are found the ruins and pyramids that attest the former presence of a religious and building race. It is certainly very remarkable, that it is said in books relating to Mexico, that the ancient name of the city of the Gods was Veitiocan. Whether that was the name of Vishnu or not, must be left to fancy. It certainly is within the region of the Serpent.

The legends of the incarnations of Vishnu are used occasionally, and some of them are transcribed in other parts of this work; but it is thought advisable, for the sake of completeness, to give them here as histories connected with America. There are nine of them, but in some works, the number is extended to above twenty, exhibiting great intercourse between America and India, or extended knowledge of its historical antiquities.

1. Matsya.—In the Satya age, all mankind was corrupt, except Satyavrata. The seven Rishis and their wives, by command of Vishnu, enter a spacious vessel, accompanied by pairs of all animals. Vishnu, in the form of a fish, fixed the ark, by a cable—a vast serpent—to his horns, till the flood subsided; when he and Brahma slew a monster named Hyagriva, who, while Brahma was reposing at the end of a Kalpa, stole the Vedas, and mankind had thus fallen into ignorance and impiety. The demon's name was Danavas. The world was re-peopled with the pious descendants of Satyavrata and his companions.

2. Kurma.—In the Satya age. To restore man, Vishnu became incarnate in the form of a tortoise. In this shape, he sustained the mountain Mandara placed on his back to serve as an axis, whereon the Gods and demons (the vast serpent Vasoky serving as a rope) churned the Ocean, to recover the Amrita or beverage of immortality.

3. Varuha.—In the Satya age. A four-handed Boar with a crescent on the tusks, containing in its concavity, an epitome of the Earth, which had been submerged in the Ocean, for its iniquities. A Daitya named Hiranyaksha, or the golden eyed, passed a long life in austerities in honour of Brahma, who appeared to him and he asked universal monarchy. It was granted, but he forgot the hog. The Daitya seized the Earth and carried it into the Ocean. Vishnu now appeared as a Boar, dived into the abyss, and after contest of a thousand years, slew the monster, and restored the Earth on the point of his tusks.

4. Narasingha or Man-lion.—In the Satya age. Two Ethereal warders of Vishnu's palace were cursed into banishment, for insolence to Sanaka, who with seven Rishis, approached to worship. Lacksmi wanted to see a battle, and Vishnu got it up for her. The sentence of eternal exile upon Earth, was mitigated to seven transmigrations. During it, if faithful, crime would be expiated. If preferred, they might have three as Daityas, as enemies of Vishnu—taking the consequences. They chose the latter, and first became Daityas of the third and fourth Avataras, and in character of Hiranyakasipa, one was slain by Vishnu, as half-man, half-lion. To account for this, there is another legend. The Daitya performed for ten thousand years, austerities for Brahma, and got exemption from all ills everywhere. His arrogance got so great, that Vishnu inspired the Daitya's virtuous son Pavaladha, to a controversy about omnipresence. "Is then the deity here," cried the father, and smote the pillar, which rent and showed the monster, Narasingha, who attacked Hiranyaksipa, and in one hour cut him up.

5. Vamana, or dwarf.—In the Tirtya age.—Mahabeli, a virtuous monarch, omitted offerings to the Gods. Vishnu resolved to punish him. He condescended to become the son of Kasyapa

and Aditi, a brother of Indra, assuming the form of a dwarf. He asked of Mahabeli a gift of the universe. As the water fell on his hand (a sign of gift) he expanded and filled the world. Vishnu, at one of three steps, deprived Beli of heaven and earth, leaving him Patala.

6. Krishna.—He was the most splendid Avatara of Vishnu. He is Vishnu and Narayana. He manifested himself in a degree of power and glory, far exceeding any of the other forms of Vishnu. Some call him an impious wretch,—an incarnate demon, now expiating his crimes in hell. His mortal parents were Vasadeva and Devaky.

7 and 8. The three Ramas—Bala Rama, Parasu Rama, and Rama Chandra.—There is confusion in the description of these three characters. They are all famed as great warriors and as youths of perfect beauty.

9. Buddha. In the midst of a wild and dreary forest, trees and flowers, and roots, lions and tigers, alone and frequented by the Munis, resided Buddha, author of happiness and portion of Narayana.

Before the subject advances, it may be necessary to furnish satisfactory evidence, that these incarnations are really connected with America. The teaching is new, and it is fair to object, that the Hindoo God Vishnu is one of the Gods of Hindostan, and nothing else. It may be considered a stretch of fancy to associate an Idol of India, with the great terra incognita, now the subject of research. But the proof is forthcoming, and that in a form the most convincing. All the Avataras of Vishnu are represented in a pictorial form. Some of the pictures are more instructive than the stories which are told concerning them. Particularly is this the case with the fourth Incarnation, that of Narasingha, the Man-Lion. The tale itself, is quite unintelligible. Who two warders of Vishnu's palace might be, would remain an eternal secret, from any thing that can be gleaned from the tradition. But when the picture is introduced, it becomes a conclusive proof, that the Incarnation belongs to Mexico, and to no other country under heaven. Accompanying the Narasingha or Lion-Man, who is engaged in putting to death a person, is a picture of a Mexican sacrifice, at the summit of a teecallis. In that scene,

MEXICAN SACRIFICE.

HINDOO NARASINGHA.

K

the bloody Mexican priests are seen holding the figure of a victim, and the chief priest is tearing open the breast of the man, to remove the heart, to be presented to the Idol, which is in an adjoining edifice.

Let the reader carefully compare the two pictures, and he will come to the conclusion, that they belong to the same subject. The Hindoo Narasingha well represents the monstrous priest. The two pillars of the Indian picture are counterparts of the Mexican temples. The stone altar, on which the victim is placed, answers to the Stone of Sacrifice on the teecallis. Then to make the comparison exact, the man-lion is opening the breast of his victim, precisely in the same manner as the priest, a form of execution so peculiar to Mexico, as to be found in the customs of no other ancient people.

The argument is, that, if one of the Incarnations is American, all the others must be so too. This is held to be sufficient evidence of the teaching of the present chapter, and it makes the following curious extracts reliable in relation to America.

Vishnu has many names. In the Puranas and other Sanscrit works, he is often called Hari, Bhaghavat, Madava, and others. Besides that, all the above incarnations are parts of himself. This can only be taken to signify, that all the names connected with Vishnu, are either ethnological or geographical as belonging to America, in prehistoric times. Most of the names, however, can be seen to belong to migrations from America into India itself, and they can be traced by many routes,— some direct from the East, some across Europe, and some through Africa.

In the Asiatic researches, there are a great number of extracts from Sanscrit works, which can be used to throw light upon ancient America. Some of these extracts may be transcribed with advantage. In Vol. VIII., 246, it is said, "The sacred isles in the west, of which Swetam dwipa is the principal and the most famous, are, in fact, the Holy Land of the Hindoos. There the fundamental and mysterious transactions of the history of their religion took place." Again, Vol. XI., 92, it is said, "All the Avataras or principal emanations of Vishnu came originally from the Sweta dwipa.

There are many forms or manifestations of Bhaghavat (Vishnu), O Muni! but the form which resides in the Sweta dwipa is the primitive one." "Rama and Narasingha are complete forms, O Muni! but Crishna, the most powerful king of the Sweta dwipa, is the most perfect and complete of all Vishnu's forms. For this purpose, Vishnu from Patala rejoins the body of Radhiceswara, the lord of Radha, who dwells in the Sweta dwipa, with the famous Snake Sesha, a portion of his essence. The Gods sent these,—portions of their own essences, to be consolidated into the person of Crishna, who was going to be incarnated at Gocala."

In the same great work there are many extracts, which disclose the fact, that, in olden times, there must have been intercourse between India and America. A specimen may be given—shortened. "In the Padma Purana Section Patala, it is said, "Suta relates the wonderful deeds of Rama Chandra, who came originally from the White Island (Sweta). Rama Chandra, having a self-moving car, performed it in a few days, in company with Mahadewa or Sambhu. They had a Muni with them, whose wife had gone to Tamobhaga Giri, where they were going. They soon arrived in the land of darkness. In the middle is Narayana Pura, and a million suns,—the Paradise of Vishnu and Lacksmi. None but those who have obtained internal knowledge can enter. On all sides were Rishis and Munis performing Puja. The four Vedas reside there, and the Romasha daya,—descendants of the holy Romashas. Rama and Siva (Sambhu) make puja to Achyuta or the incorruptible God."

"Then Narada came from heaven, with his hair tied up, with a guitar and a small crooked staff. Sambhu told him that Rama wanted to see the place. Narada went in, and announced them. Vishnu and Lacksmi, with myriads of Yogis, came out to meet them. Vishnu asked who Rama was. Sambhu said, 'a portion of your essence.' They go in, to see Lacksmi in an inner apartment. Sri devi said 'You are handsome, but Sita, your consort, is a perfect beauty.' They then left the mountains, and reached Swadadadhi or Pushcara."

To this may be added an exceedingly interesting account of the Sesha Serpent and of Vishnu reposing on it.

This scene is described in the Vishnu Purana in the following terms. It is a part of the Geography of the Puranas, or a "description of the Earth." After an account of the Patalas, which will be hereafter identified with other parts of North America, the writer proceeds. "Below the seven Patalas, is the form of Vishnu, proceeding from the quality of darkness, which is called Sesha, (N.B. He is the great Serpent, on which Vishnu sleeps during the interval of creation, and upon whose numerous heads the world is supported. The Puranas make him one with Balarama or Sankasura, who is an impersonation or incarnation of Sesha, blending the attributes of the Serpent and the demigod in their description); the excellences of which, neither Daityas nor Danavas can fully enumerate. This being is called Ananta, by the Spirits of heaven, and is worshipped by Sages and by Gods. He has 1000 heads, which are embellished with the pure and visible mystic sign. (N.B. with the Swartika, a particular diagram used in mystic ceremonies), and the jewels in his crests, give light to all the regions. For the benefit of the world, he deprives the Asuras of their strength. He rolls his eyes fiercely, as if intoxicated. He wears a single earring, a diadem and wreath upon each brow, and shines like the white mountains, topped with flame. He is clothed in purple raiment, and ornamented with a white necklace, and looks like another Kailasa, with the heavenly Ganga flowing down its precipices. In one hand he holds a plough, and in the other a pestle, and is attended by Varuni (the goddess of wine), who is his own embodied radiance. From his mouth, at the end of the Kalpa, proceeds the venomed fire, that impersonated as Radra, who is one with Balarama, devours the three worlds. Sesha bears the entire world, like a diadem, upon his head; and he is the foundation on which the seven Patalas rest. His power, his glory, his form, his nature, cannot be described, cannot be comprehended by the Gods themselves. Who shall recount his might, who wears this whole world like a garland of flowers, tinged of a purple dye, by the radiance of the jewels of his crest. When Ananta, he eyes rolling with intoxication, yawns, then the earth with all her woods and mountains and seas and rivers trembles.

Gandharbas, Apsarasas, Siddhas, Kinnaras, Uragas, and Chanavas, are unequal to hymn his praise, and therefore he is called the infinite (Ananta) the imperishable. The sandal paste, that is ground by the wives of the Snake Gods, is scattered abroad by his breath, and sheds perfume around the skies."

This very beautiful and highly poetical description of the Sesha Serpent, demands a little comment. The Sesha Serpent of the Hindoos has to be compared with the Greek Echidna. As Oceanus reposes on one, so Vishnu reposes on the other. It is the Ptolemaic Zodiac which serves to locate them both as the region lying along the west coast of North America. It will be remembered that Echidna is a monster. In the upper part she is a beautiful woman. In the lower she is a Snake. She is mother of all the other monsters. In like manner, in the Hindoo system, the Sesha Serpent is the foundation, on which the seven Patalas rest. Turned into historical geography, it shews that Mexico was the most important part of America, in the mythic ages. Echidna's monstrosity has its parallel in the thousand heads of the Sesha. Echidna's beauty has its parallel in the Oriental splendour and exaggerated beauty assigned to the Sesha. The idea got by this document, is that the country of Mexico must have been a very grand and imposing state at the time to which the description belongs. This can easily be believed from the remains it has left.

As the Hindoo mythology has never been utilized for the elucidation of history, it is not at all unlikely, that the reading public will be slow to believe, that the interesting extracts given in this chapter, can belong to ancient America, and especially to Mexico. It may be necessary, therefore, to adduce two or three things, which will afford an opportunity to judge aright of the application of the subject. In one of these extracts, it is said that "Swetam dwipa was the Holy Land of the Hindoos. There, the fundamental and mysterious transactions of the history of their religion took place." This is certainly a most extraordinary statement, and it may be challenged; but it must be recollected, that this statement relates only to the race called Hindoos. There is abundant

evidence, that the Hindoos were strangers in India. Nonnus
in the Dionusica, gives as their parent, Indus the Giant, and
Diodorus Siculus speaks of the Oceanides of the western parts,
as a part of the population of India, in his time. Under these
circumstances, it is quite credible, that the Hindoos could
have brought into Hindoostan an Oceanic religion.

Pictures are vocal. They often tell tales, when words are
unintelligible. A picture is here given of a Hindoo place of
worship, such as is found at this day, on the plains of India.
It is said of these temples,

PYRAMID OF PAPANTLA.   HINDOO KOIL.

that they are exceedingly ancient. None of them are put at
a less age than 5000 years. They are called Koils, a word
which is used on some of the Hindoo descriptions of Patala.
Accompanying this picture, for the purpose of comparison, is
a copy of one of the ancient ruined pyramids, which are found
in the region of ancient Mexico. Most of the pyramids are very
far advanced towards a state of decay, but that of Papantla
serves well to put it into comparison with a Hindoo Koil.
The resemblance of the two temples is enough to admit of a
fair argument, that the Hindoo Koil was built upon a Mexican
model, though more highly decorated and improved.

It is worthy of notice, also, that one of the Incarnations of
Vishnu may furnish evidence, that the religion of India has
been moulded or modified at some very ancient period, by

the arrival of races from beyond the Pacific and the Atlantic Oceans. In the present chapter, the legends of the Incarnations of Vishnu, have been copied from the excellent work of Major Moor, who is the English authority on Hindoo mythology. But, in a French work, which treats of the same subject, the legends of those Incarnations are very different. The pictures are the same, but the names and stories differ. In that work, one of the Incarnations is called Juggernauth. The mention of Juggernauth in the present relation is highly significant, and it throws great light upon the present question. In this chapter, a picture has been given, which leaves no manner of doubt upon the mind, that the Mexican religion must have been introduced into India.

It is true. that the modus operandi of human sacrifice practised in Mexico, has not been found in Hindoostan; but on the other hand, the religion of Juggernauth and his car was, if anything, more barbarous and more cruel, than even the sacrifices of the teecallis. At any rate, it is the same principle of religion,—blood, self-sacrifice, and unflinching self torture. The elder part of the present generation can well remember the fearful scenes which were enacted, on the plains of India, when the horrid car was drawn about, and the senseless multitude assembled in countless crowds to throw themselves beneath the wheels of that monstrous vehicle of death.

PART OF THE PTOLEMAIC ZODIAC, AS A MAP OF NORTH
AMERICA IN THE MYTHIC AGES.

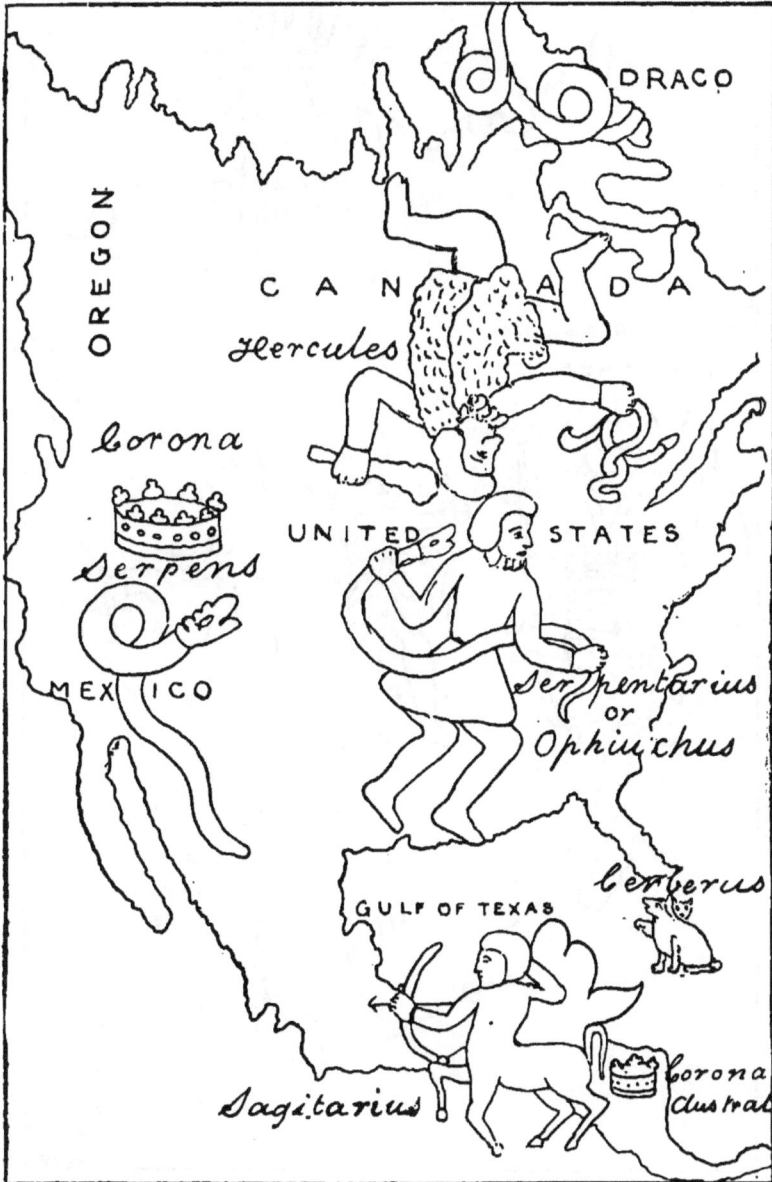

PART OF THE COPTIC ZODIAC, AS A MAP OF NORTH AMERICA
IN THE MYTHIC AGES.

CHAPTER VII.

A GENERAL VIEW OF THE FIGURES WHICH ARE EMPLOYED
TO DELINEATE NORTH AMERICA, IN THE TWO ZODIACAL MAPS,
AND THE INFERENCES WHICH ARE TO BE DEDUCED FROM THEM.

Two maps are now introduced to the attention of the reader.
They are formed upon the outlines of a modern map, and
the countries are depicted, not with the modern names only,
but with the pictorial figures of the Zodiac. By this means,
the Geography of North America is recovered, as it must have
been known in the earliest ages, by those who constructed
the maps. These maps will be used in this work, for the
purpose of drawing out the hidden histories of North America.
The plan of study proposed to be pursued is, to consider the
several pictorial figures, as appertaining to the regions which
they severally delineate. But it may be convenient to take
a cursory and general view of them, as they appear at first
sight.

Take the Coptic map first. This is a very simple portraiture
of North America; but it is highly significant. The Copts are
the genuine Egyptians; so that the map must be supposed
to comprise the special knowledge which the Egyptians had, of
North America. But the significance of the portraiture is
greatly increased, when it is observed that the Isthmus of
Central America, is drawn as a figure holding a bow and
arrow. The figure is, in fact, a Ptolemaic Sagitarius which,
is a son of Pan. But it has a name. It is called the Regnum
Arueris. Now Arueris is the elder Horus,—brother of Isis
and Osiris, and it is difficult to distinguish between Arueris
and Horus. Without going deeply into this matter, it may
be said, that Arueris and his son Horus represent the Bel or
Belus of Antiquity, and in the Greek System, Belus, with
Anchinoe, is the father of Egyptus and Danaus. This brings
the Copts into Central America as their original home.

All the rest of North America, in this map, is delineated as
Typhon; but with no less than three figures. The one most
westerly, which occupies the Region of Mexico is wound round
with serpents and spits fire. Typhon, in the Greek system, is a

Giant. In the Egyptian system, he is opposed to Horus, the son of Osiris. In pictures, he is drawn as a Bear or Hippopotamus, or some monster, with a woman's head. Looking at these figures cursorily, it can scarcely be unnoticed, that the Egyptian idea of North America is associated with the wars of Typhon and Horus.

In the Ptolemaic map, which has many figures, Draco the dragon, and Ursa Minor occupy the North, Hercules and Ophiuchus fill the whole region forming the United States, as far west as the Rocky mountains; or, at least there are no other figures. The Serpent hangs down the west coast, west of the mountains, and fairly pourtrays the country of Mexico and the lands where are discovered, at the present day, the ruined cities, temples and pyramids of Upper Mexico. The crown appears twice. In its largest form, it stands north of the Serpent. In its smallest form, it occupies that very curious and interesting portion of the Central American Isthmus, now full of ruins, and containing Uxmal, the Pompeii of America. The Sagitarius, with a bow and arrow, like the Arueris of the Copts, gives physical form to that part of the Isthmus which comprises Quiche, Petens, and the neighbouring provinces, now abounding with remarkable ruins. Cerberus stands off at the right hand of the map, if not "at the entrance to the divine abode," — certainly at the entrance to America, both North and South.

The most striking and remarkable feature, in this picture map, is that Hercules and Ophiuchus, otherwise called by the poetical astronomers, Iphicles, occupy the greater part of what now constitutes the United States. Yet, it really is not a bad idea. If it is afterwards proved that these Heroes embody the ancient inhabitants of the mysterious Earthworks of that region, it does credit both to the Earthworks and the Heroes. There is no character in the mysterious histories of Europe, Africa and Asia, so important as Hercules. He has the appearance of a Giant, nearly nude and warlike; yet, possessed of qualities of great honour and of distinguished utility, in the civilization of the old continent. It really would not be impossible to run an analogy between the character and feats of Hercules, and the honourable characteristics and the brave feats of the North American Indian,—as seen in the heroic traditions and stories of the early settlers in the great woods of the red men, in more modern times.

The story goes, that "before he had completed his eighth month, the jealousy of Juno, intent upon his destruction, sent two Snakes to devour him. The child, not terrified at the sight, boldly seized them in both his hands, and squeezed them to death, while his brother Iphicles alarmed the house with his frightful shrieks." Well! the appearance of these great heroes, as pictorial embodiment of the inhabitants of the United States in olden times, gives a funny interpretation to that story. But every bookworm knows, that the great histories of the human race have got shrunk up into nursery tales. Punch and Judy, Harlequin and Columbine, and Jack the Giant Killer, and a host of other personages, known in the nursery, cannot be put down for what the infant mind conceives of them. Science and philosophy forbid! What has become of the great histories of the vast past? Ask the baby for his last picture book.

But a little reading must be brought to bear upon this group of figures. People do not like mythology, it is unsafe. Yet, it cannot be dispensed with in the study of human antiquities. No satisfactory elucidation of any terra incognita of old geography, can ever be gained without it.

If any expert in mythological pictures should examine the group of figures that compose the present pictorial maps, he is sure to arrive at the conclusion, that North America, in the minds of the ancients, must be what they call "the Soul of the world," or "the Egg of the world," or both. Of course, it is a very silly thing, and it has always been incomprehensible and provocative of laughter. The world has no soul. It can have none, if by soul is meant the immaterial part of man. But if the ancients had a fancy for that sort of language, it cannot be helped. Perhaps, if they had lived in this scientific age, they would have called the land of their forefathers a parallelogram, or a rhomboid, or a triangle.

This symbolism is referred to very often, in the writings of many ancient nations, and to understand it, it becomes necessary to make a short collation of extracts.

In Chinese literature, it is said, that "the first man was Pouncu. This man came out of an egg, of which the yolk was taken up to heaven,—the white spread itself in the air, and the yellow rested on the earth." In Japan, the doctors say, that "the entire world, at the time of Chaos, was shut up in this Egg, which floated upon the surface of the waters." Prescott, in his history of the Conquest of Mexico, explains the meaning of the word Tezculipoca, as "the soul of the world," and supposed to have been its Creator. Champollion, in explaining the Hieroglyphics of Amon, with four heads of rams,. reads one of the legends, "Spirits of the four elements and soul of the material world." The same Egyptologist reads the legend of the Serpent-man, Cnouphis, "the great soul of the world, from which emanated the intellectual principle, which communicated movement and life to all created beings."

To these Asiatic and African quotations, a few must be transcribed from Europe and India. Dupuis, quoting Athenagoras, says, "Hercules was chief God, the same as Cronus; Cronus produced the mundane Egg." "Again, "Hercules too, like Pan, was depositary of creative power, and fecundated the Symbolic Egg." Again, "Ophiuchus, who is Esculapius, was Soul of the Eighth heaven, one of the forms of the Soul of the world." Again, "Bacchus was Soul of the world, and Spiritus, — mover of the spheres, when nature received the germ of fecundity communicated by Æther."

From India, two passages will suffice. Vain Purana. Suta says, "Prakriti and Purusha produce an Egg:—Brahm vivifies it; hence sprang Herangarbha — Brahma with four faces. This being from the Egg with a thousand heads is also called Viraj." The other passage is from the Institutions of Menu, v. 6, "The Lord first produced the waters on which he deposited a germ. (9.) This Germ became an Egg, brilliant as Gold, in which the Divine being produced himself under the form of Brahma, the grandfather of all beings."

Now, let the characters mentioned in these extracts, be compared with the constellated figures which overhang North America, and it will be found that they are the same; and therefore, that North America is the Soul of the world.

Take Ophiuchus: he is called Esculapius and Soul of the Eighth Heaven, the Soul of the world. This is the constellation that overhangs the Southern States of modern America and the region of the Southern Earthworks. Here it is curious to observe, that Prescott makes Tesculipoca to be the Soul of the world. In a future chapter, it will be shown, that Tesculipoca and Esculapius are the same God: both in name and nature,— the one in Mexico, and the other among the Mediterranean nations.

Take Hercules glossed by Cronus. Of him it is said, that he was like Pan, depositary of creative Power, and fecundated the Egg, which will be shown presently to be an inner part of the Soul of the world. Here, again, is a constellation. Hercules overhangs the modern Northern States. In the Hindoo extracts, Brahma, who is the red God of India, with four heads, is called also Viraj. There is reason to judge that the words Viraj and Eric are the same, differently spelled; and it will be hereafter shown that both are to be found in the Iroquois Indian. But Brahma is, by the Chinese, called the God Fan, and it looks a good deal as if Pan were included in the Hindoo conception of their red God, in which case, Brahma may be the embodiment of both the Iroquois and Pawnee Indians.

Take Amon. At first sight, it might be supposed that this Egyptian God has nothing to do with North America; but it is otherwise. Amon is identical with Pan. In the Egyptian mythology, Amon is the same figure as Khem, whom the Greeks recognized as Pan, who, in the above extracts, is said to have fecundated the Egg of the world. Pan belongs to Central America. He is the father of the Sagitarius itself, so that he mystically is one of the constellated figures appertaining to North America, and Amon is included in him.

Take Cnouphis, of whom it is said, that he is the great Soul of the world, from which emanates movement. Cnouphis is a form of Neph. In a later chapter there is a picture of this deity in the form of a walking serpent. In this character, Neph, the Egyptian Neptune, is the Serpent himself, who also is one of the constellations: so that a comparison of the mythic personages who compose the Soul of the world, makes them exactly identical with the group of pictorial asterisms, which overhang North America, leaving no manner of doubt, that when the ancient writers locate these deities in the Soul of the world, they do, in fact, attribute their origin, at least so far as they become divinities, to North America. The only God mentioned in the extracts, who does not appear in the Ptolemaic Zodiac, is Bacchus; but when the course of enquiry reaches Palenque, he also will present himself in a mystic identity with Neptune.

This is one of innumerable cases, in which America becomes a lamp to mythology, and mythology pays back in kind the light it receives. No doubt the argument wants confirmation. Let it be drawn from Gnosticism. A very large part of the knowledge possessed of old histories and mysteries, is drawn, not from the Pagan Greeks, but from the Church Fathers, such as Eusebius and the Gnostics. Gnosticism, being half Christian and half Pagan, is open to suspicion: yet, from the very fact that the Gnostics had not the faith nor the courage to cast away their Paganism, in the adoption of a purer system of religion, they have transmitted to posterity, unintentionally, writings and pictures which contain in them relics of the old world, in the shape of cosmogonies and diagrams, which but from that circumstance would have been totally lost. The accompanying diagram is an Ophite Gnostic Map by Celsus Origene. It is found in the very excellent work on Gnosticism by M. Matter, the French author. On a sharp-witted inspection, it will be found, notwithstanding its concealment, to be a map of America. There is a great oval with Sophia and Pronia. The explanation given of this oval is that it is "the Soul of the world." The internal Oval is called "the Egg of the world." Another oval, which answers to Central America, is described by seven small circles, which are called seven planetary powers, to whom the defunct addressed himself, going to each gate, beginning with Adonai. South America appears to be represented by Spheres for the wicked.

This curious diagram is treated as a map of America, on the following course of reasoning. A Zodiac has been proved to be a map of the world. In the Ptolemaic Zodiac, the figures, now under consideration, overhang North America.

OPHITE GNOSTIC MAP.

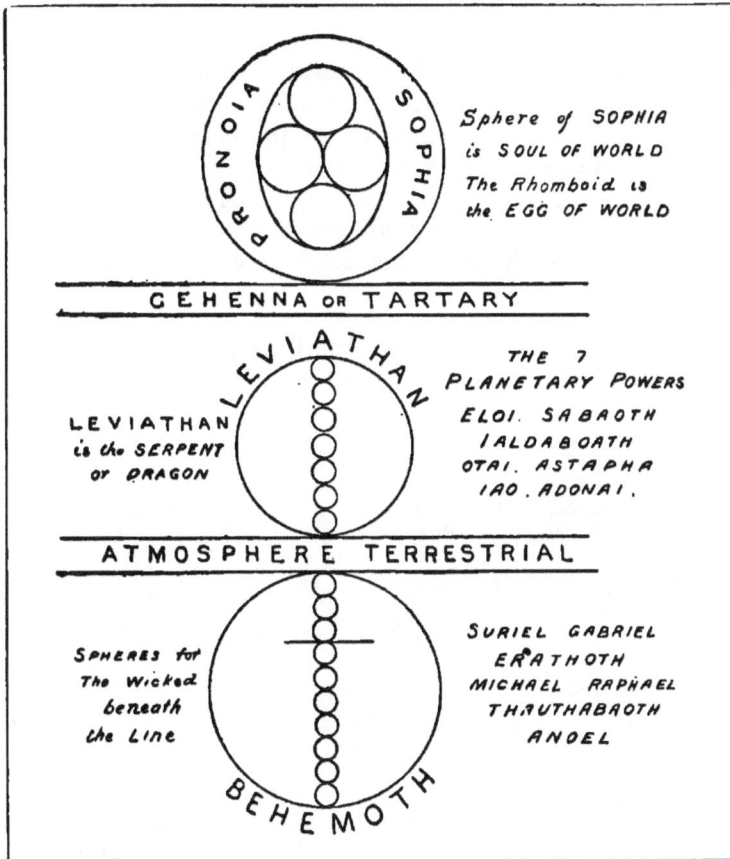

The mythology of those figures proves that they represent the
Soul of the world.

The present diagram includes a rough delineation of that
mythic region: it must therefore be a map of America. In
this diagram the Egg of the world is the internal part of
North America, and consequently the domicile of the red
men. This reasoning is strongly confirmed by the other parts
of the map. Mexico and the Serpent land are called Levia-
than or the dragon. The several provinces of Central America
are the seven planetary powers, and South America figures

for what it will afterwards be shown to be—the land of demons.

The subject of the Egg of the world is one that perhaps may be elucidated better by pictures than by words. This symbolism must have been common in ancient times, as it appears in innumerable instances, in the monuments of antiquity. In the Abraxas gems, it is a prevailing figure, and it is found, with great frequency, in mythological designs, as for instance, when it forms the bracelet of Hermione in the marriage of Cadmus. Two pictures are here given, as illustrative of the symbolism.

GNOSTIC GEM.   HINDOO PRAN.

The first picture has the Egg enclosed within the folds of a serpent. Animals of various sorts are visible in the Egg. It is dominated by a Savage, with all the marks of fury, violence and self-mortification. In view of the teaching of the present chapter, the scene presents the North American

M

Indian to the letter.   But he is in a state of Savagery, unimproved, uneducated, and addicted to barbarous customs.

The second figure is an Old Hindoo picture, and it presents an exceedingly lively conception of the subject.   The Egg appears again, and the Serpent winds round it, as it does in the other picture.   But instead of wild beasts, the Egg is girt round by a Zodiac, an emblem of high civilization.   The Egg is dominated, not by a savage, but by an astronomer,—a well-dressed man in the habiliments of civilized life.   If the former picture exhibits North America, in its incipient savagery, the present scene shews it to be under the influence of a humanising reformation.

But who is the character that dominates the Egg?   He is here termed Pran.   This is the second picture that has been given with that name.   If the reader will refer to the Third Chapter, p. 26, he will find a copy of the Zodiac, which must have been taken from a Mexican Zodiac, and called by that name Pran.   But the character carries the wings of the European Mercury.   When the subject advances to the consideration of Mexican antiquities, it will be found, that this personage is Quetzalcoatl himself, the Mercury of Europe, in Mexico.   But when Pran is put into his proper place in history, and compared with the same figure in other nations, he proves himself to be the civilizer, the inventor of arts, and the religious teacher of the old world.

It is impossible to notice, thoughtfully, the symbolism of the present chapter, without deducing from it inferences which bear more or less distinctly upon what may be called the Chronology of Antiquity.   Upon the common teaching of ancient history, it is natural to term the continent of America the new hemisphere, and to treat Asia, Europe, and Africa, as the arena of the earliest races of men, and the rise and consolidation of the oldest Empires.   But if the muses of history, in gathering up the fragmentary traditions of an earlier world, have been constrained to call the Oceanic hemisphere the Egg of the World and its Soul, the philosophical historian must pause,— recast his theories, and readjust his conceptions of Anthropology and the vast past.

CHAPTER VIII.

THE WORLD IS FULL OF TRADITIONS OF MARITIME SETTLE-
MENTS, WHICH, IN THE LIGHT OF THE ZODIACAL MAPS, MUST
BE LOCATED IN AMERICA.

All the nations of the old continent are in possession of
mysterious traditions, that relate to the intercourse between
the two hemispheres in high antiquity: but, in consequence
of the supposed loss of the Atlantic Isle, they have either
been unnoticed, or they have been misapplied to wrong
countries. It now becomes necessary to collect and examine
those traditions in the light of the present maps. But, before
that course is taken, it will be advantageous to collate the
native American traditions, which bear upon the arrival of
strangers in their lands.

Prescott, in his conquest of Peru, observes that "there is a
tradition, that the Sun sent two of his children, Manco Capac
and Mama Oello, to gather the natives into communities, and to
teach them the arts of civilized life." Brasseur de Bourbourg,
in his Histoire des Nations Mexiques, gives a Chippeway
tradition, that "they came from a distant country, west,
chased by the wicked. They passed through a long lake, full
of islands and ice." Again, speaking of Votan, the most
ancient of the American legislators, he says, that "Votan
wrote an account of the Indians and their emigrations," and
then adds, "they descended from Imos, who is of the race
of Chan, the Serpent, who drew his origin from Chivim.
His memory was held in reverence as Lord of the Sacred
Tambour." Adelung, in his Mithridates, gives a Natchez
tradition, of "a man who came from the Sun, whom they
made chief." Brinton, in his myths of the red men, says,
that "the Algonkins call their tribes living east, Abnakes—
our white ancestors." He also says of the Iroquois, that they
say, "they had two brothers Joskebha and Tawiscara, twins,
born of a Virgin." At p. 188, he says, "the last Inca was
told by his father, that the Viracochas—white men, would
come from their father the Sun, and subject them." Mr.
Brinton observes that "the central figure of Toltec mythology
is Quetzalcoatl, God of air and highest deity of the Toltecs,

in whose honour the Pyramid of Cholula was built. He was son of a Virgin in the land of Tula, of which happy realm he was High Priest. The morning Star was his emblem. He was white and clothed in a long white robe, like most of the Aztec Gods."

Commenting on these traditions, it may be observed, that they distinctly prove, that the natives, in many parts of America, North and South, considered themselves to have had among them foreigners,—white men from beyond the Pacific Ocean. They especially refer their civilization to the Sun. According to modern customs, this sort of language seems ridiculous; but, according to the habits of the old world, it can be understood. The ancients distinguished themselves by crests and banners rather than by names. It is Japan, which, by its national Heraldry, is the rising Sun. Its flag is a red sun on a white disk, and it is remarkable, that this emblazonment is exactly the same as the Heraldic head dress of the God Neph in Egypt, shewing that Neph, the Latin Neptune, is identical with Niphon, the proper name of Japan. The mention of sacred tambours points to Lapland, because the magic tambour is a superstition peculiar to that country.

The enumeration of the traditions found among the Asiatic, African, and European nations, which must be associated with an early colonization of America, may naturally begin with Japan. The American traditions themselves point in that direction. Japan is not only a maritime country, but it lies opposite the western coast of North America.

These is nothing so strong to keep alive the recollection of signal national events, in the history of a country, as religious observances. This remark, in a special manner, applies to Japan. In one of the Pagodas, there is a remarkable monument where the Bull of agriculture is pourtrayed in the act of ripping up the Egg. It might not be easy to see the meaning of that act; but, in the light of the last chapter, where North America has been shown to be the Egg of the world, it becomes quite manifest that the ripping up of the Egg, must be taken to mean the discovery and colonization of that land. But the tradition, itself, may be read with advantage. "The Bull is upon a large square altar and is of massive gold. It

JAPANESE BULL AND EGG.

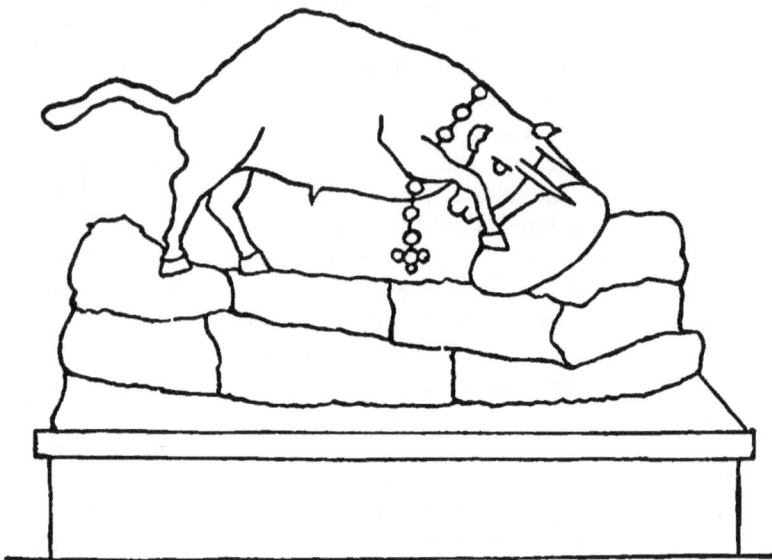

carries a very rich collar, but this is not the object of our attention. It is this Egg, which he gores with his horns holding it with his two feet. The Bull is upon a piece of rock and the Egg in water enclosed in the hollow of the rock. The Egg represents Cahos, and here comment the Doctors of Japan explaining the emblem. The entire world, at the time of Cahos, was enclosed in the Egg which swam upon the face of the waters. The moon, by the force of its light and by its influences, drew from the bottom of the waters an earthy matter, which consolidated itself, insensibly, and there the Egg stopped. The Bull finding the Egg, broke it up, and out of it came the world."

In the Japanese mythology and traditions, it is expressly said, that "Jebis, who is called the Neptune of Japan," and who must have been a very important personage, inasmuch as he is the brother of the God Tenzio, "was sent away to another Island." Where that Island was, can be confidently decided from a very curious picture, which is printed in Picard's great work on national religions.

KURMA AVATARA OF VISHNU.

JAPANESE CREATOR OF UNIVERSE.

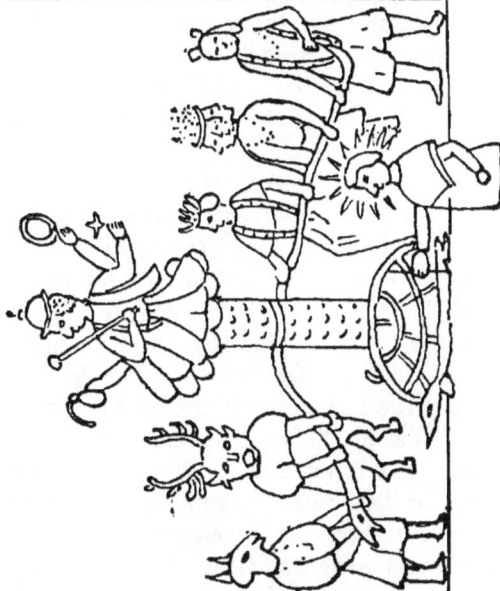

This picture is described as follows: A human figure is seated on the Capstan of a Ship. He has 4 arms holding emblems. An enormous Serpent is wound round the Capstan. Two horrid looking figures, a dog-man and a stag-man, pull the Serpent rope. The demigods of Japan have hold of the other end of the rope, pulling it. A figure which represents the Sun is in the water.

There can be no reasonable doubt, that, in this historical picture the Japanese have preserved the recollection of a former navigation of the Pacific Ocean. The navigation must have been to America, because there are demons at the other end of the rope. In the Coptic map, the Regnum demonium is the designation of the western shores of South America. It must have been a joint enterprise. In this picture, the reference to the Sun, as having sent his son to the Peruvians, receives a lively illustration.

It is most interesting to find that this Japanese picture has an exact fac simile, among the pictures which the Sages of India possess of the Avataras or Incarnations of the blue God Vishnu. A copy of it is here given for comparison. There is hardly any difference between the scenes; because the seven headed horse of the Hindoo design answers to the figure of the Sun in that of the Japanese, inasmuch as the seven headed horse is emblematical of the sun in the Hindoo system. It is driven by Surya the Sun God.

The two pictures together are most suggestive. One asks with surprise, how it could be possible for nations so far apart as Japan and India, to have the same picture among their national collections? If they are copies of the same scene, which is the original and which the copy? One thing is plain, namely, that the Hindoo picture is the most instructive. It has been already shown, that Vishnu is the Oceanus of Antiquity, and embodies the Indian conception of America. In the Kurma Avatara of Vishnu, "the Gods and the demons (the vast serpent Vasuky serving as a rope), churn the Ocean, to recover the Amrita or beverage of Immortality." Putting these circumstances together, the conclusion is inevitable, that both Japan and India have traditions of a navigation of the Pacific Ocean, in which the Asiatic nations and the natives of America

have joined. It is the Serpent in the scenes, which locates the
story. That reptile is the constellation which pourtrays the
western shores of North America; so that the settlement
formed by the navigation, must have been in that spot.

There is every reason to believe, that the traditions now given,
from Japan and India, have their counterpart in the European
myths of Ceres and Proserpine, and the rape of Proserpine,
by Pluto. This is seen by the resemblance between the
dramatis personæ. In the Asiatic stories, the Gods and the
demons join in the enterprise. In the myths of Europe,
Ceres, the Goddess of harvests, stands for the Gods, and
Pluto for the demons.

It is natural to put Ceres in Sicily, but that is manifestly
a mistake which gets corrected by the Zodiacal maps. As the
scientific professor, to shew the power of the magnet, throws
a lot of rubbish on the table and then holds the magnet
over it, to attract what iron filings are present, so the
Zodiacal maps adapted to the countries of the globe, attract
to themselves the traditions of all nations, and give them
a geographical localization.

In Poetical Astronomy, the Virgo carries the name of Ceres.
That important and extended sign, delineates the great land
of China. To put Ceres in Sicily, is late mythology, but to
put her into China, at this early time, places her in a position
fit for her grand maternity. Mr. Christie, in his work on
Etruscan Vases, has shown how the Eleusinian Mysteries are
explained by the Chinese feast of lanterns. "The Phantas-
magoria," he says, "delineated on the vases, represent the
histories of the Chinese in all lands."

As to Proserpine, Dupuis in his Treatise on the origin of
the constellations, has the following remarks on the figure
of the Crown, the sign which with the Serpent pourtrays the
west coast of America. "Above the Serpentarius is Coronus,—
in Chaldean Per-sephon. Sephon means North. The Greeks
call it Persephon. Our astronomy has only Pher Corona
Ornamentum capitis.—Mithra. Nonnus gives it as an ornament of Proserpine. Sephon is the name of Proserpine, in the
Argonauts of Orpheus. The name Sephon is part of Bel
Sephon. Sephon is the Arabic name of Janus or Bootes,—

ancient Atlas. In Arabic, it also has the name of Phatta; so Pher-phatta, another name of Proserpine among the Greeks. She has also the name of Coree. Coree is the name of the Crown of Ariadne, wife of Bacchus."

There can be no doubt whatever, that the traditions concerning Proserpine, belong to America, for an extract has already been given, from the well known fragment of Marcellus. Speaking of the Atlantic Islands, he says, that "in their times, there were seven islands situated in that sea, which were sacred to Persephone, and three others of an immense magnitude, one of which was consecrated to Pluto."

Having now located both Ceres and Proserpine, the myth relating to them is transcribed, in short. "Ceres, the goddess of corn and harvests, was daughter of Saturn and Vesta. She had a daughter by Jupiter, whom she called Phere-phatta and afterwards Proserpine. Proserpine was carried away by Pluto, as she was gathering flowers in the plains near Enna. The rape of Proserpine was grievous to Ceres, who sought her all over Sicily, and when night came on, she lighted two torches in the flames of Mount Etna, to continue her search, by night, all over the world. At last the Nymph Arethusa informed her that her daughter had been carried away by Pluto. On this, she flies to heaven on her dragon chariot, and Jupiter promised the restoration of her daughter, if she had not eaten anything in the kingdom of Pluto: but Proserpine had eaten the grains of a pomegranate, which she had gathered as she walked over the Elysian fields, and Ascalaphus, the only one who had seen her, discovered it, to make his court to Pluto. The return of Proserpine, therefore, upon earth, was impracticable: but Ascalaphus for his unsolicited information, was changed into an owl. The grief of Ceres for the loss of her daughter was so great, that Jupiter granted Proserpine to pass six months with her mother and the rest of the year with Pluto. She is the same as the Isis of the Egyptians, and is supposed to be the same as Rhea, Tellus, Cybele, Bona Dea, Berecynthia, &c."

This myth contains internal evidence, that it is not some story of a Sicilian woman, that had a daughter carried away; but that it is the damaged remains of some great history

N

belonging not to the Mediterranean Sea, but to the great Asiatic
nations of antiquity, and embodies in itself national movements, by which the western shores of North and South
America were colonized, in high antiquity, by Chinese and
Mongolidan races. Ceres is a form of the great mother of
the Gods, with emblems of the Chinese dragon. Her daughter
is a colony from the mother country. A nymph that is an
Oceanide, reveals to her its localization; and Ascalaphus is
manifestly the Mexican God, Tesculipaca, who will hereafter
be identified as Esculapius—the Serpent God. Nay! prominent
among the Mexican deities, Ceres herself appears. She is
Tonacacique, whose picture stands first in the collection of Lord
Kingsborough. Her colour is Mongolidan. She is seated on
a Chinese stool. She has on her head the turreted crown
of Cybele. She is the only Goddess crowned. She is called
the Seven Serpents, so that she embodies in herself the
constellation of the Serpent, and carries on her head the
Seven Serpents, so that she embodies in herself, the
constellation of the crown.

Perhaps the greatest objection that can be made to the
present argument affects navigation. It may be said, that
in ancient works, there is no mention made of the navigation of the Pacific. Let a collation of quotations be
made. Orpheus makes Pluto carry Proserpine across the
sea. In Emeric David's work on Neptune, the author
shews, that Neptune was the horse, which carried Ceres on
his back. At page 8, he says, "Ceres, who is Terra, took the
form of a mare, to avoid Neptune: so he became a horse
and had a daughter whose name is unknown, and Arion.
He was nourished in the Stables of the Nereids, and went into
the hands of Oncus." At page 20, he says, "The Nereids are
in the Stables of Ocean." Nonnus makes Ceres attach her
dragons to her car and she goes away with her daughter
to sea. There she hides her daughter in a cave, and con-
fides her to dragons. Again, Ceres was a Cabiric deity. She
was Demeter in heaven, and Ceres Chthonia upon Earth, receiving in her bosom the bodies of the dead and decomposing
them to be formed anew. Pluto remained in the inferior
hemisphere. He never changed. Proserpine is the representa-

tive of Souls descending to Enfer and returning from Enfer to the light again. Mercury was the Servitor. He conducted the Souls to Enfer and back."

It must be noticed that these extracts relate to what must be called the northern route, that is to say, the route by the Crown. In Poetical Astronomy, there is a Southern route, hanging on to the Libra. The Scales perform the same part as the Crown. They, too, constitute a sort of flying bridge. Sometimes they are in the hands of Virgo, and sometimes they hang on to the folds of Scorpio. The same process of Souls descending and being regenerated and then returning to Virgo is described. In Zoroastrian books this navigation is called the Tchinavar bridge. These two routes, together, constitute the navigation of the Pacific in the mythic ages. Of course they are mythic: but the concealed histories included in them are too manifest to escape detection.

The hypothesis that Pre or Proserpine is indicative of a Chinese colonization of the west shores of America, is sustained by a reference to the old Hindoo map of the world, given in the second chapter of this volume, page 8. On reference, it will be seen that the Hindoo artists have put both the words Para and Parvam, on the Eastern limits of the country, which occupies the place of China. Supposing the Chinese to have colonized America, in the name of Pre, it makes Proserpine to be a daughter of Ceres, a daughter colony from a motherland.

However that may be, it is observable that the Egyptians have in their legends and pictures, the identical navigation now described, and in the same name. This is seen in the accompanying picture, which is called the boat of Phre. It may be observed, that the form of the boat bears great resemblance to a Peruvian raft, as given in works relating to that country, having the rudder in the like position. The details of the naval scene, shew that it belongs to the history comprised in the mythology of Proserpine. It is said to relate to the ritual of the dead, which, in the Greek system, is the service of Proserpine. A ghost kneels in the fore part of the vessel, giving honour to the divine hawk, that is to say, to Phre, who is the captain of the ship—a harpy or man-bird. The names of the passengers are given.

The Boat of Phre.

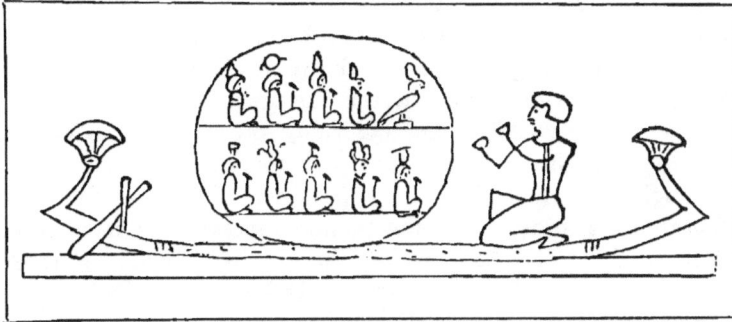

They are Atmou, Soon, Tafne, Seb, Netpe, Osiris, Horus
Isis and Nephtys.   An Egyptologist will notice that these
passengers constitute the Amenti Gods and Goddesses.   They
are on their passage to Amenti.   It is true, that that country,
wherever it was, is put in the west: but a more accurate
knowledge of the structure of the globe than the ancients had,
explains that it is accessible also from the East.

The Egyptians, in addition to the navigation of Phre, have
a large number of pictures, which represent the Asiatic races,
in their descent to what must now be called America.

Tiphe.   Urania.   Cœlum.

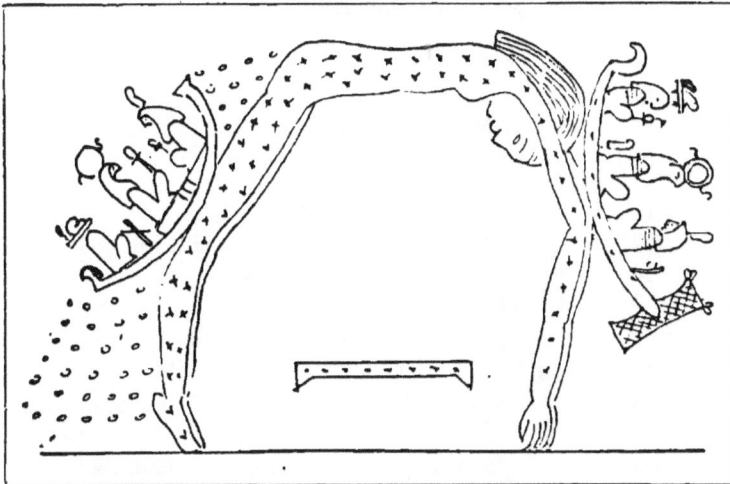

One of them is here given as a specimen. This scene is even more significant and explanatory than the boat of Phre. It is called Tiphe, and glossed by Urania and Cœlum. The human figure that gives form to the vault of heaven · is Urania, the heavenly Venus, who in the classics is transformed into a serpent, or as it is sometimes said, into the Marine Venus. The scene might be taken for an astronomical sign, as it is bespangled by stars: but the appearance of two vessels, full of passengers, proves that the picture represents a navigation upon Earth. The boat is on its way to Tiphe. Further research will reveal the country of Tiphe, as the Copts have in their Zodiacal map given the name of Typhon to both North and South America. Thus the scene is plainly indicative of an Asiatic colonization of America.

The same navigation to America, is apparent in the Deluge tablet, unearthed from the subterranean palace of Assyria.

1. I will reveal the concealed story,
2. The city Surrippak, God's city
3. Ana, Bel, Ninip, Lord of Hades,
4. Surrapakite, son of Ubaratutu.
5. Made a great ship, for thee,
6. Hea, my lord, I will perform it,
7. It was 14 measures, with roof and Altars,
8. Panizu, the pilot.
9. Silver, gold, seeds and beasts,
10. A flood, Shamas made.
11. I entered the ship,
12. Buzzursadiribi the pilot,
13. Vul, thundered in the storm,
14. Nebo and Saru went in front.
15. The destroyer Nergal, overturned
16. Ninip went in front, swept the Earth,
17. The Gods feared the tempest, and sought refuge
18. Then ascended to the heaven of Anu
19. Ishtar spake, &c.

Later studies will shew, that this ship went to South America.

The navigation traced in this chapter, is visibly pourtrayed in the Ptolemaic Zodiac, in the constellation of the Ship Argo, which when reduced to localization, must be put in the Erythrean Sea. It is a large, handsome, well equipped ship, with a compass nailed to the mast head. This ship and its uses have been very much misunderstood. It forms a very important feature in the historical antiquities of Asia, and it has a very large number of myths connected with it. But the subject can be better understood, in connection with Asia, than with America. It is sufficient here to refer to it. There are other traditions, which shew that the Asiatic races have colonized America, in ages past; but this enumeration of them is held sufficient to establish the fact itself. The Scandinavian and Russian traditions, will appear in the next chapter, and those of Persia, in the chapter on the Crown.

CHAPTER IX.

The Geography of Ancient America and its Asiatic Settlements lie concealed in the Icelandic and Scandinavian Mythology.

The settlements which must have been formed in prehistoric America, in connection with the navigation described in the last chapter, are best elucidated by Scandinavian Sagas. Before, therefore, the histories of America which have been transmitted by classical authors are introduced, it is necessary to study the Northern legends.

It may be said, that mythology is history in disguise. In the prose Edda, that doctrine is distinctly stated. The work is called "the deluding of Gylfi." King Gylfi, of Svithiod, was amused with a parcel of funny stories, dressed up in all the vulgarity peculiar to rough sea-faring people, and they read like the adventures of individual men. But, when the acknowledged delusion is removed, and the stories are put into comparison with the traditions of other nations, it is found that they form a Cosmogony, second to none in the Ancient World. Its heroes swell into histories,— its Gods into

nationalities,—its journeys into migrations; and it becomes
a Gazetteer of the old world's geography. Instead of being
limited to Iceland and Sweden, it contains in it an allusion
to America.

America figures in the Prose Edda, as the land of the
Giants. This appears in the story of Thor's adventures, on
his journey to the land of the Giants. He and his companions
"proceeded Eastward, on the road to Jötunheim, until they
came to the shores of a vast and deep sea, which having
passed over, they penetrated into a strange country." This
must have been America, because there is no other great and
deep Sea, eastward of Scandinavia and Russia than the
Pacific. This is in accord with the Classics, where the Giants,
the Titans, and the Aloids locate in the same land. In this
tradition, the land is called Jötunheim. the home of the Jötnes.

It is in the tradition called the "Origin of the Hrimthursar,
or frost giants, that North America is described. After speaking of the formation of the rime, Har says, "That part of
Ginnungagap that lies toward the north, was thus filled with
heavy masses of gelid vapour and ice, whilst every where
within were whirlwinds and fleeting mists. But the southern
part of Ginnungagap, was lighted by the sparks and flakes,
that flew into it from Muspellheim." The being that was
formed by this process, was Ymir; but the frost giants call
him Örgelmir. From him descend the race of the Hrimthursar.

Now, it will be shown, in the chapter on the Mound cities,
that Ymir, the Giant, is Hercules in an earlier form; so that
Ginnungagap must be the name, by which North America
was known to the ancient Icelanders. Then it is said that
the sons of Bör dragged the body of Ymir into the middle
of Ginnungagap, and of it, formed the earth and heaven. It
is also observed that they were themselves descended from the
frost giants, and that is mentioned as the reason why they
were strong. From this it may be gathered that the Rime
giants were Greenlanders or Esquimaux, or races in the high
North of America who had crossed the Atlantic at an early
period and formed an element in the Icelandic and Norwegian
population. This is called "the mingling of the races."

Another piece of geography is in the myth of the supreme deity, where it is said, that "all that are righteous shall dwell with him in the place called Gimli, or Vingolf; but the wicked shall go to Hel and thence to Niflhel which is below, in the Ninth World." Gimli is uncertain, but, in a future chapter, Hel and Niflhel will be shown to locate in the great forests of the region of the Ohio and Miami, and which must have been the area of the Empire of Saturn, in the earthworks, which must once have constituted the domicile of the race of Cronus and Hercules in the underground hemisphere.

Mention is also made of a place called Muspellheim. "But the southern part of Ginnungagap was lighted by the sparks and flakes that flew into it, from Muspellheim." There is nothing said, that serves to locate Muspellheim; but the description of it is sufficient to shew, that while Niflheim is intended for the northern part of the region, at present constituting the United States of America, Muspellheim completes the geography as forming the Southern part of the same great country.

This is sufficient for the present, as it serves as an introduction to the valuable legend of Loki and his progeny. "There is another deity," continued Har, "reckoned in the number of the Æsir, whom some call the calumniator of the Gods, the contriver of all mischief and fraud, and 'the disgrace of Gods and men. His name is Loki or Loptur. He is the son of the Giant Farbauti. His mother is Laufey or Nal. His, brothers are Byleist and Helblindi. Loki is handsome and well-made; but of a fickle mood and most evil disposition.—His wife is called Siguna and their son Nari. Loki has likewise three children by Angurbodi a giantess of Jötunheim. The first is the wolf Fenrir,—the second Jormungand, the Midgard Serpent,—the third Hela. The Gods were not ignorant, that these monsters continued to be bred up in Jötunheim, and having had recourse to divination, became aware of all the evils they would have to suffer, from them.— All—father therefore deemed it advisable to send one of the Gods to bring them to him. When they came, he threw the Serpent into that deep Ocean, by which the Earth is engirdled. But the monster has grown to such a size, that, holding his tail in his mouth, he encircles the whole Earth.

Hela he cast into Neflheim, and gave her power over nine worlds (regions) into which, she distributed those who are sent to her, that is to say, all who die through sickness or old age. Here she possesses a habitation, protected by exceedingly high walls, and strongly barred gates. Her hall is called Elvidner, hunger is her table,—starvation her knife,—delay her man,—slowness her maid. The one half of her body is livid,—the other half the colour of human flesh. She may, therefore, be easily recognised,—the more so, as she has a dreadfully stern and grim countenance. The wolf Fenrir was bred up among the Gods, but Tyr alone had the daring to go and feed him."

It is quite safe to treat this tradition as a deluding story, which contains in it great histories, which must have taken place in times of high antiquity, by which America was colonized by Asiatic races; and the three children of Loki represent three great centres of colonization in that land. Odin manages it. Who is Odin? As the myth says, he is All-Father—the great colossal deity of the Eastern world.

On the principle of this treatise, two of the settlements can be located with accuracy. The serpent and the wolf are in the Zodiacal map. The first delineates Mexico,—say, the western shores of America, and the wolf pourtrays the upper waters of the Amazon—call it for want of a better name, Peru. Hela may, for the present, be put into the great woods of the red men. These three characters have to be compared with the three Gorgons of the Classics. One of them is plain. The Medusa, with Serpents for hair, is equivalent to the Midgard Serpent. The wolf answers to Euryale, and Hela to Stheno. They may also be compared with the three judges of the infernal regions, Sarpedon, Minos and Rhadamanthus. As the Icelandic legend is much the most geographical, it will form the basis of the localizations of future chapters.

The tradition of Loki and his progeny, receives great light from some of the Russian songs. Mr. Ralston, in his work on the Songs of the Russian People, at p. 106, speaking of the demigods and fairies, says, "When Satan and all his hosts were expelled from heaven, some spirits fell into the lowest recesses of the underground world, where they remain, in the shape of Karliki, or dwarfs. Some were received by woods, as Lychie, like the Faunes and Satyrs." At p. 107, the author observes, "After death, the soul had to begin a long journey to sail across a wide sea. A road led to the other world. Sometimes it was a rainbow or the milky way. The abode of death had three names—the house of the sun, lying eastward beyond the Ocean." Further on, he refers to the many-headed Snake. "A hero penetrated into the castle of the snake, and conquered him."

Commenting upon these songs and their resemblance to the traditions of Loki, it may be noticed, that the simple hardening of the *ch* in the word Lychie, brings the two names together, in identity, as if they were ethnological and real. Satan here mentioned may be supposed to be Saitan, God of the Barabinsky. It has already been observed that Loki must have gone to America, as he passed over a wide Ocean in the East. Here is exactly the like movement. Then, these spirits become dwarfs and faunes and satyrs. The two last have been shown to embody the North American Indians. The first remain to be discovered. The many-headed Snake has shown his horrid fangs. His capture awaits study.

This fitly introduces the history of America, and it will be worked out, not by writers of myths, but by real historians, of Sicily and Phœnicia.

CHAPTER X.

THE HISTORY OF THE ATLANTIC ISLE, BY DIODORUS SICULUS, AND THE COSMOGONY OF SANCONIATHON, ARE THE HISTORIES OF THOSE ASIATIC COLONIES IN AMERICA, REFERRED TO IN THE LAST CHAPTERS.

Let the threads of evidence now be caught up, by way of recapitulation. The course of enquiry has disclosed the fact, that America is depicted in ancient maps. Among the Mediterranean nations it was mystically called Oceanus. By

Oriental writers, it was called Mount Caf. Among the Sages of India, it was designated Sweta dwipa and Suvarna, where resided Vishnu, the Hindoo Water God, who is both in name and nature identical with the European Oceanus.

It has been further proved that the vast Insular hemisphere has been called the Atlantic Isle, the domicile of a race called Oceanides, or Nymphs. Among these Oceanides are the Titans, the chief of whom are the Atlantides, a race that has undeniably mixed itself largely with the histories of the old continent. This race carries the name of a mythic character that stands out prominently, in history, as an Astronomer, who invented Zodiacs. By some extraordinary blunder, this Isle has been supposed to have sunk, and with it have sunk the histories of by far the larger part of the antiquities of the world.

By a course of sharp investigation and reasoning on myths and symbolism, the only sort of writing handed down from high antiquity, it has been further discovered, that this Isle has been visited and colonized by Asiatics, who must have come in Japanese and other vessels. It now remains to be seen, whether there are any histories or descriptions of these colonies, extant among the writings of the ancients themselves, either in the form of simple narrative, or in that of allegory, as common to all nations. The present chapter will be limited to the acknowledged documents of the learned.

This new enquiry is full of interest, inasmuch as it discloses the fact that two very important historical documents, which no one has ever been able to understand, contain the identical information now sought. The first is no less than an actual history of the Atlantic Isle itself, written by an acknowledged historian, Diodorus Siculus, and setting forth in plain language, that it belongs to that Island. But for the theory of the Sunken Isle, this document must have been always taken for the history of America. The second is what is termed the Cosmogony of Sanconiathon. This paper, being the Cosmogony of the Phœnicians, might be treated otherwise; but its internal contents prove it to be a similar history to the other.

It is remarkable, that these two documents are written neither by Romans nor Greeks, yet the details of both the histories and the names that appear in them, are the same as those which constitute the Theogonies of both those learned nations: so that there can be no reasonable doubt, that they are based upon facts well known to all nations. It is to be observed that the personages mentioned in them are neither obscure, nor unknown names; on the contrary, they belong to the highest rank of mythic beings, well known to European writers.

In the transcription of these interesting documents, it is not necessary to give them verbatim, partly because they are both very confused, and partly because they are overlaid with interpolations. The parts which belong to America are uncomfortably mingled with what appertains to the old continent. A succinct Epitome, with a slight comment, will most conduce to edification.

ATLANTIS, FROM DIODORUS SICULUS.

The Atlantides inhabited a rich country, bordering upon the Ocean, and were esteemed to excel all their neighbours, in civil reception and entertainment of strangers; and they boast, that the Gods were born among them, and say, that the most famous poet among the Greeks confirms this their assertion, when he brings in Juno speaking thus

> "The utmost bounds of Earth, far off, I see
> "Where Tethys and Ocean, boast to be,
> "The parents of the Gods."

They say, that Uranus was their first king, who caused the people, who then wandered up and down, to dwell in towns and cities, and reducing them from a lawless and savage course of life, taught them to use and lay up the fruits of the earth and many other things useful for man's life. It is said, he had under his dominion, the greatest part of the world, especially towards the west, and the northern parts. And that, being much addicted to Astronomy, he prognosticated many things that were come to pass in the world, and measured the year, according to the course of the sun, and the months, according to the motion of the moon, and divided the days into hours, and therefore the people, as at that time ignorant of the constant motion of the stars, did so admire his prognostications, that it grew into a common opinion among them, that he was a God: and when he was dead, by reason of his deserts and art in Astronomy, they honoured him as a God.

The starry heavens were called after his name, because that he was so familiarly acquainted with the rising and setting of the stars and other things happening in the Ethereal world, and for that, his memory had all the honours that could be attributed to him; he was called the Eternal King of the Universe.

They report that this Uranus had forty-five children by several wives, and eighteen of these were by one Titea, who, for her benevolence and wisdom was, after her death, reported a Goddess, and called Terra. Of Uranus and Titea, were born several daughters, of whom two were most famous, Basilea and Rhea, by some called Pandora. Basilea, being the eldest, bred up her brothers with the care and affection of a mother, and therefore was called the Great Mother.

After the death of her father, by the general suffrage of the people and consent of her brothers, she was elected Queen, being as yet a Virgin and remarkable for her modesty and chastity. She was long unwilling to marry; but afterwards desiring to leave heirs of her own body, to succeed in the kingdom, she married Hyperion, one of her brothers, whom she most dearly loved, by whom she had two children, Helio and Selene, who for their beauty and modesty, were the admiration of all her other brothers. They say, partly out of envy at the issue and partly out of fear, lest Hyperion should assume the kingdom entirely to himself, they committed a notorious act; for entering into a conspiracy, they assassinated Hyperion, and drowned Helio, then a tender infant, in Eridanus.

Upon the discovery of this disaster, Selene, who passionately loved her brother, threw herself down headlong from the house top, and the mother, while she was seeking for her son at the river side, dreamed that she saw Helio standing by her, to comfort her, and wished her not to grieve too much for the death of her children, for the Titans should execute dire revenge upon the malefactors, and that he and her sister, by the providence of the Gods, were to be deified; so that which was before called "the holy fire in heaven," should be

then called Helios, and that which before, had the name of
Mene, should then be termed Selene.

Presently, afterwards, in a furious rage of madness, she
wandered up and down, with her hair dishevelled about her
ears, and playing like a mad woman, upon a timbril and
cymbal, she was even a terror to the spectators. And while
everybody pitied her miserable condition, there arose on a
sudden a terrible storm of rain, thunder and lightning, and
she was seen no more. The people, hereupon, admiring the
prodigy, began to transfer the name of Helios and Selene (in
honour of them) to the Sun and Moon, in the heavens, and
being persuaded that the mother was a goddess, they erected
altars, and with the noise of timbrils and tinkling of cymbals
offered sacrifice and instituted other divine rites and ceremonies in honour of her.

The writer then identifies Selene with Cybele, in Phrygia.
As this passage does not belong to the history, it may be
omitted.

After the death of Hyperion, they report that the children
of Cælus divided the kingdom among them. Atlas and Saturn
were the most renowned. The country bordering the Ocean
fell by lot to Atlas, who called the people there, Atlantides, and
the greatest mountain in the world, after his own name. They
say, that he was an excellent astrologer, and was the first
that discovered the knowledge of the sphere, whereon arose
the common opinion, that he carried the world upon his
shoulders, noting by this fancy, his invention and description
of the sphere. The most eminent among his sons was Hesperus,
for piety towards the Gods and justice and kindness towards
his subjects. Being upon the top of Mount Atlas, to observe
the motion of the stars, he suddenly vanished in a tempest.
The people, thereupon, much lamenting the loss of him, that
they might for ever honour him, called the brightest star
in the heavens after his name. Atlas likewise had seven
daughters, who were all called after their father's name,
Atlantides: but their several proper names were Maia, Electra,
Taygete, Asterope, Merope, Alcyone and Celœno. All these
were got with child by several heroic princes, and even by
some of the Gods themselves, and bore divers sons, who

were the first ancestors of several nations, and for their virtuous qualifications, were afterwards called Gods and demigods. So Maia, the eldest, was got with child by Jupiter, and bore Mercury, the inventor of many arts and sciences, for the use of mankind. All the rest, likewise, had sons, who were famous in their times, some of which gave beginning to whole nations,—others to some particular cities, and therefore, not only some of the Barbarians but likewise some among the Greeks, refer the original of many of the ancient heroes to these daughters of Atlas; for they were in great reputation for wisdom and justice, and therefore, when they were dead, were adored as Goddesses and fixed in the constellation of the Pleiades.

Nymphs were commonly called Atlantides, because Nymphs is a general term in this country, applied to all women.

They say, that Saturn, the brother of Atlas, was profane and married his sister Rhea. He had Jupiter (Olympus). There was another king of Crete, inferior to the latter. The ancient Jupiter was only king of Crete and father of ten sons— Curetes, and called the name of the Island Ida, after the name of his wife.

Saturn reigned over Sicily, Africa and Italy, and enlarged his dominions over all the western parts of the world, and by garrisons and strong forts, kept his subjects: so in Italy they were called Cronia.

Jupiter, they say, was the son of Saturn, who, contrary to what his father did before him, carried himself justly and courteously towards all, and therefore he was called father by all his subjects. He succeeded to the kingdom, either as given up to him by his father, or set upon the throne by his subjects, out of hatred to his father. And though Saturn afterwards, by the help of the Titans, made · war upon his son, yet Jupiter overcame him in a battle, and so gained the kingdom, and because he was of a strong body and endowed with all virtuous qualifications of mind, he easily conquered the whole world. He chiefly made it his business to punish the impious and to do good to all his people. And, therefore, after he left the world he was called Zena (Zeus) from life, because he was the first that taught men to live well, and therefore, they, of whom he had done well, rewarded him with their honour, that he was unanimously by all, placed in the highest heavens, and called a God and Supreme Lord of all the Earth. And this is the full account distinctly related, of all the Gods mentioned and recorded by the Atlantides.

Here is a history of America. It will be noticed, that Diodorus expressly identifies Oceanus with the Atlantis; and he quotes an Homeric verse to prove it. It is a rich country in the Ocean. Until the appearance of one Uranus, the people are savages, wandering up and down in a lawless life, destitute of agriculture. To suppose that histories so important as those narrated in the document, belonged to some island in the Atlantic that sunk and disappeared, is the height of improbability, not to say, impossibility. When applied to America, one of the largest and most beautiful parts of the habitable globe, it opens up one of the noblest and grandest chapters in human history. It restores to its proper place in the antiquities of the world, one of the fairest portions of God's earth.

The details of this history will be considered elsewhere. The general scope of them, belongs to matters and names that are quite common in the ancient literature, both of Europe and Asia. So much so indeed, is that the case, that it becomes the main impediment to its understanding, Accustomed to treat the great characters mentioned, as appertaining to Europe, it requires some effort of mind, to adjust them to their proper country. Taken as a whole, the story exhibits the American races as having received among them, the blood of Asiatic people, and in the course of ages, the joint races have migrated into the old continent and laid the basis of the modern world.

THE COSMOGONY OF SANCONIATHON.

The Cosmogony of Sanconiathon is said to be "a history, taken out of the sacred books of the Phœnicians; and it is composed of three fragments, out of the writings of Philo,— one out of a work called Phœnician history, one concerning the Jews, and one relating to Phœnician letters." After referring to the Chaos, there is the following paragraph.— "All these things, the son of Thabion, the first Hierophant of all among the Phœnicians, allegorized and mixed up with the occurrences and accidents of nature and the world, and delivered to the priests and prophets, the superintendents of the mysteries, and they, perceiving the rage for these allegories increase, delivered them to their successors and to foreigners, of whom one was Isiris, the inventor of three letters,—the brother of Chna, who is called the first Phœnician. These things were found written in the cosmogony of Taautes, and in his commentaries, and were drawn from his observations and what he had discovered, by which we have been enlightened.

GENEALOGIES.

"Of the wind Colpias and his wife Baau, which is interpreted Night, were begotten two mortal men, called Œon and Protogonus. Œon found fruit on trees. The immediate descendants of these were called Genus and Genea, and they dwelt in Phœnicia, and when there was a great want of rain, they stretched out their hands towards the sun, in heaven, supposing him to be God, calling him—Baalsamin, which in the Phœnician language, signifies the Lord of heaven. [As Zeus among the Greeks, Philo or Eusebius]. Afterwards, by Genus were begotten mortal children, named Phos, Pur and Phlox. These found out the method of producing fire by rubbing pieces of wood against each other, and taught them the use of it.

These begat sons of great bulk and height, whose names were conferred upon the mountains which they occupied. Thus, from them, Cassius and Libanus, and Antilibanus and Brathu, received their names. Memrunus and Hypsuranius were the issue of these men. Hypsuranius inhabited Tyre and he invented huts, constructed of reeds and rushes. He fell into enmity with his brother Usous, who was the inventor of clothing for the body, which he made of the skins of wild beasts. And Usous, having taken a tree and broken off the boughs, made a boat, and first ventured on the sea. And he consecrated two pillars to fire and the wind, and worshipped them and poured out upon them the blood of wild beasts, which he took in hunting; and when these men were dead, consecrated rods to them and worshipped the **pillars and held anniversary feasts, in honour of them.** And

P

in time, long subsequent to these, were born of the race of Hypsuranius, Agreas and Halicus, the inventors of hunting and fishing, from whom huntsmen and fishermen derive their names.

Of these were begotten, two brothers, who discovered iron and the forging thereof. One of these, called Chrysaor, [which is the same as Hephæstus], exercised himself in words and charms and divinations: he invented the hook—the bait, the fishing line and boats of light construction: and he was the first of all men who sailed, wherefore he was worshipped as a God, after his death, under the name of Daimichius. And it is said, his brother invented the art of building walls with brick. Afterwards, of these races were born two youths, one of whom was Technites and the other Genius Autochton. These discovered the mode of mingling stubble with the clay of bricks, and baking them in the sun. They also invented tiles. By these were begotten others, one named Agrus, the other Agruerus or Agrotes, of whom in Phœnicia there is a statue, held in great veneration, and a temple drawn by yokes of oxen, and at Byblus he is called the greatest of the Gods. These added to their houses, courts, porticoes, and arches. Agriculturists and those who hunt with dogs are derived from these—they are also denominated Aletæ and Titans.

From these men, descended Amynus and Magus, who taught men to construct villages and tend flocks. By these men were begotten Misor and Sydyc, that is secure and just, and they discovered the use of salt. From Misor descended Taautes who invented the Alphabet [the Egyptians call him Thoor,— the Alexandrians, Thoyth, and the Greeks Hermes]. From Sydyc descended the Dioscuri or Cabiri, or Corybantes or Samothraces, who built the first perfect ship. From these descended others, who were the discoverers of medicinal herbs and the cures of poisons and charms.

At that time lived Elioun, called Hypsistus, and his wife Beruth, who dwelt at Byblus. By these were begotten Epigeus, or Autochton, whom they afterwards called Ouranos—heaven, [so that from him, that element which is over us, by reason of its excellent beauty, is named heaven], and he had a sister of the same parents, who was called Ge,—earth, and by reason of her beauty, the earth was called by her name. Hypsistus, having been killed by wild beasts, was consecrated, and his children offered libations and sacrifices to him. Ouranos succeeding his father in his kingdom, married his sister Ge, and by her, had four sons, Ilus called Cronus, Betylus, Dagon which signifies Siton (bread corn) and Atlas.

Ouranos, by other wives, had much issue, at which Ge, being vexed and jealous, reproached him, and they separated from each other; but Ouranos returned to her by force, whenever he pleased, and then, again left her. He also attempted to kill the children he had by her; but Ge defended herself by the assistance of her friendly powers. When Cronus arrived at man's estate, by the advice of his secretary, Hermes Trismegistus, he opposed his father Ouranos to avenge the indignities offered to his mother. To Cronus were born Persephone and Athena. The former died a virgin; but, by the advice of Athena and Hermes, Cronus made a crooked sword and a spear of iron. Then Hermes addressed the allies of Cronus with magic words, and excited in them a strong desire to make war against Ouranos, on behalf of Ge. And Cronus having overcome Ouranos, drove him from his kingdom, and succeeded him in his imperial power. In battle, was taken a well-beloved concubine of Ouranos, who was pregnant. Cronus bestowed her upon Dagon, and while she was with him, she was delivered of a child, and they called his name Demarous.

After these events, Cronus surrounded his habitation with a wall, and founded Byblus, the first city of Phœnicia. Having suspicion of his brother Atlas, he threw him into a deep cavern and buried him by the advice of Hermes. At this time the descendants of the Dioscuri, having built some light and more complete ships, put to sea, and being cast away over against Mount Cassius, there built a temple. But the auxiliaries of Ilus, who is Cronus, were called Eloeim, and were the allies of Cronus, having a son called Sadidus, killed him with his own sword, because he suspected him, and with his own hand, deprived his child of life. He in like manner cut off the head of his own daughter, so that all the Gods were astonished at the disposition of Cronus.

In process of time, Ouranos, when in banishment, sent his daughter Astarte, being a virgin, with her two sisters Rhea and Dione. to cut off Cronus by treachery. Cronus took them all and married them, notwithstanding they were his sisters. When Ouranos understood this, he sent Eimarmene and Hora with other auxiliaries, to make war against Cronus; but Cronus gained the affections of these also, and took them to himself.

It was the God Ouranos, devised Betulia, contriving stones that moved as having life.

By Astarte, Cronus had seven daughters called Titanides. By Rhea, seven sons, the youngest of whom was consecrated from his birth, and by Dione, he had daughters, and by Astarte he had two sons, Pothos and Eros. Dagon, after he had found out bread corn, was called God of agriculture. To Sydyc, who was called just, one of the Titanides, was born Asclepius, and to Cronus, there were born in Perea three sons called after himself, Zeus, Belus and Apollo. Contemporary with these, were Pontus and Typhon, Nereus the father of Pontus. From Pontus, descended Sidon, who, by the excellence of her singing, first invented the hymns of odes or praises, and Poseidon. To Demarous, was born Melicarthus, who was first called Heracles.

Ouranos then made war upon Pontus; but afterwards relinquishing the attack, he attached himself to Demarous, when Demarous invaded Pontus, who put him to flight, and Demarous vowed a sacrifice for his escape. In the 22nd year of the reign of Cronus, he, having laid an ambuscade for his father Ouranos in a certain place, situated in the middle of the earth, and having taken him prisoner, dismembered him, over against the fountains and rivers. When he was consecrated, his spirit separated, and the blood of his parts flowed into the fountains and rivers. Then Astarte, called the greatest, and Demarous, named Zeus, and Adobus, called the king of the Gods, reigned over the country by consent of Cronus: and Astarte, having put upon her head as a mark of sovereignty, a bull's head, by travelling about the world, she found a star, falling through the air, which she took up and consecrated in the holy island of Tyre. [The Phœnicians say, Astarte is the same as Aphrodite].

Cronus, visiting the different regions of the habitable world, gave his daughter Athena the kingdom of Attica. After this, Cronus gave the city of Byblus to the goddess Baaltis, which is Dione and Berytus to Neptune and the Cabiri, who were cultivators of the soil and fishermen, and they consecrated the remains of Pontus at Berytus.

But, before these things, the God Taautes, having pourtrayed Ouranos, represented also the countenances of the Gods, Cronus and Dagon, and the sacred character of the elements. He contrived also for Cronus, the ensign of his royal power, having four eyes in the parts before, and parts behind, two of them closing, as in sleep, and upon the shoulders four wings, two in the act of flying, and two reposing as at rest. The symbol was, that Cronus, while he slept, was watching, and reposed while he was awake. And, in like manner with respect to the wings, that he was flying while he rested, yet rested while he flew. But, for the other Gods, there were two wings only to each, upon his shoulders, to intimate that they flew under the control of Cronus. And there were also two wings upon the head, the one as the symbol of the intellectual part, the mind—the other for the senses.

And Cronus visiting the South, gave all Egypt to the God Taautes, that it might be his kingdom.

These things the Cabiri—the seven sons of Sydyc and their eighth brother Asclepius, first of all, set down in the records, in obedience to the command of the God Taautes."

This cosmogony, like the story of the Atlantis, is manifestly a history of America. There is much about it that would lead a thoughtless reader to suppose that it is a history of Phœnicia: and in all probability, Philo and Eusebius thought so. They are copying three documents, the application of which they do not thoroughly understand. But when the fragments are compared with those of Diodorus Siculus, the real nature of the history comes out to view: and it is seen to be a description of a race, that came into Phœnicia, at times of high antiquity and laid the basis of the kingdom. The race must have come from America.

These conclusions are reached by comparing the cosmogony

with the Sicilian document and with general mythology. Thus, the cosmogony early introduces the Giants, who must have lived in the land of the Giants. Then appears Chrysaor, who, in the Classics, springs from the blood of the Gorgon Medusa, whom Hesiod puts beyond the Ocean in the West. Then come the Titans. There were no Titans in Phœnicia. They were an Atlantic race. Then comes Ouranos himself, the same as Uranus in name and nature. To make the two documents absolutely identical, Atlas, the astronomer, appears in his own name. Then Cronus has a son Zeus, just as Saturn, in the other document, has a son Jupiter.

CHAPTER XI.

Prehistoric America elucidated by the details of the Atlantis and the Phœnician Cosmogony.

THE SIGN OF THE CROWN AND ITS MYTHOLOGY.

It is now time to introduce the several constellated figures, which compose the ancient mystic or pictorial maps of America, at page 7z, and to try to educe from them, the secret histories that belong to the separate settlements described in the tradition of Loki and his progeny.

The Crown comes first. The Crown is a figure, which surmounts the Serpent. In the picture it looks as if it belongs to the Serpent. As portraiture of a country, it must be taken to represent the region lying North of Mexico. Perhaps it may be intended to include the great district lying between the Rocky mountains and the Ocean. From the position it occupies in relation to Japan and China, it may fairly be looked upon as the earliest Asiatic colony. Like Connecticut and Massachusets in modern times, which were the first settlements of the Pilgrim Fathers, the spot now mentioned would be the first colonized. The situation is convenient for boats, even of a primitive construction, as they could conveniently coast by the Aleutian Islands; and this is in accordance with the traditions of the Americans themselves, which refer the advent of the first civilizers to the north-west, to islands and to ice.

The teaching of Poetical Astronomy, in relation to the Crown, has been referred to, (p. 88), when studying the story of Ceres and Proserpine. The crown bears the name of the daughter. This agrees well with the present hypothesis. The Crown is also called Mithra. In the pictures of Mithra, he is represented as holding the Keys of the underground world. It gives a lively and natural interpretation of that symbolism, to find him at the entrance of the mysterious region which forms the subject of the present work. Again, in mythological monuments, there is little or no difference between Mithra and Œon. Œon also holds the key of the under world. In the Cosmogony of Sanconiathon, Œon is put at the top of the Genealogies. In that document Œon is vastly earlier than Ouranos.

The constellation of the Crown appears in one of the Classic myths. It is that of the daughters of Orion, and is as follows: "The daughters of Orion distinguished themselves as much as their father, and when the oracle had declared, that Boeotia should not be delivered from a dreadful pestilence, before two of Jupiter's children were immolated on the altars, they joyfully accepted the offer and voluntarily sacrificed themselves for the good of their country. Their names were Menippa and Metioche. They had been carefully educated by Diana; and Venus and Minerva had made them very rich and valuable presents. The deities of hell were struck at the patriotism of the two females, and immediately two stars were seen to arise from the earth, which still smoked with the blood, and they were placed in the heavens, in the form of a crown. According to Ovid, their bodies were burned by the Thebans, and from their ashes arose two persons, whom the gods soon after changed into constellations."

This myth belongs to a category of ancient world-wide traditions, which the Greeks have misunderstood and wrongly applied to their own histories. That it is mythical and not a personal and real narrative, is proved by what is said. These ladies were children of Orion and educated by Diana. If so, where could they have lived? Orion and Diana did not live in Boeotia. Those great characters are impersonations of the great and ancient nations of Eastern Asia. If so, these young ladies must have been Asiatics. Then, the deities of hell were witnesses to their patriotism. But was Greece in hell? Then, they were turned into the constellation of the crown. It requires no argumentation to shew that this myth, and traditions of a similar character, are the floating, uncertain stories of the past world, which the Greeks have turned into myths, just in the same way as at the present day, ancient histories of great magnitude are turned into nursery tales.

It is not difficult to find out the historic meaning of this interesting myth, by submitting it to the principle of interpretation adopted in this work. Menippa and Metioche are daughters of Orion. Orion, the giant, overhangs the great country of Iran or Persia. He embodies Iran in the histories of the world. Two daughters of Iran, could be nothing else than two colonies, migrating from Iran. They immolate themselves, a sort of immolation that is very common in these days, where emigrants from their native land are never more heard of. The ladies die. They go abroad. That is a common meaning of a mythic death.

It is equally easy to see to what part of the habitable globe they went; inasmuch as they were turned into the crown, a constellation which delineates the north-west shores of America. In other words, the inhabitants of the Orient must have joined in the general colonization of America, which has been already traced. This colonization from the Orient is very natural, as there is a direct water-way from the Persian gulf to the land in question, by coasting. From what is said of the presents made by Venus and Minerva, it may reasonably be inferred, that these colonists must have visited China and Japan on their route. If so, they must have acquired their cargo and their outfit, from lands quite competent to supply a divinely furnished ship.

But who are these daughters of Orion? There is nothing

very definite to answer that question. It may be a matter
of debate. They are now traced to the Crown; but, in all
probability, the immigrants to that region must have spread
themselves abroad East and West, North and South, just as
has been the case with modern emigrants, on the Eastern shores
of the same continent. Judging from their names, it is natural
to suppose, that they mean Mexico and Peru. Mythology,
though uncertain in its stories, is geographical in its names.
Metioche is the proper pronunciation of Mexico. The name
Menippa is only recognizable as a Thibetan Idol; but as Thibet
is a land of monks, it is plain that an Idol is not Thibetan.
It looks as if the name were but another version for Menalippa,
who is said to be a daughter of the Centaur Chiron. If that
were so, then Metioche and Menippa stand very well for
Mexico and Peru.

The sign of the Crown is a sort of clue by which to trace
the prehistoric histories of America. It forms a convenient
point, from which to calculate the mythic chronology
of the hemisphere. It seems to have been the custom of
Hierophantic map makers, to require that the name of the
picture, be it man, beast, or thing, should agree with the land
or king. That must be noticed here. In the story of the
Atlantic Isle, Uranus is made to be the first king of the
Island. His name is the same as the Sign, though differently
spelled. The words clang together. Not only so: but the
Crown itself seems to have been chosen because it designates a
King. Uranus wears the Crown as first King of the Atlantic
Isle. This agrees well with the mythology of the Crown as
just stated, as the Crown is found to be the landing place
of the first colonists, and the spot from which to extend them-
selves over the length and breadth of the hemisphere.

The name of Uranus, of Diodorus, tallies exactly with the
Ouranos of Philo. They are the same in name and nature.
Ouranos has a son called Ilus. He is glossed by Cronus.
Here again Cronus clangs with the Crown. Cronus is a sort
of second Uranus or Ouranos. He carries on the history
which begins with the others. Both of them are spoken of
as builders: Uranus builds cities, and Cronus erects walls.

Orion, the mythic representative of Irania, has the same

name as Uranus, the first King of the Atlantic Isle. His daughters make a settlement in America, and they call it by the same name as their old country, just as in modern times, the English settled in Connecticut and the neighbouring States, and called it New England. There is no difference between the Persian, Phœnician, and the Greek pedigrees. They all have Ouranos and Ge at the top of their cosmogonies. In the second fargard of the Vendidad, Aryana and Gau tally with Ouranos and Ge. Gau is said to be the dwelling place of Sughdha (Scythia). In the Scythian Cosmogony, Vrindus is glossed by Ouranos and called water, pointing plainly to the Oceanic hemisphere as his domicile.

Using the Crown as a Chronological Epoch, and putting that Epoch at the top of American histories, as known to the Sicilians and Greeks, the Phœnician Cosmogony exhibits a much earlier history. The wind Colpias and his wife Baau, beget Æon and Protogonus. They have Genus and Genea, and they, Phos, Pur and Phlox : they, the Giants, Memrunus and Hypsurianus, whose issue was Usous.

It would not be very wrong to call this, the Antediluvian period of Prehistoric America, but that term does not go deep enough into the vast antiquity of the human race. The characters that stand at the top of this curious cosmogony, belong to a period far anterior to Uranus. It is in the light of the Mosaic cosmogony, that this subject has to be studied. It may here be noticed, that the opening passage in the Phœnician cosmogony, runs parallel with the second verse of the first chapter of Genesis. This is not the place to study the Mosaic cosmogony,—although that splendid epitome of the world's vast antiquities even yet in the 19th century remains to be developed. It is sufficient here to observe that the mystic characters of Colpias and Baau, have their correspondents in the second verse of Genesis.

There is reason to think, that the very early form of Prehistoric America, comprised in the opening passages of the Cosmogony of Sanconiathon, appertains to the woods and forests of the red men. Æon and Protogonus were immediate descendants of Colpias and Baau. Mythologists consider Æon to be analogous to Cronus, Hercules, and Phanes.

All these mythic personages belong to the woods and prairies. Ymir is the old name of the constellation, Hercules, who overhangs those regions. Cronus becomes a savage, and Phanes is but another spelling for Faunes, already shown to be the North American Indians. But as Protogonus is son of Colpias, and as Ymir is more ancient than Hercules, they must impersonate the red men at times far earlier than Uranus.

The same conclusion is reached, when the passage now under review, further says that these begat Giants. Memrunus and Hypsurianus were the issue of these men, as was Usous. Dr. Movers, in treating of the Cosmogony, considers both Hypsurianus and Usous, as synonymous with Hercules. Moses treats the Giants as a race that sprang from the union of Gods and men. It was a race, in which the people of the two hemispheres combined in the formation of the Giant race. The constellated figures of the Giants, Hercules and Ophiuchus, localize the Giants, as the occupants of the region in which are found at this day the great earthworks.

This brings back the history to the Crown, because both the documents put Uranus or Ouranos, as commencing what may be called the Post-diluvian part of the history. By comparison of the documents, it is plain, that these two personages are the same, and that they belong to the same location,—the region of the Crown. Here it will be noticed that Uranus is credited with Astronomy. As Uranus is stem-father of Atlas and the Atlantides, it must be inferred that the Astronomy of Uranus is the Aztlan astronomy, which the Spaniards found in Mexico. Both the documents then exhibit the movements of the race, or, say, the immigrants. Uranus has many wives. It wants no penetration to see that that expression means that the race separates and passes off into many parts of the country. Forty-five children spring from that marriage. This is quite analogous to the immigrations of the Pilgrim fathers. They spread over the land. In the other document, it is the same with Ouranos. He has many wives, and much issue. It may be convenient to follow the story of Ouranos.

Ouranos is called Epigeus or Autochthon, and he had a

sister Ge. They had four sons, Cronus, Betylus, Dagon, and Atlas. Here, again, it may be convenient to follow Cronus, who seems to retain his father's name. Ouranos leaves the country and comes back again when he pleases. From this it must be inferred, that there were numerous arrivals of colonists from the mother country. This is in accord with the Greek myth of Ceres. But there must have been disagreements among the colonists, for Ouranos attempts to kill his own children, and when Cronus arrives at man's estate, he opposes his father Ouranos. All this is very natural. It is the common result of colonial settlements. The thirst for land creates disagreements and strife. The issue of it is, that Cronus drives his father Ouranos from the kingdom.

Cronus, who is a most interesting character in history, has two daughters Persephone and Athena. This must have been in the region of the Crown; because this sign carries the name of Persephon. These two daughters assume great consequence in the underground world, and it throws great light upon the obscure mythology of Europe, to discover the origin and nature of those deesses. Persephone is the wife of Pluto. She is the Amenti Isis,—Queen of the Manes. Athena is Queen among the Furies. She is decorated with the bloody head of the Medusa, which Perseus cuts off in one of the wars, which must have sprung out of these settlements, because Medusa locates not far from the Crown.

It is interesting to follow Cronus, and to try and find what became of him in these Atlantic histories. Of course, it is somewhat dubious; but still, there is enough said about him, to trace him further. "Cronus surrounds his habitation with a wall." "Having suspicion of his brother Atlas, he threw him into a deep cavern and buried him." "Then Cronus, who is called Ilus, slays his son Sadidus and his daughter, and all the Gods are astonished at the disposition of Cronus." "Ouranos then sends Astarte, Rhea, and Dione to cut off Cronus by treachery; but Cronus takes and marries them." There is another quotation, but that can be deferred.

From the last of these statements, it may be inferred, that many more arrivals of colonists appear on the sea coast of the Crown. They come under three names, and try to cut off Cronus. Instead of that, he marries them all. That was, perhaps, the best thing he could have done. Instead of colonial quarrels, they settle down in amicable agreement. Then, it is said, that "he throws his brother Atlas into a deep cavern and buries him." Fortunately this can be understood and located. Atlas has the centre of the Atlantic Isle; so that this portion of the colonists must have gone to Central America. That seems a long way to go; but, that only shews the magnitude and extent of these histories; and it gives a hint for the correct interpretation of the whole story. It embraces the entire continent.

But it is the remaining clauses of these quotations that serve to shew what became of Cronus himself. He turned savage, and surrounded his habitation with a wall. If he turned savage, he must himself have migrated from the Crown into the land of Savages. That this was so, is presumable from the statement, that "all the Gods were astonished at his disposition." Under these circumstances, it is hardly conjectural to conclude that he and his followers must have crossed the Rocky mountains, and descended into the great prairies and forests of the vast region that now forms the United States of America. This teaching is strongly confirmed, from the remarkable circumstance mentioned, that "he surrounded his habitation with a wall." It would certainly be difficult to find the solution of that mysterious statement, simply from the cosmogony itself; but when the tracing of these myths, with the assistance or rather compulsory leadings of the Zodiac, carries Cronus into the land of the mound cities of America, it can scarcely be doubted, that Cronus must be credited with the erection of those vast earthworks.

This is not the only argument: it is sustained by two other things, which are worthy of notice. On a critical inspection of the Cosmogony of Sanconiathon, it may be observed, that the proper name for Cronus is Ilus. Ilus is glossed by Cronus. It does not appear who did that; but it may fairly be assumed, that it was done by those who had sufficient authority for it. In this work, there is a close adherence to names. Identifications, where the name is dissimilar, are rejected, except when the ancients themselves make the gloss.

That is the case in the present instance. There is no Cronus
in what can be detected concerning the mound cities; but
their erection is ascribed to the ancient race of Alli, in the
work of Mr. Schoolcraft upon the subject of the North
American Indians. Take away the Greek terminal *us*, and
the name is the same.

The other thing, that gives countenance to the present
theory, that the Earthworks of North America are attributable to Cronus, is, that the Latins have no Cronus. They
gloss the name by Saturn. There can be no question that
those two Gods are one and the same. In a small work,
published in the Biddle Library, entitled the Life of Tecumseh,
the noted Shawnee Chief, of modern times, it is said, that
"the Iroquois name of the Shawnees is Satanas." That is,
certainly, a very curious fact; and if it can be relied upon,
as there is no reason to suppose it cannot, it goes very far
to confirm the mythic tracing, which brings Cronus into
the lands of the Shawnees.

To close the life of Cronus, it will be observed that he is
guilty of parricide. In his 22nd year, he lays an ambuscade
for his father, Ouranos, in the middle of the Earth, and
dismembers him over against the fountains and rivers. He
then has three sons, Zeus, Belus, and Apollo, and then he
is found in Phœnicia giving Byblus to Baaltis.

It certainly is a most surprising thing, to find the great
Gods of Greece and Syria, in the lands now called the
United States. It is freely admitted that no one would
look for them there, unless they were obliged to by some
justifiable mode of mythic interpretation. It wants confirmation. The cosmogony of Sanconiathon is a document
acknowledged by all learned men to be very valuable, and
the Mediterranean nations appear to have employed it, in
the construction of their several systems of mythology. It
must be referred to another chapter, to introduce a series
of myths or group of myths, which can be used to test the
conclusions here reached, having relation to the great European and Asiatic Gods, that have just made their appearance.

The reader must now retrace his steps to the Crown, to
get a further view of the movements, by which pre-historic

America must have been peopled. The Sicilian historian introduces the next piece of history, when he makes Pandora marry her brother Hyperion, and they together have two children, Helio and Selene. As the Crown is contiguous to the Serpent, but more northerly, Hyperion must be placed along the west coast of North America. This throws him into the region, which modern maps call New Mexico; and it is in that region where are found the temples, pyramids, and other ruins, which are the wonder of modern times.

Hyperion is a son of Cœlus and Terra—Pandora is both sister and wife of Hyperion. She, in the classic myths, is daughter of Japetus and Clymene. This relationship is in accord with the Phœnician document, but it is more explanatory. It reduces the personages to Ethnology, as Japetus stands for the Zapotec race. Pandora, in Asiatic life, is the great mother. In Mexico she is Tonacacique. This mystic marriage opens out into the appearance of Helio and Selene. At length, Hyperion is assassinated, and Helio is drowned in Eridanus. This assassination of Hyperion is one of the most notorious incidents in mythology. All the writing nations of the Earth have a tradition of it in some form or other. As the Eridan is the Nile, some great expulsion must have taken place from Mexico to Egypt.

Still pursuing the comments on these two documents, it must be observed, that after the death of Hyperion, the children of Cœlus divided the kingdom. The reconstruction of the Atlantic nationalities, makes Saturn and Atlas to be most renowned The Sicilian Saturn is the Phœnician Cronus, so that what is said of Saturn, takes up the history of the woods and prairies of the red men. Mexico is lost sight of, and the story introduces the mysterious histories of the mound cities in the North, and of Central America on the South. Here the Aztlans and Atlas appear. It is curious to notice what is said of Saturn. "He was profane and married his sister Rhea and had Jupiter (Olympus). Jupiter was good and so called father. He succeeded to Saturn, and was set on the throne, by his subjects, out of hatred to Saturn. Afterwards, by the help of the Titans, Saturn made war upon him, but Jupiter overcame him in battle." This will be worked out by the means of other myths in later chapters. It is sufficient here to notice, that the vast race of the North American Indians must have now become civilized. The good Jupiter follows the savage Saturn; and a God of Europe arises out of the race of civilized Indians. The two divisions of the race fight, and a battle ensues, which is famous in the myths of Greece.

The story then proceeds to people Central America proper. Atlas is located there—in the country bordering the Ocean, and he calls the people Atlantides. He has seven daughters. It is not necessary to pursue this history at any length, here, as it will come up again in the study of Central America. This ultimate settlement of the Uranian or Aztlan race in Central America, is delineated in the Ptolemaic Zodiac by the Austral Crown, which appears to pourtray Quiche and Yucatan. It is unfortunate, that the daughters of Atlas here mentioned, cannot all be located. "They all became first ancestors of nations." That saying seems to imply, that they left their oceanic domicile, and by migration across the Atlantic, they became stemparents of Asiatic, European, and African nationalities. This can readily be believed, because the mythological dictionary of the Greeks is full of them. They are the nymphs of classic authors. Though these names are obscure, the relations of Atlas and his wife Electra, are more than usually distinct.

The Cosmogony of Sanconiathon supplies further details concerning the historical antiquities of the Atlantic Isle, especially in relation to the Titans; but as that race is very important, it will be convenient to reserve that subject for a separate chapter.

CHAPTER XII.

THE ETHNOLOGY OF MEXICO AND THE SURROUNDING COUN-
TRIES, FOUND TO BE IN ACCORDANCE WITH THE PEDIGREE
OF TITAN.

In the Fifth Chapter, the Titan Giants have been treated
as a general equivalent for the Oceanides. In the Cosmogony
of Sanconiathon, they acquire a more limited localization.
"By Astarte, Cronus had seven daughters, called Titanides."
"To Sydyc, who was called just, one of the Titanides bore
Asclepius." In this work, it will be satisfactorily proved,
that Esclepius is the Mexican God Tezculipoca, in name and
nature. This fact suggests an enquiry into the Ethnology
of Mexico, to see if there is any resemblance between the
races of the country and the ancient Greek pedigree of Titan.
There is no part of the Greek mythology more important
and less ambiguous than that family; so that it is possible
to make a fair comparison between the descendants of Titan
and the known inhabitants of Mexico and Central America.
This process is the strongest possible test of identity. Long
ages have intervened, between the composition of classical
myths and the present day: so that there can be no suspicion
of forgery, or unfairness in the comparison. If, therefore, it
should be found, that the actual Ethnology of America agrees
with the Pedigree of Titan, the identity will be established
irrefragably.

The following is the pedigree of Titan—

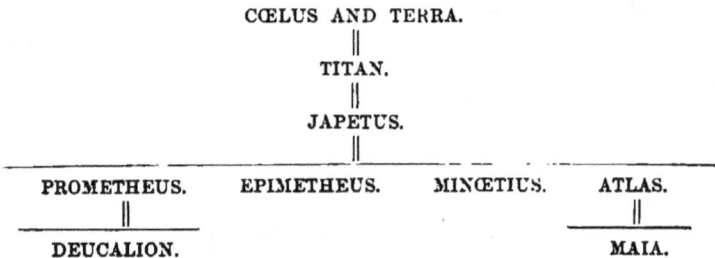

```
                    CŒLUS AND TERRA.
                           ‖
                         TITAN.
                           ‖
                        JAPETUS.
                           ‖
_____

PROMETHEUS.    EPIMETHEUS.    MINŒTIUS.    ATLAS.
     ‖                                        ‖
_____                                  _____
DEUCALION.                                   MAIA.
```

who marries PYRRHA.

This has to be compared with the actual Ethnology of
Mexico and Central America, and the statements of travellers,

R

concerning the races of men found in that land. The most convenient book for making this comparison is Adelung's Mithridates—a German work, containing the languages of all the world, studied by means of the Paternoster. The advantage of this work for the purpose, consists in its giving the Ethnology of the Country, checked by Philology. It will be observed, that Titan is the stem-father of the family. Supposing, therefore, that the theory is correct, which puts the Titans in Mexico or thereabouts, there ought to be some race of that name in the land.

This requirement is met, exactly, in Adelung's description of the races. He says that "the Totonaques were the oldest inhabitants of Anahuac. The Totonaques are situated about Vera Cruz, and they were formerly on the sea-coast of Tezcuco. They had a mythology, comprised of two kinds, one of men-offerers, and one of flower-offerers, in which the last prevailed. The language consists of four dialects."

In this extract, there is a surprising agreement with the Greek Pedigree, now under consideration. Titan is found in the Totonaques. Here Titan and Toton are the same—a most surprising circumstance at this great distance of time. It might be discredited, were it not a known fact, that language and names have more tenacity than bricks and mortar. But Adelung expressly says, that "the race is the oldest in Anahuac," and it must have been very ancient, to have divided itself into four dialects. This nominal agreement cannot be accidental, because Typhon, who delineates the country of the Totonaques, is one of the Titans.

Dropping down the Pedigree, it will be seen that the son of Titan is Japetus; so that there ought to be some race in Mexico and Central America, that answers to that personage. As the Greeks are said to have looked upon Japetus, as "the father of all mankind," and, as in other myths, he is son of Cœlus and Terra, the parents of the Giants, the required race ought to be prominent and wide spread. These conditions are well fulfilled in the Zapotecs, in which the name of Japetus is found exactly. Adelung says "In the East are the Zapotecs, bordering the Talasca and Guatamala." In the traditionary histories of the country, they are found at Quiche. The Zapotecs are said to be identical with the Toltecs, the civilizers of the land. M. de Paix, the French traveller and artist, has given the best account of the Zapotecs. He has made it plain, that the Zapotecs are older than the Mexicans. "They were the artists of the country, and famous for sepulchral tumuli." Nothing can be more complete than this identification, and nothing can be more material to the elucidation of Mexican antiquities; because the Toltecs, here identical with Japetus, were the builders of the great edifices and wondrous temples, now in ruins.

In the present pedigree, Japetus is the father of four sons. Let them be taken separately. Prometheus stands first. In another chapter, it will be satisfactorily proved, that Prometheus stands for Mexico itself. The syllable Pro is evidently an affix. When it is thrown away, the remaining word is the native name of the Mexicans. Adelung writes the word—Mixteca; and he puts the Mixtecas south-east of modern Mexico. He observes that "the Mexicaner call themselves Azteken." The terminations are German in both instances. Prometheus, in Greek mythology, is tied to the Caucasus. When the histories of Asia get studied in the light of poetical astronomy, it will be found that that teaching is correct. The histories of Mexico transfer themselves bodily to the Caucasus.

The next son of Japetus is Epimetheus. In an Ethnological point of view, there is no difference between Prometheus and Epimetheus. Like Pro, the syllable Epi, must be thrown away, as affix. There is the same distinction between the two Mexicos at the present day. Mexico is divided into Upper and Lower Mexico.

In the history of the Atlantis, Pandora, the great mother, marries Hyperion. In the Greek myth she marries Epimetheus. There is nothing to shew whether there is any difference between the two; but certainly, the great ruins of the land, are discovered in the northern parts of Mexico. In the present comparison, Prometheus and Epimetheus equally stand for the Mexicans. This identification of the two eldest sons of Japetus makes the Aztecs or Mexicans to spring out of the older or generic race of the Zapotecs.

Atlas may be mentioned next. This is exceedingly plain.

Atlas and the Aztlans answer to one another in name and
nature.   Atlas is the mythic astronomer, and the Aztlans
the real astronomers of the Atlantic Isle.   The Aztlans were
found in Mexico: but, according to a well-known native
picture, they seem to have originally migrated from somewhere else.   In another chapter, Atalaa, in the mountains
of Quiche, will appear to have been the central location of
the kingdom of Atlas, and the name will be found stamped
upon the nomenclature and race of the region, in Central
America proper ; appearing to justify the language of Sicilian
mythology, which makes Atlas to occupy the centre of the
Isle.   The classic myth puts Atlas in North-Western Africa.
There is no objection whatever to that allocation.   It is a
part of the mythic life of Atlas.   The Aztlans bring their
astronomy across the Atlantic Ocean.

In this pedigree, Atlas has a son, called Maia.   Turned into
Ethnology, Maia is even plainer than that of Atlas and his
brothers.   Adelung places the Mayas in Tabasc and Yucatan.
He says, that " perhaps the Mayas speech could be understood over the great Antilles."   At the present day, Maya
is the name of the inhabitants of Yucatan and other adjoining provinces.   The descendants of Atlas are the Atlantides,
who are spoken of as the Pleiades.   There can be little
doubt, that these Atlantides, of whom Maia is one, represent seven provinces in Central America.   If the Mayas are
one of these sisters, they were placed in the most convenient
situation for the passage of the Atlantic Ocean into the
old hemisphere.

Prometheus, in this Cosmogony, has a son, by name Deucalion, and he ought, also, to be among the races that
inhabited the western shores of America : for, although he
is a navigator and visits other quarters of the globe ; yet,
the harbour from which he sails must have been in the
land of the Titans.   It is pretty plain, that the name of
Deucalion must be treated in the same way as Prometheus.
The first syllable must be thrown away, to get at the real
Ethnology of the character.   So treated, it is Calion, almost,
if not the exact name given to Cortez and his companions
by the natives of Mexico, as their native name.

The only remaining son of Japetus, is Minœtius. This personage, unfortunately, has no myth, with that spelling; and he does not appear to be connected with Mexico and Central America either by tradition or Ethnology. But, the myth of Minos assists the student to understand him. "Minos was the father of Androgeus, Glaucus and Deucalion, besides two daughters Phœdra and Ariadne." The mythology of Minos is very plain. In the later parts of this work he will be found located in Peru; so that one has to look to South America, for the Ethnology of Minœtius. Adelung puts the Mainas upon the upper waters of the Amazon. He says, "the Romainas and the Mainas speak the same dialect." Specimens of their language are given, which, in a marvellous manner, exhibit some mysterious connection with Europe.

On the whole, it would be very difficult to deny, that the pedigree of Titan, compared with the real Ethnology of Mexico and Central America, exhibits a very close resemblance. It is sufficiently close, to create the theory, that the myths of the Greeks concerning the family of Titan, are really derived from the real histories of this part of America.

CHAPTER XIII.

MEXICO, No. 1.—MEXICO IS THE GREAT DRAGON OF THE ANCIENT WORLD.

THE SIGN OF THE SERPENT AND ITS MYTHOLOGY.

Perhaps, in all the transformations which the classic writers have handed down to posterity, to preserve a record of old histories, there is none so striking, or so well composed, as the following. It may be called the master myth of antiquity.

" Taurus, draconem genuit, et Taurum, Draco."

The Bull begat the Dragon, and the Dragon the Bull.

The elucidation of the first part of this mysterious line, has been educed by the concealed histories, traced in the foregoing pages. The Bull mentioned is the Japanese Bull (a picture of which has been given at page 85,) ripping up the Egg of the world. The outcome of that act was the production of the dragon. The mingling of the blood of Asiatic races with those of Western America, created the dragon, or at least, entered into its constitution. The complement of the classic line will receive its elucidation, when the subject passes from Central America. It is this dragon which now awaits attention.

The discovery of Mexico and its conquest by the Spaniards, was one of the most remarkable incidents in modern history. It took the world by surprise, and revealed the circumstance, which Europeans were very slow to believe, that there were other portions of the habitable globe besides their own, in possession of civilization and social institutions. The account and description of the country, its people and its religious customs, seemed incredible. Europe asked with astonishment, for some explanation of the mystery. One had a right to enquire of the learned, who and what these people were. Was there any account of them in ancient literature, which could throw light upon their histories? But the enquiring world got no reply; nor has it done so to this day. It is proposed now to shew, that the country was not only well known in ancient times, but that the traditions and histories connected with it were all down in the common school books of Europe—that, in short, it was the dragon of the ancient world. Before the draconic myths are introduced, it may be necessary to collect a few particulars, concerning the country and its institutions. Brasseur de Bourbourg is a good authority to consult.

"Before the Olmeques, the region was occupied by the Quinames, or Giants, and Tlalac was one of their divinities. With the Olmeques were the Totanaques and Othomies. The name of the ancient city of the Gods was Toetiuacan, which was founded by the Totonaques. This city was more anciently called Veitiocan. Quetzalcoatl is at the head of the Toltec race, which race is glossed by Nahoas; but this deity had no Idols. He introduced monasteries. To him was erected the vast pyramid of Cholula, the base of which was twice as great as that of Cheops in Egypt." Mention is also made of pyramids of the sun and moon, in the centre of a plain. Somewhat inconsistently with this description of Quetzalcoatl, it is said, that he set up a new Toltec state in Huitzelcapan (Puebla de los Angelos). Near it was the mountain of Tlalac, and a statue to that Idol. More inconsistently still, there is an account of a temple erected by Quetzalcoatl, which was circular, and the entrance represented the throat of a serpent, which filled with fright, those who approached it for the first time.

A few more particulars may be gleaned from other sources. The proper name of Mexico was Anahuac. The state of civilization among the Mexicans, when they were first known to the Spaniards, was much superior to that of the Spaniards themselves, when they were first known to the Phœnicians. The ancient Mexicans had more fire, and were more sensible to the impression of honour, more intrepid, and more industrious than those of modern times; but they were at the same time more superstitious and cruel.

Perhaps the best idea that can be got of Mexico, is what is said of Montezuma. All his palaces were surrounded with pleasant gardens, in which was every kind of beautiful flower, odoriferous herb and medicinal plant. It had, likewise, woods enclosed by walls, and furnished with variety of game, in which he frequently sported. In one of the royal buildings, was an armoury filled with all kinds of offensive and defensive arms, and he employed a number of artificers, in manufacturing these, and also artists, such as goldsmiths, mosaic workmen, sculptors, painters and others. One whole district consisted, solely, of dancing masters, who were trained up to entertain him.

Of one Emperor, it is said, that during his time the power and wealth of the crown had arrived at such a height, that he undertook to construct a temple to the tutelary god of the nation, which was to have surpassed in magnificence all the temples of that country. He had prepared a vast quantity of materials for this purpose, and had actually begun the structure, when death interrupted his projects. His successor completed the temple. This work was diligently prosecuted for four years, and on occasion of its consecration, he is said to have sacrificed 72,344 persons.

The Mexican temples, or teecallis,—houses of God, as they were called, were very numerous. There were several hundreds, in each of the principal cities. They were solid masses of earth, cased with brick, or stone, and in their form, somewhat resembled the pyramidal structures of Ancient Egypt. The bases of many of them were more than 100 feet square, and they towered to a still greater height. They were distributed into four or five stories, each of smaller dimensions than that before. The ascent was by a flight of steps, at an angle of the pyramid on the outside. This led to a sort of terrace, or gallery, at the base of the second story, which passed quite round the building, to another flight of steps, commencing, also at the same angle as the preceding, and directly over it, leading to a similar terrace; so that, one had to make the circuit of the temple several times, before reaching the summit. The top was a broad area, on which were erected two towers, forty or fifty feet high, the Sanctuaries in which stood the sacred images of the presiding deities. Before these towers, stood the dreadful stone of sacrifice, and two lofty towers on which fires were kept, as inextinguishable as those in the temple of Vesta. The description of the sacrifice is too terrific for transcription. A picture of the scene is given in the chapter on Vishnu, page 65.

One detestable feature of the Aztec superstition was its cannibalism, though, in truth the Mexicans were not Cannibals, in the common acceptation of the term. They did not feast on human flesh, merely to gratify a brutish passion; but, in obedience to their religion. Their repasts were made of the victims, whose blood had been poured out on the altar of sacrifice.

Here is the great dragon of the ancient world! It is true, that the foregoing extracts are a description of modern Mexico, when discovered by the Spaniards; but it requires only a slight acquaintance with the literature of ancient nations, to recognise in the description,—the dragon of traditionary history. This horrible creature must have been known to all the people of the old world: for it is more largely mentioned and delineated in pictures, than any thing which has come down to modern times.

As an illustration of these observations, it may be mentioned, that in the classics there is a myth of Draco, or something which looks very much like one. "A celebrated lawgiver of Athens, when he exercised the office of Archon, he made a code of laws for the use of his citizens, which, on account of their severity were said to be written in letters of blood. By them, idleness was punished with as much severity as murder, and death was denounced against the one, as well as the other. Such a code of rigorous laws, gave occasion to a certain Athenian, to ask of the legislator,— why he was so severe in his institutions, and Draco gave for answer, that, as the smallest transgression had appeared to him, deserving death, he could not find any punishment more rigorous for more atrocious crimes."

This may be real history—perhaps it is. It looks a good deal more like Montezuma than an Athenian lawgiver for it is said of him, that " he was inexorable in punishing those who resisted his orders, or transgressed the laws of the kingdom. He was an implacable enemy to idleness, every species of which he restrained or corrected." But, if it be historical, it only shews, that the great dragon had saturated the human mind with principles of rigour, cruelty and blood.

Much the most vigorous and graphic description of the Great Dragon is found in the twelfth chapter of the Book of Revelations. " And there appeared a great wonder in heaven, —a woman clothed with the sun, and the moon under her feet, and upon her head a crown of twelve stars. And, she being with child, cried, travailing in birth and pained to be delivered. And there appeared another wonder in heaven, and behold a great red dragon, having seven heads and ten horns and seven crowns upon his heads. And his tail drew the third part of the stars of heaven, and did cast them to

s

the earth; and the dragon stood before the woman, which was ready to be delivered, for to devour her child, as soon as it was born. And she brought forth a man child, who was to rule all nations with a rod of iron, and her child was caught up to God and to his throne. And the woman fled into the wilderness, where she hath a place prepared of God, that they should feed her there a thousand two hundred and threescore days. And, there was war in heaven, Michael and his angels fought against the dragon, and the dragon fought and his angels, and prevailed not, neither was their place found any more in heaven. And the great dragon was cast out,—that old serpent called the Devil and Satan, which deceiveth the whole world, and he was cast out into the earth and his angels were cast out with him."

This remarkable passage of Scripture is singularly in accord with the mythic tracings of the present work, and it discloses much which must have had relation to Mexico, at times of high antiquity. It will be observed, that the passage is Zodiacal. It is based upon the Ptolemaic Zodiac. The dragon has seven heads and ten horns, and seven crowns upon his heads. Here the dragon is the Serpent of the present map. In the modern Zodiac, the Serpent has only one crown; but, there is reason to suspect, that older copies of the spheres had more crowns. The Sesha Serpent, so often referred to in this treatise, has seven heads, and in the picture given of that Serpent at page 60, Brahma has four crowns, and he springs from the navel of Vishnu, who reposes on the Serpent.

Then, again, the dragon sweeps the third part of the stars of heaven. This reference to the stars shews that the writer is drawing his imagery from the Zodiac. The constellations which, in this work, are localized over America, compose about that proportion of the whole starry heaven. America, itself, is about one-third of the terrestrial globe. The passage now under review, may be adduced as a very distinct proof of the theory educed in former pages from the tracings of poetical astronomy, and it also fixes with minuteness, the present allocation of the great red dragon.

The subject of the woman clothed with the sun and having the moon under her feet, is one of great obscurity, as it is commonly read; but, in its present relation, it receives not a little elucidation. It happens to come up as the very next subject, which presents itself in this study of the dragon. In the cosmogony of Sanconiathon, Hyperion is the impersonation of the monster.

Hyperion may be taken to be the embodiment of ancient Mexico as the Great Dragon of the world. The present portrait of him gives a lively conception of the notions entertained of old, concerning that mysterious land. He, in this picture, is drawn black to make him horrid. He is surmounted with the seething pot crown, as the king of hell. He sits upon the gridiron—fit emblem of the cruel practices of the country. In one hand, he clenches a serpent, and he has a bow and arrow in the other. He has nine horrid heads, in which he differs slightly from the representation of

HYPERION OR PHŒBUS.

the Sesha Serpent, with which he corresponds, and which has but seven. This picture is taken from Dr. Clarke's valuable book of travels.

The myth of Hyperion, in the Classics, is limited to his relationship. "Hyperion, a son of Cœlus and Terra, who married Thea, by whom he had Aurora, and the Sun and Moon. Hyperion is often taken by the poets for the Sun itself."

Much the best idea of what the ancients mean by Hyperion, is gained from the Atlantis of Diodorus Siculus, already presented to the reader. That author makes Pandora marry her brother Hyperion, and they together have Helio and

Selene, otherwise called the Sun and Moon. The historian then says, that Hyperion arrogated to himself universal dominion. This can readily be believed, from the manifest greatness of the Mexican Empire, when discovered by the Spaniards under Cortez, as well as the astonishing ruins it has left. It would seem, however, that the great power of Hyperion excited the envy of his family, who became afraid that he would assume the whole kingdom. They, therefore, conspired against him and assassinated him, and they drowned Helio in Eridanus.

This is not a bad description of what may be taken to be an epitome of the Asiatic colonies in what may be called— Mexico. Hyperion is a brother of Oceanus with varying pedigrees. The mingling of the Asiatic and American people leads to the formation of a powerful state, which in process of time suffers from intestine commotion, issuing in the end in the dismemberment of the Empire, and the flight of some portion of the people into Egypt. The histories and events which must have filled up the period of time, between the marriage of Pandora and Hyperion and the flight of Helio, or his drowning in the Nile, is obscure; but there are numerous traditions that supply a large number of particulars,—tho most prominent of which will be noticed in this and the following chapters. The traditionary history of the country, as published by Brasseur de Bourbourg, furnishes the native remembrance of the same facts.

The most curious thing in the myth of Hyperion is his family. He is father of Aurora, and the sun and moon, or, he is the sun itself. As the sun was worshipped in Mexico, as the second God of the Empire, it might be supposed that Hyperion's parentage of the sun and moon is drawn from the natural phenomena of those orbs: but the story is against that supposition, inasmuch as Hyperion is slain. Helio is drowned in Egypt, and Selene wanders over the Earth. It must be symbolic Ethnology.

It would seem that the fancy of the ancients in making the great dragon and his wife to be the parents of the sun and moon, is in a sense, correct and true. The sun race of Asia, in settling upon the western shores of America, in a land of barbarian philosophers, has created for succeeding ages and in other lands, a God and a Goddess, with the Solar and Lunar emblems. In Europe, it was Apollo and Diana, or perhaps, more accurately, Phœbus and Phœbe. In Phœnicia and the Orient, it was Baal and Astarte, or Ashtoreth. It is not to be denied that the demon Sun and Moon have constituted a practical religion for many nations.

This fact is well illustrated by one of the Abraxas Gems, or Amulets, scattered so widely over Europe and Western Asia, and retained long among the early Christians, who found it difficult to throw away their old pagan amulets.

The present is the most common form of an Abraxas Gem, and there can be no mistake about its signification, as both the symbolism and the inscription explain it. It is called Iao—that is to say, Jove, and it has the inscription, "the sun spread abroad." The com-

IAO. SEMES. EILAMPSE.

ponent parts of the figure shew that it belongs to Ancient Mexico. It is a bird man—a composition so common in Mexican pictures, as to be characteristic of them. The serpent legs localize the figure in the serpent land. The figure of Typhon in the Coptic Zodiac is drawn in the same manner.

Typhon, in the Egyptian system, is the Dragon Sun. He is Helios himself. In the following collation of extracts concerning him, he is so called. The picture is in the Coptic Zodiac itself, delineating Mexico and called Regnum Typhonis. It is at page 73. Plutarch says, "the Egyptians esteem Typhon as no other than Helius the chief deity. He burst into life, obliquely through the side of his mother." Bryant. "The head of a Typhonian monster, is found on vases, brought as part of the tribute from Asia, to the kings of the eighteenth dynasty. It is something like a Medusa's head." Wilkinson. "Typhon is the son of Earth and chief of darkness, and takes the form of a serpent. His seat is in the Scorpion, over which sign he triumphs. He is red. He is the bad Genius. He cuts the body of Osiris into fourteen pieces." Dupuis. "Typhon is son of Hera alone—had 100 fiery dragons' heads. He tried to rule Gods and men; but Zeus bound him and cast him into Tartary. By Echidna he begot the dog Orthos, Cerberus,— the Chimæra, and the Harpies." Apollodorus.

These extracts give a very lively idea of the mysterious histories of ancient Mexico. They shew that the aboriginal dragon race must have been visited by Asiatic people, who, by mixing with the natives, had become savage and had turned red. The extracts also shew that the Typhonian and dragon race in Mexico must have spread itself into South America, and conquered the upper waters of the Amazon.

It appears to have been the custom of the ancients to affix particles to the names of places and people. It is these affixes, which obscure the histories of olden times. Among the Titans, of whom, in fact, the present subject treats, there are several affixes of this kind. Prometheus, Epimetheus, and Deucalion are specimens. As the syllables Pro and Epi are evidently affixes to the names of Metheus, so in all probability the word Hyper is an affix in the name of Hyperion. This teaching gains colour when it is observed, that the removal of the affix brings out to view a personage of singular importance to an enquiry into the probable histories of Mexico and its sur-roundings. It has been already pointed out, that the name of Ion or Eon is used extensively in old literature, for America in general.

It looks a good deal as if the Hyperion of the classics, were the Æon of the Cosmogony of Sanconiathon. In that document Æon is put at the top of the races, which, by study, have been found to be American. Æon and Protogonus are the parents of Genus and Genea, who again become the stem fathers of the Giants. This makes Æon to be very similar to Hyperion, if he does not actually coalesce with him. A picture is here given of Æon. Let him be examined. He is a human being, wound round by serpents. He has the wings which the Phœnician cosmogony assigns to Taautes and Cronus. He holds a staff or rod, and at his feet, is the Caduceus of Mercury. He also holds the key of the lower regions. The picture is taken from Millin's extensive collection of mythic personages, where he is said to be analagous to Heracles or Phanes of the Orphics. All this suits Hyperion very well. But if the identification is wrong, Æon must be put into Mexico by the emblems which he carries.

ÆON.

There is another character among the mythological monuments of antiquity, which answers to Æon, and by consequence to Hyperion, the dragon. It is Mithra, and he is a figure of such importance, as to make it necessary to study him with more than common care. Perhaps, he may throw light upon the obscure histories of Mexico. A picture is here given of him. Let the image of Mithra be examined and compared with that of Æon. Here it must be admitted, that the two figures bear great resemblance. They are both human beings wound round with serpents. They both hold the key of the lower world, and they both have wings. Yet, there are some differences, and Mithra, in this picture, has the four wings

which the cosmogony of Sanconiathon assigns to the god
Taautes, while Æon has only two.   Both Mithra and Æon

MITHRA.   VICHLIPUCHLI.

have lion's heads: but that can be accounted for; as Mithra
was known to European authors and sculptors as a Persian
God.   This study leads to the conclusion that Æon and
Mithra are the same characters, when carried back to their
original home.

At the side of Mithra, another picture is here given of the
great war god of the Mexicans—Vichlipuchli.   It is for comparison.   Let the two figures be examined.   It cannot be denied
that the two images, as they appear, at first sight, are very
much alike.   They both stand upon the globe,. a position very
uncommon for the gods of the old world.   The globes are
also put upon pedestals, which are very much alike.   The

Mexican globe and pedestal are adorned with the barbarous paraphernalia peculiar to half civilized people. But the real resemblance between the figures, does not consist in the form of the pictures. That may or may not be accidental, or a mistake of the Spanish artists, who must have copied the Mexican war god.

The identity of the two gods, consists in the symbols by which they are distinguished. They are both of them represented as men-bird-serpent. Mithra has those peculiarities in a very marked form. They are not so easily distinguishable in the Mexican God; but they are present. He is a man. The bird is upon his head, and he holds the serpent, in form of sceptre. Admitting the identity, the question arises, which was the original? For the purpose of deducing historical conclusions a rule has already been laid down that the natural is father to the unnatural. In the present case, the natural is with Vichlipuchli—the unnatural with Mithra. The first sits upon a throne,—the bird is his ornamental head dress and the serpent a stick. Under these circumstances, admitting an identity, Mithra must be a copy of Vichlipuchli. Hence it would follow, that the Persian deity, for such is the status of Mithra, is a remembrance—a deified remembrance of ancient Mexico.

The conclusion now reached, is one that may be challenged. It is contradictory of all common conceptions of ancient Asiatic history. To make the Medes and Persians to have been a race which had crossed the Pacific Ocean, and to make them emigrants from Mexico into Iran, looks problematical. But the real histories of the Central Empires of the Orient need illumination almost as much as those of America itself. Yet there is a mode by which this teaching can be tested. If the practices of the Mithraic religion were found to be dissimilar to those of Mexico, it would explode the notion. On the other hand, if they were found to tally, it would be the strongest proof possible, of consanguinity and ethnological identity. Let therefore the initiations of the two countries and religions, be put into comparison.

There is a valuable American work, on Freemasonry, by A. G. Mackay, which can be utilized for this purpose. The

T

author says, that in Mexico, were mysteries, with cruelty and bloodshed. There were long fastings to the initiated in a heightened form. All the terrors and sufferings used in the East were there. They were scourged, wounded, and cauterized. A groan would unfit the initiated to pass the trial. In the temple of Vichlipuchli, the ceremonies were grandest. They represented the wanderings of the God. The caverns were the path of the dead. The initiated was conducted through the caverns, till he came to the lifeless body of a man, thrown down from under the high altar. After many horrors, he got to a fissure and out into the open air, when vast multitudes received him, as born again. Another higher degree was for priests, and they were symbolic, referring to the deluge and subsequent settlement of their ancestors on the lake of Mexico.

This has to be compared with the mysteries of Mithra. The aspirant was purified by water, fire, and fastings. He was then introduced into a cave, representing the world; on the walls and roof of which were the celestial signs. He was there baptized, and had a mark made on his forehead. He was then presented with a crown, on the point of a sword, which he refused,—saying—"Mithra, alone, is my crown." He was then anointed with oil, and crowned with olive, clothed in enchanted armour, for the seven stages of initiation to be passed. *First*, he was introduced to a cavern, where were the howlings of wild beasts. *Second*, enveloped in darkness except by lightning. *Third*, He was hurried to the spot whence the sounds came, and suddenly thrust through a door, into a den of wild beasts, where he was attacked by the initiated, in the disguise of lions, tigers, hyænas, &c. He was then hurried through the apartment into the second cavern, again shrouded in darkness. Then there was thunder. He then was led through four other caverns with the same fright. In the *seventh*, he came to the light, and was introduced to the Archimagus on a throne, and surrounded by the dispensers of mysteries. Here secrecy was enforced, and he was made acquainted with sacred words, among which was the infallible name of God, and taught the doctrines and rites of Mithracism, of which the history of creation formed a part.

On comparison of these two processes of religious initiation, it is quite plain, that the Mithraic of Persia were imitations of those of Mexico. Tested by the same rule as was applied to the two figures of Mithra and Vichlipuchli, that conclusion is inevitable. The initiations of Mexico were ceremonies, to keep up the remembrance of the wanderings of the forefathers of the people. The initiations of Mithra, in another land, were the same ceremonies; but they have got turned into a religion. But the lesson to be drawn from the comparison, is that the Medes and Persians must have drawn that religion from Mexico and the great God Vichlipuchli.

This study has brought out prominently to view, that Vichlipuchli, the great war god of modern Mexico, is the Dragon of the ancient world, of which all the nations of the earth have stood in fear. When Mexico was discovered by Cortez and his companions, they came upon the dragon in all the habiliments of fright and horror, which had long ago alarmed the inhabitants of other parts of the earth. He had lost nothing of the cruelty and blood-thirstiness, which had characterised him in times of old. According to all appearance, he must have gone from bad to worse, and assumed features of malignity, much in excess of those which had rendered him a terror to the world in the mythic ages. If the monster has occupied his den, all the time since the Apostle John wrote of him, and has slain his thousands at the same ratio as that mentioned in an extract, where it is said, that the victims slaughtered at the dedication of a temple amounted to seventy thousand, how vast must have been the number of victims of the dragon, during all that long period!

Mr. Prescott, in his conquest of Mexico, thus describes Vichlipuchli. In enumerating the Gods, the author says, "At the head of all stood the terrible Vichlipuchli, the Mexican Mars, although it is doing injustice to the heroic war god of antiquity, to identify him with this sanguinary monster. This was the patron deity of the nation. His fantastic image was loaded with costly ornaments. His temples were the most stately and august of the public edifices, and his altars reeked with the blood of human hecatombs, in every city of the Empire. Disastrous, indeed, must have been the influence of such a superstition on the character of the people!"

There is a tradition in the European collection which seems to belong to this war god, and it may therefore be transcribed, as the embodiment of the ideas which must have floated about, in ancient Europe, concerning Mexico and its Gods. It is as follows—

"Cacus, a famous robber, son of Vulcan and Medusa. He is represented as a three-headed monster and vomiting flames. He resided in Italy and the avenues of his cave were covered with human bones. He plundered the neighbouring country, and when Hercules returned from the conquest of Geryon, Cacus stole some of his cows and dragged them backwards into his cave to prevent discovery. Hercules departed without perceiving the theft; but his oxen having lowed, were answered by the cows of Cacus, and the hero became acquainted with the loss he had sustained. He ran to the place and attacked Cacus, squeezed and strangled him in his arms, though vomiting fire and smoke."

Cacus, in this myth, is put in Italy, and mention is made of Geryon, who belongs to Spain: so that the story must relate to the movements of the warlike races, that Plato brings into Europe, from beyond the pillars of Hercules. Those races comprise the people who came into Europe from beyond the Atlantic. But the parentage of Cacus reveals the particular spot in America, whence they came. They must have been Mexicans.

Cacus is here called the son of Vulcan and Medusa. Leaving Vulcan out of the pedigree, as rather a general character, hard to localize, this myth makes Cacus to be a Mexican, If he is the son of the Medusa, he must have been so. The Gorgons were beyond the ocean in the west; so that Cacus must have been an American. In the following chapter, it will be proved, that the Medusa stands for Mexico: so that Cacus must be put there in the first instance. But the myth discloses the den of the dragon. It was covered with human bones. The monster had three heads and vomited flames, an evident allusion to the great fires kept always lighted at the summit of the teecallis. As to the name of Cacus itself, the word is but a different spelling for Gorg or Gorgon, the Gog and Magog of later histories. Cacus answers to the riddle of 666.

THE DRAGON'S WIFE.

It seems that this great red dragon had a wife—a beautiful Lady: at least, in her upper parts. Well! he is not the only monster that has had a beautiful wife. This wants looking to. It may turn out instructive.

KRISHNA DESTROYING THE SERPENT, HIS WIVES THE NEREIDS INTERCEDING.

This picture of the Hindoo dragon and his wives shews at a glance, who this lady was. She turns out to be the Mermaid of the ancient world. In the European mythology, "the Nereids were nymphs of the sea, daughters of Nereus and Doris. They were fifty, according to the greater number of the mythologists. The Nereids were implored as the rest of the deities. They had altars, chiefly on the coasts of the sea, where the piety of mankind made offerings of milk and honey and often of the flesh of goats. When they were on the sea shore, they generally resided in grottoes and caves, which were adorned with shells. They were subject to the will of Neptune. They are represented as young and handsome virgins sitting on dolphins and holding Neptune's trident in their hands, or sometimes garlands of flowers. They were particularly fond of alcyone."

But who were these wives of the serpent? Must they be considered as natives of the serpent land, or must they be intrusive races, who had come into the land and married the great Dragon? It is in the power of comparative Idolatry, to answer that question. Indeed, the description of the Nereids, just read, supplies an answer. "They were subject to the will of Neptune." Who was Neptune?

In the Japanese Idolatry, the great God of Japan is Amida, a human being, with a dog's head, riding a seven headed horse. This divinity resolves himself into two other forms. One is a figure, which bears a close resemblance to an European Minerva, and the other is a Nereid. This change of nature, reduced to history, simply means that the Japanese made a settlement on the west coast of America. They gave existence to a colony, which, by its sea-faring habits and capacity for navigation, has figured in the pictures and traditions of the world as Nereids or Mermaids.

In the Hindoo system, Nereus the father of the Nereids, has a counterpart in the very curious figure of Narayana. Narayana floats upon a leaf. When looked at closely, it can be seen that this personage is, in reality, Vishnu himself in another name. Without troubling the reader with a dissertation upon this obscure subject, it may be noticed, that these characters, Nereus and Narayana, appear to be geographical in Mexico. In any good map of the country, the region is called Nayarit. Whether that is to be considered the real name of the land of the Nereid or not, it cannot be denied that it is the same word. If it were so, it would throw great light upon the antiquities of Mexico, as it has just been shown that the Nereids had for parent a Japanese God.

As Japan or Niphon is the Neptune of the old world, and as Poseidon had the Atlantic Isle as his portion, he ought to be found in Mexico. That this God, if he is to be called by that name, had been in the land of the Serpent, is a part of the symbolic teaching of the Egyptians, wherein Nef, the Egyptian Neptune, is transformed into a Serpent.

This figure is too plain for mistake, especially when it is understood that the legs ought to be red. Nef has several other figures to represent him; so that when he appears as a walking snake it brings Neptune or Poseidon into the Atlantic Isle. One of the names of the Egyptian Nef is Nou. This name is found in Mexico as the Naohas, who are the Toltecs, the builders and civilizers of the land.

But there is another picture which teaches the same doctrine. If the reader will turn once more to the frontispiece of the present work, he cannot fail to notice, that the throne of Neptune is supported by the dragon. The God himself is supposed to be behind the curtain, veiled in secrecy; but on the face of the picture, it might be said, that the dragon is the God. The scene bears analogy with the Egyptian figure of Nef, in form of Serpent. From all this it may be inferred, that the wives of the Serpent were a very different race from that of the people who embody the dragon.

It is certainly very curious to find these "young and handsome virgins" to be the wives of the dragon, when it is remembered, that the women-fishes of all the great nations of antiquity, are the teachers of the world. This is particularly the case in Chaldea. In the cosmogony of Chaldea, they are called Oannes. The Oannes came into the Persian gulf in boats. By day, they gave instruction in the arts and sciences, and retired by night. It was not a casual visit paid to the Persian Gulf. They made repeated visits, and so important must have been the influence they exerted on the inhabitants

NEF SERPENT.

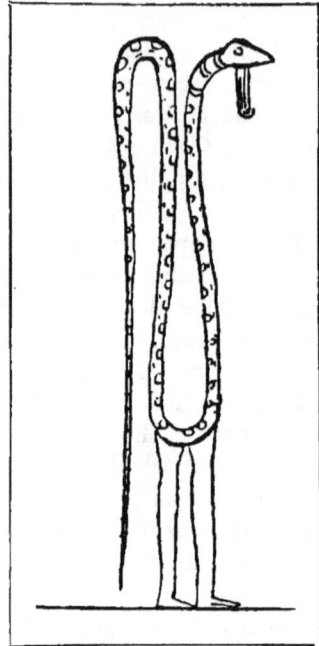

of the valley of the Euphrates, that the most beautiful temple in Assyria carries their name. They performed the same offices in many other lands of the old continent—in Egypt—in Syria—in Gaul, and in Ireland. One is at liberty to suspect that there must be some mistake in the identification of the Oannes with Mexico, as the harbour whence they swam; but it is much in favour of the hypothesis, that the name Oannes is the same as the Æon of this chapter.

The tracing of the myths of the dragon and his wife as illustrative of ancient Mexico and its inhabitants, is well sustained by the descriptions given by the Spaniards of the state of the country and its institutions. The monstrosity and cruelty which is embodied by the great Red Dragon, has its counterpart in the bloody practices of the Mexican priests: while, on the other hand, the highly favourable features appertaining to the Oannes, as teachers of the arts and sciences has its counterpart, likewise, in the description given of the mercantile, artistic, and social condition of the province. The repulsive side of this subject has received sufficient notice. The beautiful reverse claims a few extracts.

The Mexicans, says Clavigero, could boast of many inventions, worthy of immortalizing their name. Such as besides those of casting metals, and mosaic works of feathers and shells, the art of making paper—those of dyeing with indelible colours,— spinning and weaving the finest hairs of the rabbits and hares—making razors of a stone called "itzli," which they manufactured with such expedition, that in an hour, an artist could finish more than 100—making beautiful looking glasses of this stone set with gold,—the cutting and polishing of gems, —breeding of the cochineal, &c. Add to this, the well established fact, that the science of astronomy had its birth and most correct development in Mexico. As to the art of painting, it is only necessary to look at the great work of Aglio, to see that the art must have been fostered in an eminent degree, if it were not created in the land. The Oannes had something to carry with them to the Persian gulf.

CHAPTER XIV.

MEXICO, No. 2.—MEXICO AS PROMETHEUS AND THE MEDUSA.

In search for the real histories which underlie the mythic traditions of the classics, an identification is scarcely satisfactory, unless the name of the mythic personage and the country he represents be the same, making allowance for spelling and pronunciation. In the present instance this requirement is found in two characters—Prometheus and Medusa.

The following is the myth of Prometheus. "A son of Japetus, by Clymene, one of the Oceanides—he surpassed all mankind in cunning and fraud. He ridiculed the Gods, and deceived Jupiter himself. He sacrificed two bulls, and filled their skins, one with the flesh and the other with the bones, and asked the father of the gods, which of the two he preferred as an offering. Jupiter became the dupe of his artifice, and chose the bones, and from that time the priests of the temple have ever been ordered to burn the whole victims on the altars, the flesh and the bones together. To punish Prometheus and the rest of mankind, he took away fire from the earth, but the son of Japetus outwitted the father of the gods. He climbed the heavens by the assistance of Minerva, and stole fire from the chariot of the sun, which he brought down upon the earth at the end of a ferula. This provoked Jupiter the more; he ordered Vulcan to make a woman of clay, and after he had given her life, he sent her to Prometheus, with a box of the richest and most valuable presents, which she had received from the Gods. Prometheus who had suspected Jupiter, took no notice of Pandora, or her box; but he made his brother Epimetheus marry her, and the god, now more irritated, ordered Mercury, or Vulcan, according to Æschylus, to carry this artful mortal to Mount Caucasus, and there tie him to a rock, where, for 30,000 years, a vulture was to feed upon his liver, which was never diminished, though continually devoured. He was delivered from this painful confinement about thirty years afterwards, by Hercules, who killed the bird of prey. Prometheus had received the gift of prophecy, and

U

all the Gods, and even Jupiter himself, consulted him as an infallible oracle. To him mankind are indebted for the invention of many of the useful arts: he taught them the use of plants, with their physical power, and from him they received the knowledge of training horses and different animals, either to cultivate the ground, or for the purposes of luxury."

This tradition is transcribed at length, on account of its intrinsic importance, in an historical point of view. It reads like the story of some individual man; but, when looked at in the light of the present treatise, it swells into great histories, which link together the two hemispheres in times of high antiquity.

There need be no time occupied by arguments to prove that Prometheus in the first part of his mythic life, is an impersonation of ancient Mexico. That has virtually been done in a former chapter, where the Ethnology of Mexico and Central America was put into juxta-position with the Greek pedigree of Titan. It is there shown, that Japetus stands for the Zapotec race. Prometheus and Epimetheus stand for Lower and Upper Mexico.

The myth of Prometheus must be divided into two parts. Vulcan is ordered to take the artful mortal to Mount Caucasus, where he is tied to a rock. This takes Prometheus into Media, a country the history of which is so ambiguous and uncertain, that something is wanted to explain it. That something is discovered in the present myth. Media must have had its birth in the arrival of people from Mexico. The boats of the Oannes must have brought into the Orient, the forefathers of a nationality, which appears in the history of the Orient as Media, and in that of the World as the birth of Freemasonry. They must have been Mexicans. Yet the greater part of the tradition belongs to Mexico, and the details of it in that relation can be compared with the national characteristics of the people and the arts to which they appear to have devoted themselves. One of the characters attributed to Prometheus, is that of a prophet. Not only was he a prophet himself, but the very gods themselves consulted him. It will be remembered that Nereus also had that office. This ascription of religion to Mexico, reads strangely; but a more extended knowledge of the subject, shews that the Mexican people were in possession of religious sentiments, which will compare advantageously with the most orthodox Christianity.

One of the peculiar feats ascribed to Prometheus, is that of bringing fire down from heaven. To bring fire down from heaven requires a mirror of great power; but in an extract already given concerning the Mexican arts, it is said, that "they had the most beautiful looking glasses made of itzli." In the figurative language, common to ancient literature, this is called "stealing fire from the chariot of the sun." But, when the fire is put at the end of a ferula, it seems rather to refer to the production of fire, by the friction of wood. In the pictures of Mexican antiquities, this particular method of creating fire, is exemplified by numerous specimens. In fact, it is so common, as to give it prominence in the customs of the land.

Then it is said, that "mankind is indebted to Prometheus, for many of the useful arts." If so, Mexico must have occupied a position in the early civilization of man, which is not commonly attributed to it. One naturally supposes that this famous State must have received its useful arts from some extraneous people; but the myth reverses the movement. The writings of the Spaniards make it manifest, that the arts of life were in the highest possible state of successful cultivation. Even the short extract given at the end of the last chapter, is sufficient to prove that fact.

The reference to human sacrifice, contained in the myth, looks something like a parody upon what is now looked upon as a serious matter. They played a trick upon the father of the Gods—rather a poor compliment to such an elevated God! But though the story is funny, it is plain enough. Prometheus got the flesh and the God got the bones. This is the exact thing which is described in accounts of the practice of human sacrifices among the Mexicans. They slaughtered the victims at the summit of the teccallises, and then threw the bodies down to the bottom of it, to be taken away and eaten!

On the whole, it must be admitted, that this story in its present application, reads very naturally. Without straining it

at all, it educes many important points in the long lost
histories of the west coast of North America. This is not
exactly the place to consider the bearing of the subject on
Asia and its histories. It would take a volume to trace the
influences of America upon the old continent. In the present
work, such influences can only be referred to in a casual manner.

One curious character mixed up with Prometheus demands
notice. It is that of Pandora. "Pandora, a celebrated woman,
the first mortal female that ever lived, according to the opinion
of the Poet Hesiod. She was made of clay, by Vulcan, at
the request of Jupiter, who wished to punish the impiety
and the artifice of Prometheus by giving him a wife. When
this woman of clay had been made by the artist, and received
life, all the Gods vied in making her presents. Venus gave
her beauty and the art of pleasing: the Graces gave her the
power of captivating. Apollo taught her how to sing. Mercury
instructed her in eloquence, and Minerva gave her the most
rich and splendid ornaments. From all these valuable presents,
which she had received from the Gods, the woman was called
Pandora, which intimates that she had received every necessary
gift. Jupiter, after this, gave her a beautiful box, which she
was ordered to present to the man who married her, and by
the commission of the God, Mercury conducted her to Prometheus. The artful mortal was sensible of the deceit, and
as he had always distrusted Jupiter, as well as the rest of
the Gods, since he had stolen away fire from the sun to
animate the man of clay, he sent away Pandora without
suffering himself to be captivated by her charms. His brother
Epimetheus was not possessed of the same prudence and
sagacity. He married Pandora, and when he opened the box
which she presented to him, there issued from it a multitude
of evils and distempers, which dispersed themselves all over
the world, and which, from that fatal moment, have never
ceased to afflict the human race. Hope was the only one that
remained at the bottom of the box, and it is she alone who
has the wonderful power of easing the labours of man and
of rendering his troubles less painful to life."

In the Atlantis, by Diodorus Siculus, Pandora is made to
be a daughter of Uranus and Titea. "Of Uranus and Titea

were born several daughters, of whom two were most famous Basilea and Rhea, by some called Pandora." This puts Pandora into the Atlantic Isle and its histories. Not only so, but it puts her into what has been called in this treatise, the region of the Crown, the country north of the serpent land. It follows, therefore, that the myth belongs to the histories of the settlement in America of the Asiatic races, which have been traced into that land. In this view, and with these localizations, it is not difficult to understand Pandora, and the story fills up an hiatus in this remarkable history, which is most material to the elucidation of America's obscure antiquities.

The first question that arises from this myth is, what do the mythologists mean by the *gods* that sent this interesting personage to the west coast of America? This question can be answered easily enough. There are no such things as Gods, and never were. The gods of the ancient world are the nations of the ancient world, and they are great or small, according to the dimensions of their territories. In the present case, it can easily be understood as it has been sufficiently proved, that the Asiatic nations have colonized America in high antiquity. Pandora is the classic reproduction of the Chinese Puzza. She is sent across the Pacific Ocean, decked out in all the habiliments of Asiatic life.

This myth shews that there must have been two Mexicos in ancient times, and that circumstance helps to clear up a perplexity which hangs about the ruins of the country. The present location of Mexico is not that in which the ruins are found. The present myth exhibits two Mexicos, in the persons of Prometheus and Epimetheus.

After Venus and the Graces had trimmed her out and put her into receiving order,—after Apollo had given her a sufficient number of music lessons,—after Mercury had got her up in rhetoric and public speaking—and especially after Minerva had filled her boxes with a superabundance of rich drapery—she takes ship.

She tries Prometheus first; but he would not have her. Perhaps he was a believer in the Munro doctrine. At any rate, he was well furnished already. He had no need of Asia

or its refinements! So she went to Epimetheus. He had an
eye to business, or the Lady, and he married her. He took
the silks of China,—the vases of Japan,—the jewellery of India,
—the learning of Thibet, and the beauty of Scythia, and with
what result? Let the ruins of Upper Mexico tell—a pyramid
twice the size of the largest in Egypt, and ruins which
constitute one of the wonders of the world.

Another tradition, which belongs to Mexico, and is illustrative of its ancient histories, is that of Medusa. It is
unnecessary to prove the location of the Medusa, in this place,
as she is one of the Gorgons, and that subject has been
sufficiently handled before. But a picture is here given, by
which it is indubitably proved, that Medusa is the mythological
Mexico.

The picture at the right hand is the European portraiture
of the Gorgons. It is taken from Millin's Collection, and is the
most characteristic picture to be found. It will be seen that
they are woman-birds or winged women. One of them is
the Medusa herself. She is decapitated, and Chrysaor and
Vulcan start from her neck in a form so peculiar, as to define
the personage, wherever she may be discovered.

At her side is given a part of a large Mexican scene, which
appears in Aglio. It must be pronounced the Medusa herself
in propriâ personâ. She also is a woman-bird or winged
woman. The Mexican artist has given great prominence to
the bird. She also is decapitated, and a figure starts from her
neck, in a form exactly like that of the Greek figure. On
a comparison of the two scenes, it is hardly possible to deny
that one must have been taken from the other, and the story
of the Medusa makes it evident that the Mexican picture is
the original.

The tale is as follows: "Medusa, one of the three Gorgons,
daughter of Phorcys and Ceto. She was the only one of the
Gorgons, who was subject to mortality. She is celebrated
for her personal charms, and the beauty of her locks. Neptune
became enamoured of her, and obtained her favours in the
temple of Minerva. This violation of the sanctity of the
temple provoked Minerva, and she changed the beautiful locks
of Medusa, which had inspired Neptune's love, into serpents.

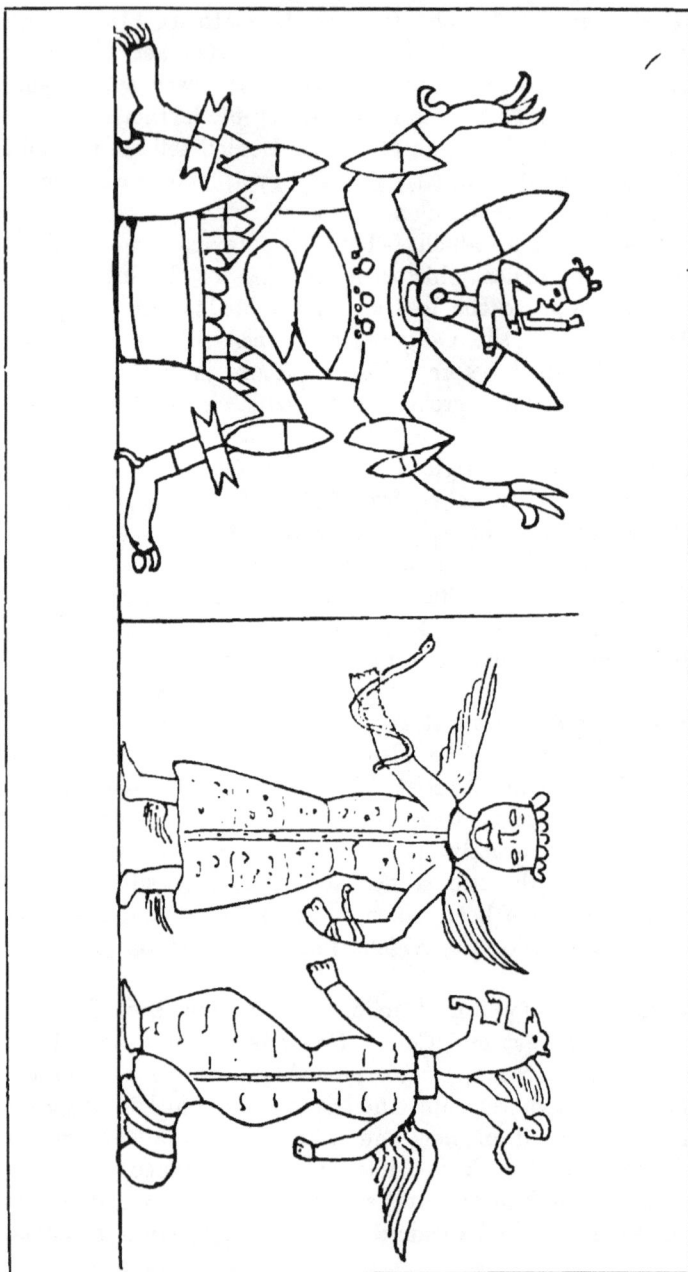

MEXICAN FIGURE.

TWO GORGONS.

According to Apollodorus and others, Medusa and her sisters came into the world with snakes on their heads instead of hair, with yellow wings and brazen hands. Their body was also covered with impenetrable scales, and their very looks had the power of killing or turning to stones. Perseus rendered his name immortal by the conquest of Medusa. He cut off her head, and the blood that dropped from the wound, produced the innumerable serpents that infest Africa. The conqueror placed Medusa's head on the Œgis of Minerva which he had used in his expeditions. The head still retained the same petrifying power as before; as it is well known, in the court of Cepheus. Some suppose that the Gorgons were a nation of women, whom Perseus conquered."

Commenting on this myth, it must be noticed that it suits the present course of treatment of Ancient Mexico, in every detail; but it also shews that the histories of it have been retained only under misconception and misapplication. In this myth, Neptune appears again. He takes a fancy to the Medusa. All the myths agree that it was Neptune, that is to say, Niphon, that colonized the country. Then the description of the Medusa suits well the barbarous costumes and cruel practices of the land. The people, dressed as wild beasts and birds, must have conveyed to such strangers as visited the land, the zoomorphic form described in the story. If the priests served foreigners in the same way as they treated their prisoners, it must have turned to stone all that visited the place. Now appears Perseus. His myth is very long. Only the chief points of it, and such as relate to America, need be transcribed in this place.

"Perseus, a son of Jupiter and Danae, the daughter of Acrisius. Perseus was no sooner born, than he was thrown into the sea with his mother Danae, and they were driven by the winds upon the coasts of the Island of Seriphos. Perseus was entrusted to the care of the priests of Minerva's temple. Polydectes was the king of the place. This king sends Perseus to bring him the head of the Medusa. Then the Gods appear in the tale. They give the hero a combined outfit. He first goes to the Graiæ, sisters of the Gorgons, and he steals their eyes and gets information of the location of the Gorgons.

Perseus flies there, which was beyond the western ocean. He finds them asleep, and cuts off the Medusa's head with one blow. From her blood sprang the Libyan serpents, Chrysaor also with his golden sword, as well as the horse Pegasus, which immediately flew through the air and stopped on Mount Helicon, where he became the favourite of the Muses."

This is perhaps the most curious tradition of the old world, and it requires only the localization practised in this work, to turn it into genuine history. Perseus himself is an impersonation of Persia. He delineates that land in the Ptolemaic Zodiac. On study, it will be found, that on return to Persia, he is the great Feridoun, that built the city of Persepolis. His mother Danae is uncertain, but she accompanies him, and in the chapter on Central America, she will be found there.

It might be supposed that Perseus was some Persian hero, who alone performed the feat of striking off the head of the Medusa, but the story will not admit of that interpretation; for all the Gods join in the enterprise, and they furnish the hero with the needed equipment. From this, it must be inferred, that the barbarities and inhuman customs of ancient Mexico were well known all over Asia, and they must have excited an amount of indignation, that would not be satisfied without the destruction of the blood-thirsty race. The myth of Perseus is not the only one that treats of some former destruction of Mexico. Thor does it in Scandinavian myths—Horus in those of Egypt—Krishna in those of India—and Perseus in those of the Classics.

But in those days, the snake must have been scotched only. Its heads grew again as soon as they were cut off. The lust of blood is not easily satisfied. It is fed by its own drops. It was reserved by Providence for the heroic Cortez in modern times, effectually to deprive the monster of her remaining head, and to terminate the powers of a state and priesthood, which had excited the wrath of Earth and Heaven.

Perhaps the most remarkable part of this marvellous story, is that which the Muse has reserved till the last. It is said, that from the blood of the Medusa, sprang the serpents of Africa,—Chrysaor with the golden sword, and the horse Pegasus, which flew to Mount Helicon. These astounding facts, if true,

v

must have very much affected the histories of ancient Africa and Europe. They must have linked together the two hemispheres, in some of their most interesting and material histories. Take them separately.

The Serpents of Africa comprise a page of history which would be beyond research, if it were not for the Zodiacal map. Perhaps there is no part of the globe so dark as Africa, in regard to early history; but when the great dark continent is studied, these Serpents make their appearance. The present land of Dahomey comes out in a marvellous way, as having been visited by the Serpent, who, for ages, has been worshipped there, and whose bloody practices have rivalled those of Mexico, and have not yet been abolished.

The next character that sprang from the blood of the Medusa, is Chrysaor. "He is a son of the Medusa by Neptune. Some report that he sprang from the blood of the Medusa armed with a golden sword. He married Callirhoe, one of the Oceanides, by whom he had Geryon, Echidna, and the Chimœra." It is said of Geryon that he lived in the Island of Gades. If so, there must have been historical connection between Mexico and Spain.

But, by far the most important character mentioned, is the horse Pegasus, a mythic figure, that belongs exclusively to Greece. The horse Pegasus, in the Ptolemaic Zodiac, delineates Greece itself and the surrounding parts. Not only so. This surprising animal is on the banner of ancient Greece, as its national heraldry. That being so, there must have been direct communication between Mexico and Greece. But this is the teaching of the story, for the horse flew to Mount Helicon.

After what has now been said, it will create no surprise to be told, that two of the Gods who were worshipped by the Mexicans, on the arrival of the Spaniards in the land, are European gods. There is no test of Ethnological relationship so strong as that of the Gods. Like people, like priest. The customs of religion stick to a nation longer than speech or feature. The first of these Gods is Tezculipoca, a picture of whom is now given.

Tezculipoca, in Mexico, was the God of penitences and self-mortification. His priests are represented cutting themselves with knives, and to him were offered human sacrifices. The picture, now before the reader, gives a vivid conception of this God. His temple is ornamented with skulls and cross bones, and he is surrounded with all the barbaric paraphernalia, which indicate the savage.

This Mexican God Tezculipoca is manifestly the Esculapius of the Greeks, who had a temple erected to his honour, in Epidaurus.

TEZCULIPOCA.

ESCULAPIUS AND TELESPHORE.

At that place, he is called the Serpent God. Living serpents were kept in the precincts of the temple, just as they were in Mexico. Under these circumstances, the name becomes material to the identification. In this case, the two names are virtually the same. It is true that the Mexican God has the letter T at the commencement of the name: but Esculapius is often written with a diphthong Æ. In the ordinary transformation of names and words a diphthong implies a lost consonant.

But to make the identity certain, it is to be noticed, that, in the mythological monuments of Europe, Esculapius is nearly always accompanied by another God, if he is to be considered as entitled to that tall epithet. This is Telesphore—a little fellow, who must be pronounced a dwarf. Unfortunately there is no myth of Telesphore; but as Esculapius is commonly accompanied by Telesphore, so in Mexico, Tezculipoca had a brother God—Tlalec. One temple sufficed for the two gods. This is a strong point in the identity, because Gods do not very often admit their little brothers to equal rights.

Esculapius has a tradition, so that he can be studied. "Æsculapius, son of Apollo, by Coronis, or, as some say, by Larissa, daughter of Phlegius. He was God of medicine. After his union with Coronis, Apollo set a crow to watch her, and was soon informed, that she admitted the caresses of Ischys of Omonia. This God, in a fit of anger, destroyed Coronis with lightning; but saved the infant and gave him to be educated by Chiron the Centaur, who taught him the art of medicine. Æsculapius was physician to the Argonauts. He restored many to life, of which Pluto complained to Jupiter, who struck Æsculapius with thunder. Apollo, angry at the death of his son, killed the Cyclops, who made the thunderbolts. Æsculapius received divine honours after death, chiefly at Epidaurus, Pergamos, Athens, &c."

This myth is difficult, but there is enough about it to shew that Esculapius, the Asclepius of Egypt and of Phœnicia, was half Asiatic—half North American. He was the Serpent God in the old continent.

But Esculapius is better understood from the position he occupied in the old continent, where he has a remarkable connection with Belus and the Syrian Bel. Thus, it is said, that the tower of Babel was consecrated to Bel; but the upper story of the edifice,—the special place of honour,—was devoted to Esculapius. This is certainly very strange, and it might be thought a mistake: but the same thing is said of the Bursa of Carthage, another great temple of Bel. Thus Esculapius and Bel are very nearly the same God. Now the myth says, that he is the son of Apollo, who is a form of Bel.

The position and character of Bel, in the ancient world, is rather a difficult subject, not because he cannot be seen, but because he is seen too much. There are so many Bels, that one has to be cautious in the identification of them. One thing is very certain, that the religion of Bel was the religion of human sacrifice. Without enter-ing deeply into this subject, enough has been said to shew that the religion of Bel and Esculapius in the old continent, was that of Tezculipoca the Mexican God. Under those circumstances, much light is thrown upon the histories of ancient Mexico, by the Idolatry of Bel.

QUETZALCOATL.

The other God of Mexico belonging to the Old Continent is Quetzalcoatl.

The description of Quetzalcoatl has been already given. "He is the Lord of the Eastern light and winds. He was born of a Virgin in the land of Tula, or Tlapallan, in the distant East, and he was high priest in that happy land. He bore as a sign of office,—a mace like the cross of a bishop. One of his symbols was a flint. One fell from heaven in the beginning of things, and broke into 1600 pieces, from each of which sprang up a God."

It is impossible to misunderstand Quetzalcoatl.   He comes from the distant East under the Virgo. He carries the mace or cross, commonly seen in the hands of a Chinese Bonze,—the origin of the Caduceus.   He builds Pyramids, which in Eastern Asia, are erected to hold the relics of the Spirit of heaven. He is the God of the Toltecs, or Nahoas, the civilizers of the land.   In the traditionary histories of Mexico and Central America, by Brasseur de Bourbourg, he seeks to correct the abuses of the Empire—to restrain the sanguinary priests,—to disseminate that tender regard for human life, which is the distinguishing peculiarity of Eastern Monachism.   In those histories, the party headed by Quetzalcoatl, actually wrest the reins of dominion from the bloody priests on one occasion.

Now, this God, as the Mexicans called him, or Monk, as he ought to be called, is the European Mercury.   It is not necessary to exhibit a picture of Mercury, in his European form: he is too well known.   But a native picture is here given from Aglio, which must be pronounced an admirable specimen of an European Mercury.   It is highly characteristic.   There are many other specimens. Some hold the purse and some have the caduceus, better drawn than in the case produced.   They all have the winged feet. The present specimen has the Sun upon his head, and the cross upon his back.

MEXICAN FIGURE.

It is that last symbol which identifies the two characters. In the picture of Quetzalcoatl just given, the dress of the man is covered with the cross. In the case of Mercury, the Caduceus is a cross, but, by time and change, it has lost its proper form. The cross is the emblem of Eastern monachism wherever it is seen, and the movements of the monastic races all round the world can be traced by its means.

When the history of religion comes to be written and understood, it will have to be acknowledged that the Mexican Gods referred to in this and the previous chapter, have had the most material influence in the formation of the religious systems prevailing during the long period of religious darkness that characterized the mythic ages. The Serpent worship of India—the human sacrifice of Baal—the fire rites of Persia—and the philosophy of Hermes, have all to be traced to Mexico. Under these circumstances, it is impossible that America could have been unknown to the other quarters of the Globe. Its people must have mingled with all nations and its histories must have been known.

That it was so, is proved by the innumerable pictures that constitute the mythological collections of Montfaucon, Inghirami, and Millin. The Etruscan Vases and the Græco-Etruscan fictile Vases form quite an historical picture gallery of the scenes and incidents comprised in the traditions of American life. Those mysterious works of art as well as the enlarged gravings of the Abraxas gems, constitute the pictorial literature of America.

A specimen is here given, as an illustration of this fact. It is taken from Millin's splendid work on the Etruscan Vases, and is called Minerva among the Furies.

This celebrated picture is full of symbols; so that any expert in mythological designs can easily detect the several personages that compose the group. Minerva is recognizable by the Medusa's head, which hangs upon her breast. One of the Furies stands at the left hand of the company. He is wound round with Serpents, like Typhon, Æon, and Mithra, and like them, he is winged. The dwarf, who answers to the Aztec dwarf, is on a sort of sedan chair. In Mexican native pictures, the dwarfs are always carried on sedans, but in a form more simple. The noble figure, richly clad, out of whose head the tree springs,—emblem of Saca the Thibetan Buddha, answers to Quetzalcoatl.

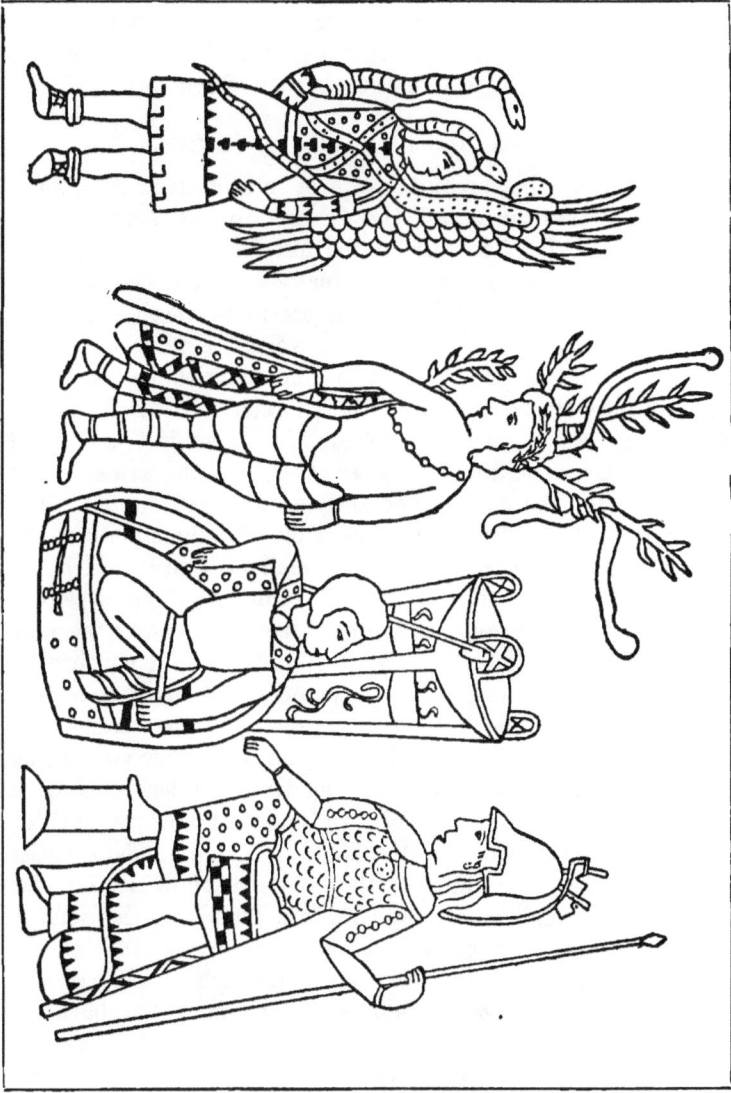

MINERVA AMONG THE FURIES.

CHAPTER XV.

THE VAST EARTHWORKS, SCATTERED OVER THE NORTHERN PARTS OF NORTH AMERICA, MUST HAVE CONSTITUTED AN EMPIRE, WHICH IN THE HISTORY OF THE ATLANTIC ISLE IS REFERRED TO SATURN OR CRONUS, AS ITS EMPEROR.

THE SIGN OF HERCULES AND ITS MYTHOLOGY.

It is putting the present mode of elucidation of obscure histories by traditions and the Zodiac, to the severest test, to apply it to the discovery of the lost histories of the Earthworks that are found scattered over the United States. The Mound cities are involved in darkness more dense than any other of the remains of the ancient world. On one hand, the savage inhabitants of the woods and prairies had not the slightest idea of the history of their forefathers : on the other, the civilized world has long considered the subject as beyond research. Let it be understood, however, that the writer is not responsible for the conclusions reached in these studies. The theory itself must be held responsible for them. Given an ancient map : given a series of national pedigrees, which are found to be geographical : given a number of tales which, though fragmentary and incomplete, hang on both to the map and the pedigrees ; and the only question is, to what conclusions do they lead. So long as the argument is kept perspicuous, and the materials used honestly, let it come to what it may.

The first thing to be done, is to collect particulars concerning the mound cities themselves. The following condensed account of them is taken from the work by Squier and Davis, entitled Ancient Monuments of the Missisippi. "The mounds are vast earth structures, something of the character of British circular mounds, but much greater. They are found on the sources of the Alleghany west of New York. On the east, they extend along the shores of the lake Erie, through Michigan and Winconsin to Iowa and Nebraska. There are none above the great lakes. There are some as high as 46 N. lat. They are found on the river Missouri, 1,000 miles from its junction with the Mississippi. They are found in Kansas and on the Platte river and all along the intermediate country, and down to the

W

Mexican gulf. They extend from Texas to Florida: but they are less frequent in South Carolina. There are great numbers of them in Ohio, Indiana, Winconsin, Missouri, Arkansas, Kentucky, Tennessee, Louisiana, Virginia, North and South Carolina. They are situated on rivers only. Bordering the lakes in Michigan, Iowa, and Missouri, but most in Winconsin, these remains are found in a singular form. They are Earthworks in the form of beasts, birds, reptiles, and even men, forming gigantic Bassos Relievos. On Ohio and its tributaries are more advanced works. There are Pyramidal mounds, terraced with gradual ascents, like the Teecallis of Mexico, with enclosures of earth and vast stones. They extend to the Gulf of Mexico, increasing in size and regularity. Conical mounds are less frequent, but those in the shape of Teecallis more so. Enclosures diminish and there are traces of brick. The valley of Sciot is the favorite seat. There are 100 enclosures in Ross County, Ohio, 10,000 tumuli in Ohio, and 1,500 in Kenhawas in Virginia. There is a mound in Cahokia, Illinois, six acres in extent. The greatest "ancient fort" is in Ohio, on the little Miami River. It has four miles of embankment, 20 feet high, and is impregnable. In Adams' County, Ohio, there is a great Serpent work, 700 feet long, with its mouth opening swallowing an Egg."

Before entering upon the argumentation arising from the principle of localization, this subject admits of a little reasoning *a priori*. It is impossible to deny, that the foregoing description of the mounds indicates a former state of society in North America, very different from that which was discovered by the early settlers in the same land, in modern times. Judging from the known habits of North American Indians, it may safely be inferred, either that they could not have been the builders of the mounds, or, that their forefathers must have been much more civilized than they themselves. Again, the extent of these erections, their multiplicity and dimensions, reveal a state of society which can be descriptive of nothing less than a vast Empire or Empires; and it is unreasonable to suppose, that the history of such an Empire can be wholly blotted out of existence: it must exist somewhere, however hidden. Supposing the mounds to have been an Empire, the great fort on the Miami river, with four miles of embankment, must have been the capital. Again, many of the erections mentioned shew great resemblances with those that have been found in modern times, in Mexico and Central America: there must therefore have been affinity between the acknowledged civilization of the Serpent lands and the population of the mounds. In this view, it is to be noticed, that the red men of the Northern woods, in modern times, called the Great Spirit, Manitou. They had two Manitous, the Quichemanitou or Good Spirit, and the Matchimanitou or Bad Spirit. Now, it is remarkable, that these two words contain in them, both Quiche and Mexico, so that their conceptions of the Spirit may have been drawn from those two Empires. But the word Manitou itself, and the idea of a Spirit, hangs on to the Shang-ti of the Mantchou Tartars. Again, the existence of walled towns, in the form of cities, points to the presence of some extraneous race, that was accustomed to walled towns. Europe could hardly have supplied a model for such erections. One is obliged to look to China and Tartary for walled cities. When therefore the mythology of former chapters has· exhibited in America, the presence of Uranus and his descendants, and when Diodorus Siculus attributes to Uranus the gathering of savages into cities in the Atlantic Isle, there is a *primâ facie* evidence, that the mounds were his cities, or those of his descendants.

Two constellations overhang the region of the mound cities: one is that of Hercules, dressed in a Bear-skin Coat, and with his head downwards. The other is that of Ophiuchus. Both figures hold serpents. Hercules has them in his hand, and Ophiuchus, who assimilates himself to Iphicles, the brother of Hercules, seizes a great snake. The subject is large and interesting; let it be divided into two parts, the northern mounds with Hercules as their exponent, and the southern mounds with Ophiuchus.

THE NORTHERN MOUNDS.

At first sight it creates surprise to find Hercules, whom all ordinary conceptions of ancient history put in the old continent, depicted as representative of the United States; but research will be found to justify the allocation of Poetical Astronomers.

M. Bergman, drawing his information from Northern Sagas, observes that "the Giant Ymir sleeps with his head to the South and his feet to the North. A boy and a girl were born at his left arm." As this suits nothing human, it may be supposed to belong to the constellation of Hercules, where the Hero has that attitude. This makes it necessary to transcribe the myth of Ymir in short. Thridi says "whilst freezing cold and gathering gloom proceeded from Niflheim, that part of Ginnungagap looking towards Muspelheim was filled with glowing radiancy, the intervening space remaining calm and light as wind still air. And when the heated blast met the gelid vapour it melted into drops, and by the might of him who sent the heat, these drops quickened into life and took a human semblance. The being thus formed was named Ymir, but the Frost Giants call him Örgelmir. From him descend the race of Frost giants (Heimthursar) as it is said in the Voluspa, "From Vidolf came all witches, from Vilmeth all wizards, from Svarthöldi all poison seethers, and all Giants from Ymir." And the Giant Vafthrudner, when Gangrad asked "Whence came Örgelmir, the first of the sons of the Giants, answered, "The Elivagr cast out drops of venom that quickened into a Giant. From him sprang all our race and hence we are so strong and mighty." Afterwards he added, "We call Ymir the old Frost giant." Another part of the myth says that "the sons of Bör slew the Giant Ymir and they dragged the body into the middle of Ginnungagap and of it formed the Earth."

This tradition shews that Ymir of the Icelanders and Hercules of the Romans are the same. Ymir is called Örgelmir. The Icelandic myths commonly have a syllable added to the name. Let the syllable mir be thrown away and Ergel or Hercule remains. Then it is explained, that it is the Frost giants themselves that call Ymir Örgelmir. It would appear from this circumstance that the constellation must originally have been called Ymir. Then the Icelanders say, that this Giant was their own forefather. If so, there must have been intercourse between the two hemispheres, in high northerly latitudes, at a period exceedingly early.

This introduces Hercules, whose myth has been referred to

in an earlier chapter. It is only necessary here to study his pedigree.

Hercules was the son of Jupiter and Alcmena. He had hardly entered upon his career than Juno sent against him serpents. He and his brother Iphicles seize them. Unfortunately Alcmena is uncertain. Her location has to be decided by secondary evidence. The first wife of Hercules seems to have been Hebe, who locates in the northern regions of Asia. In his symbolism, Hercules carries a club and a Lion's head. The Lions give portraiture to Eastern Siberia, Thibet, and Tartary, and the great tribes of men that go by the names of Tungoose and Goths. This, in all probability, is the correct localization, because it makes Hercules to be the Red Eric of Scandinavian Sagas. He would be a good embodiment of the Irkutsk and Kamtschatka portion of Asiatic people, who appear to have colonized America in early times. They may have crossed the Pacific Ocean in very northerly latitudes, and settled in the northern parts of America. They mix with the people, or they conquer them. They seize the serpents.

This interpretation of the myth of Hercules is strongly corroborated by the myth of Echidna, a most extraordinary character, whom he marries. "Echidna is called a celebrated monster, sprung from the union of Chrysaor and Callirhoe, the daughter of Oceanus. She is represented as a beautiful woman in the upper part of the body, but as a serpent below the waist. She was mother of Typhon, Orthos, Cerberus, &c. According to Herodotus, Hercules had three children by her, Agathirsus, Gelonus and Scytha."

This curious myth throws more light upon the mysterious histories of the mound cities of North America, than any thing else. Notice who this second wife of Hercules is. Nothing can be plainer. She is the daughter of Chrysaor who springs from the blood of the Medusa. Callirhoe is a daughter of Oceanus. She is half-a-serpent and half-human. This sort of language constitutes the Ethnology of the ancient world. She is a half-caste. In other words, she is the outcome of the union of races produced by the arrival of Asiatic people in the Atlantic Isle.

Hercules marries her and has children by her. This shews

that he must be a late arrival in the mound cities. He does not build them. This was done by Uranus, a character much earlier in these hidden histories. He comes into the Earthworks at a time, when they were inhabited by the half-caste race of Echidna. But who are the children of Hercules and Echidna? He has three sons by her,—Agathirsus, Gelonus, and Scytha. Here the veil of mist which the ancients have contrived to cast over their Ethnology is too gauze-like to hide the characters. They are the Goths, Gauls, and Scythians or Scotch. From this it is impossible to draw any other conclusion, than that the races inhabiting the northern mounds must have been the ancestors of those European races, which, in historic times, inhabited the west and north of Europe.

There is every reason to believe, that the mound cities of North America are described in the records of the ancient world, as Hel, or Hela, or some word that answers to it. In a former chapter, devoted to the Geography included in the tradition of Loki and his progeny, that doctrine was propounded. The settlements of the sons of Loki in the land of the Giants are three. The serpent and the wolf being appropriated by the Ptolemaic Zodiac to Mexico and Peru, there is no other location for Hela, except the Earthworks. But the description given of Hela suits the mounds to the letter; while the graphic portraiture of the Lady, and her character and household, suit the people whom modern exploration found to be the residents of the forsaken mounds.

It is said of Hela, that "she was banished into the lower region, with the government of nine worlds, or regions." The expression lower region is too expressive to be misunderstood, while the very large extent of her dominion requires some very large domain equal to the area of the earthworks, described in the early part of this chapter.

If there is any one thing more noticeable than another, in the collation and comparison of ancient traditions, it is the singular resemblance there is between the mythic systems of all the writing nations of antiquity. That peculiar feature is discoverable in the description given of what is called the lower region. There is in Niklas Muller's work, called Glauben

Wissen und Kunst der Alten Hindus, a curious diagram, which gives visible form to these Mounds.

DIAGRAM OF PATALAM.

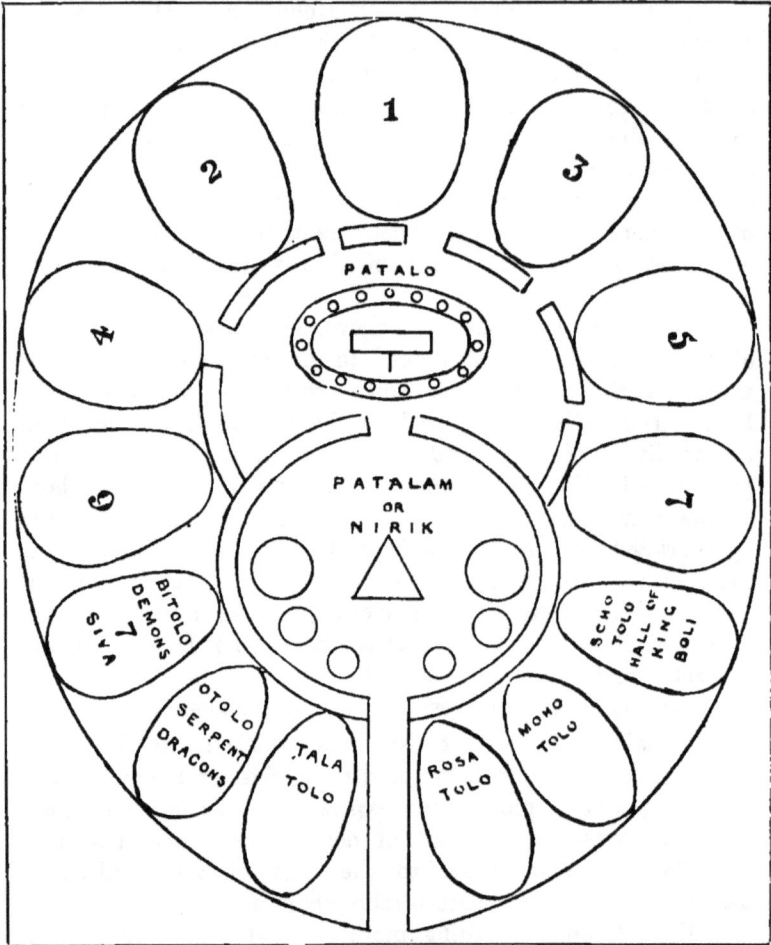

DESCRIPTION OF THE SEVEN REGIONS OF PATALA BELOW THE EARTH.

"Patala. Its depth is 70,000 yojanos,—each of the seven regions extending down 10,000 yojanos. These are Atala, Vitala, Nitala, Gabhastimat, Mahatala, Sutala, and Patala.

Their soil is white, black, purple, yellow, sandy, stony and gold. They are embellished with magnificent palaces, in which dwell numerous Davanas, Daityas, Yakshas and great snake Gods. The Muni, Narada, after his return from those regions to the skies, (the Mahabarat mentions Narada's and Matala's visit to Patala) declared amongst the celestials, that Patala was much more delightful than Indra's heaven. "What," exclaimed the sage, " can be compared to Patala where the Nagas (serpents) are decorated with the brilliant and beautiful and pleasure—shedding jewels"? Who will not delight in Patala, where the lovely daughters of the Daityas and Danavas wander about, fascinating even the most austere,—where the rays of the sun diffuse light and not heat by day, and where the moon shines by night, for illumination, not for cold.—where the sons of Danu, happy in the enjoyment of delicious viands and strong wines, know not how time passes. There are beautiful groves and streams and lakes—where the lotus blows and the skies are resonant with the Koil's song. Splendid ornaments—fragrant perfumes—rich unguents—the blended music of the lute and pipe and tabor;—these and many other enjoyments, are the common portion of the Danavas, Daityas and Snake Gods, who inhabit the regions of Patala." Vishnu Purana.

In a note, it is said, that "Bali the Daitya is sovereign of Patala, according to some." This makes it probable that the above description and diagram include Central America.

This diagram is called Patalam, with seven Hell Kingdoms and Patala, with seven Halls of purification or Niriks. Then it is surrounded with numerous circles and ovals, some of which are named as Bitolo, Demons, Otolo, Serpents and Dragons, and Schotolo, Hall of King Boli.

This diagram must be taken to be a Hindoo map of the mound cities of the United States—an ancient picture of the nine worlds of Hela. It is not a stretch of fancy, but a fair inference, to see in the two large circles what is here called the Northern and Southern mounds. In the north is the great Earthwork, a capital of the Empire. The mounds are varied in form with a pyramid. The ovals all round, delineate the numerous mounds. In the description of the existing works, mention is made of some in the form of serpents and other animals. Even those animal forms are specified, and as if to make the identification certain, one of the ovals is called the Hall of the King Boli, the very character put there, both by the Scandinavians and the Hindoos,— the former as Baldur and the latter as Beli. This latter person is one of the Incarnations of Vishnu. He loses his kingdom in Asia and gets only Patala.

It is not improbable that some readers will demur to the use of mythology for the discovery of the early inhabitants of the Mound cities. Certainly that class of elucidation requires confirmation from other sources, if possible. In a recent chapter the pedigree of the Titans was subjected to a comparison with the actual Ethnology of Mexico and Central America. Let the

MAP OF INDIAN COUNTRY.

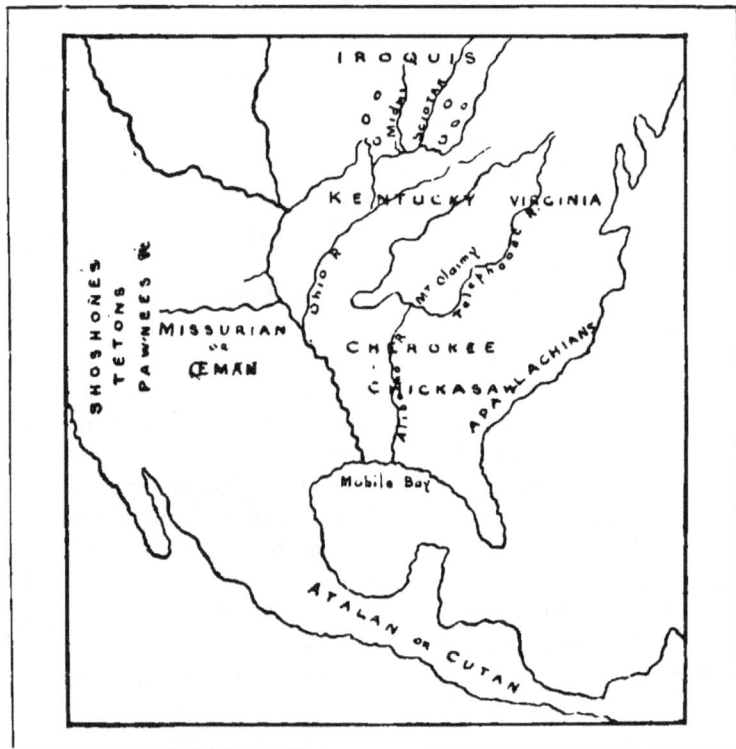

x

same process now be adopted in regard to the arena of the Earthworks. A map of the region with the native tribal names is here presented, as the basis of the comparison.

Take Hela first—the governor of the nine regions which form the area of the mounds. Her name is stamped upon the large district of the Alleghany mountains and rivers. Alli is said to be the name of the oldest tribe of Indians known to enquirers, and it is that tribe which is said to have constructed the Earthworks themselves.

Take Saturn, who assumes a position so imposing in the history of the Atlantic Isle, that Diodorus says of him, that "after the division of the country on the assassination of Hyperion, he and Atlas were the most renowned." He is found in the Shawnees, who, by the Iroquois are called Satanas. In this tribe one also sees the Satyrs, a class of compound figures commonly classed with the Pans in the mythological monuments of Europe.

Hercules or Heracles has his name very strongly marked in the Iroquois tribe, situated in the identical region which may fairly be considered as marked out by the constellation of Hercules. This tribe is commonly divided into seven nations, and called the Lenni Lenape.

The Faunii or Fauns of European mythology, the myth of whom was transcribed in the chapter on Oceanus and the Oceanides, are next. Their name is discovered exactly in the Pawnee tribe of Indians, whose locality is commonly fixed westward of the Missisippi, and who play so great a rôle in the modern stories of North American Indians, in novels and adventures.

The Eumenides, who are also called Erinnys and Furies, and who form in the classical dictionary an exact counterpart to the graphic description of Hela in the Northern Saga, are found by name in the Missourian Indians. In the enumeration of Indian tribes by Professor Rafinesque, the Missourian Indians are glossed by Œman.

The Sesha Serpent and the Titans have their names in the Shoshones and Tetons, who are said to have inhabited the most westerly parts of the Indian country.

Later studies will introduce to the reader's notice the

important Greek divinity Apollo, in a position somewhat
unexpected. That name is fixed upon the large and important
tribe of Apalachian Indians, occupying the lands of the modern
state of Virginia.

The Giant Aloeus and the Aloides, who occupy perhaps the
most distinguished place in the description of the Gigantes,
and whose name is sometimes used to designate the Giants
in general, is found in the ancient race of Alli on the Alleghany
mountains and river, and which has been already pointed out as
the counterpart of Hela.

To complete the list, it may be mentioned, that Atlas and
the Atlantides have their name in the Atalans or Otalans,
which race the learned American professor already mentioned,
places in the Isthmus which connects the great Insular continents of North and South America.

It may be instructive and interesting to get a peep into the
Earthworks. The imagination must be called in to fill up the
great histories that must have intervened between the time
when the mounds were thrown up and at length forsaken.
If that latter event were put at 9,000 years before Plato,
who will venture to assign a period for their erection, and
the events that must have occurred in them? Yet a few
particulars may be gleaned from Northern Sagas. There is
the story of Hermod.

Hermod is sent to Hela to seek Baldur, who is resident
there. Hermod pursues his journey, till he comes to the
barred gates. Here he alights, girds his saddle tighter, and
remounting, claps both spurs to his horse and clears the gate
by a tremendous leap. Hermod then rides to the palace,
where he finds his brother Baldur, occupying the most distinguished seat in the hall. The next morning he besought
Hela to let Baldur ride home with him, but in vain.

The best tale in these myths, is the visit which Thor
and Loki pay to the King Utgard Loki. They set out in a
car, drawn by two he-goats, and after some adventures, they
go eastward on the road to Iötunheim and pass over a vast
and deep sea. They then get into an immense forest and
sleep in a very large hall, with more adventures. They dress
and start on a long way to a city called Utgard, where live men

taller than they—followers of Utgard Loki, and their road
leads northward to rocks. Towards noon, they descry a city
standing in the middle of a plain. It was so lofty, that they
were obliged to bend their necks quite back on their shoulders,
ere they could see to the top of it. On arriving at the walls,
they found the gateway closed, with a gate of bars, strongly
locked and bolted. Thor, after trying in vain to open it, crept
with his companions through the bars. Seeing a large palace
before them, with the door wide open, they went in, and
found a number of men of prodigious stature, sitting on
benches in the hall. Going further, they came before the
king, Utgard Loki, whom they saluted with great respect.
Their salutations were returned by a contemptuous look, &c.

Here is a mound city. The travellers go eastward. They
arrive at a sea, which in that direction could be nothing but
the Pacific Ocean. They cross and reach Rocks, evidently
the Rocky mountains, and then have adventures in the land
of the Giants. They then reach a city with walls so high,
as that it strains their necks to see the top. So completely
do these facts agree with the mounds, that it is hardly a stretch
of fancy to see in Utgard the vast mound described above,
on the little Miami river, Ohio, where the remains of the
enclosure are still so high as to be put at 20 feet high,
with four miles in length.

There is then a long account of feats that Thor and Loki are
put to perform. First, there is a feat of eating. Then a race
is run. Then there is a feat of drinking. Then is a trial of
lifting a cat. Then they wrestle with an old woman. Some
authors have seen in these feats of Thor the works of Hercules:
and it is certainly curious to find, that the present identification
leads to that conclusion. The works of Hercules have always
been incomprehensible. Perhaps by shifting the locality of
their performance to America, they may be better understood.
Undoubtedly, the cast of the story is better suited to Indian
practices than to those of Europe. The part Erectheus plays
in these works has always been a mystery. A divine hero
with a King over him, is unintelligible, but an Iroquois warrior,
sent out on the war path by a superior chief, is quite Indian.

From all that has now been advanced, it must be inferred

that Saturn who was one of the most renowned "Kings of the Atlantic Isle," and who stands for the Satanas was sovereign of the whole region. As his domains were spacious and numerous, it is no straining of language to call him the Emperor of the Mound Cities. A passage from Dr. Mover's Work on the Phœnicians belongs to this localization. He says that the Persians and Arabs say, that "Saturn dwelt in the Seventh heaven, in a high, well guarded Castle, a protector of all thieves and robbers. In Phœnicia as King, he strengthened his dwelling with a wall." He then quotes authors, who say, "that the tower of Babel was built after the model of the city in the Seventh heaven, in the sphere of Saturn." This he compares to the walled city described by Enoch, in the book of Enoch. "I went forward till I came to a wall, built out of crystal. A flickering flame surrounded it, which began to frighten me. I trod into the flame and drew near a roomy dwelling, built also of crystal. It was as hot as fire and as cold as ice."

The myth of Saturn adapts itself wonderfully to the present localization, and is meaningless elsewhere. "Saturn, a son of Cœlus or Uranus, by Terra, called also Titea. He was naturally artful, and by means of his mother, he revenged himself on his father, whose cruelty to his children, had provoked the anger of Thea. The mother armed her son with a scythe, which was fabricated with the metals drawn from her bowels, and as Cœlus was going to unite himself to Thea, Saturn mutilated him, and for ever prevented him from increasing the number of his children, whom he treated with unkindness and confined in the infernal regions. After this, the sons of Cœlus were restored to liberty, and Saturn obtained his father's kingdom, by the consent of his brother, provided he did not bring up any male children. Pursuant to this agreement, Saturn always devoured his sons as soon as born, because, as some observe, he dreaded from them a retaliation of his unkindness to his father: till his wife Rhea, unwilling to see her children perish, concealed from her husband the birth of Jupiter, Neptune, and Pluto, and instead of the children she gave him large stones, which he immediately swallowed, without perceiving the deceit. Titan was some time after informed, that Saturn had concealed his male children : therefore he made war against him, dethroned and imprisoned him, with Rhea and Jupiter, who was secretly educated in Crete."

As this myth is difficult to understand, a few words of explanation may be tolerated. Cœlus here answers to Uranus, who stands for the Asiatic Colonies. Saturn dismembers this Deity by colonizing the infernal regions. He and his race become savages and perhaps cannibals.

In process of time a separation takes place, and his sons form a new State. Titan makes war with them, and they are driven out of the region of the mound cities into Europe.

But what is meant by the sons of Saturn and the concealment of their birth ? In the myth these sons are called Jupiter, Neptune and Pluto : but in the cosmogony of Sanconiathan, Ilus, who here coalesces with Saturn or Cronus, has Zeus, Belus and Apollo. What can the birth of Zeus mean and how could it have happened in the mound cities ? Here the study of the Northern Mounds ends. The place of concealment of the Gods of Greece and Europe must be sought by a critical investigation of the myths that belong to the Ophiuchus.

CHAPTER XVI.

THE EARTHWORKS WHICH ARE FOUND IN THE SOUTHERN STATES OF NORTH AMERICA, MUST HAVE BEEN INHABITED BY RACES, WHOSE TRADITIONS SHEW A CLOSE RELATIONSHIP WITH EUROPE AND PHŒNICIA.

THE SIGN OF OPHIUCHUS AND ITS MYTHOLOGY.

The constellated figure which overhangs the southern portion of the Mound cities,—agreeing tolerably well, with the Southern States of North America,—is called Ophiuchus, or Serpentarius. It is sometimes also called Esculapius, Cadmus, and Ophion.

It is a remarkable circumstance, that in the pictures which adorn the Antiquities of Mexico, there is a capital specimen of an European Ophiuchus. It must be admitted to be far superior to the figure of Ophiuchus in the Ptolemaic Zodiac, and it is set in Stars. This fact makes it unreasonable, if not impossible to deny, that there must have been a close connection between America and the old continent, in times of high antiquity. The picture is at page 24.

The region covered by the Ophiuchus has many things about it, that exhibit a more advanced state of civilization, than that delineated by Hercules. The Earthworks, themselves, are described as more substantial and artistic. The Alleghany mountains and river are in the region. This is more noticeable, inasmuch as Mr. Schoolcraft says, that it was there that the ancient tribe of Alli resided, who are credited with the erection of the Earthworks themselves. In the same region were the Cherokee and Chikasah Indians, who appear to have been, in later times, remarkable for superior characteristics. So, again, in the description given of the state of Virginia and its natives, on the first discovery of America, mention is made of images and practices in advance of the more northerly tribes.

It is under these conditions, that the search must be made for the concealment of Zeus. The myth of Ophion, in Pauly's Cyclopedia, is as follows:—" One of the oldest Titans, who with his wife Eurynome, a daughter of Oceanus, ruled over Olympus, till they retreated before Chronus and Rhea; and both threw themselves into the floods of Ocean." The myth of his wife is as follows:—" Eurynome, daughter of Oceanus, who with Tethys drove Vulcan from Olympus." In the Dionusica of Nonnus, it stands thus, " Eurynome, an Oceanide, spouse of Ophion, one of the five Giants that escaped from the battle of Olympus." Pauly has the following, " In the oldest Theogony, Eurynome, with her husband Ophion, possessed the rule of the world before Chronus." To these myths must be added. " Eurynomous, God of the under world."

This cluster of myths is very consistent with the theory of an historical base for such writings. They hang together well, and there is no fear of misunderstanding them. Ophion and Eurynome are rulers of the region now under examination, before Cronus.   This, explained in the light of an Asiatic colonization under Ouranus, and afterwards under Cronus, shews that Ophion is to Ophiuchus, what Ymir was to Hercules,—a preoccupant of the lands of the red men.   It is equally plain that Cronus drives away the Giant and his wife by a battle, and takes possession of their Empire.   But when it is said that this battle took place at Mount Olympus, one is obliged to pause.   Olympus, in Lempriere, is said to be "a Mountain of Macedonia and Thessaly.   The ancients supposed that it touched the heavens with its top, and from that circumstance, they have placed the residence of the Gods there, and have made it the Seat of Jupiter.   It is about one mile and a half in perpendicular height, and is covered with pleasant woods, caves and grottoes.   On the top of the mountain, there was no wind, no clouds, no rain, but an eternal Spring."

Of course, the present enquiry comes to a dead stop, at the sight of the word Olympus.   If Olympus and the Olympic Gods were in Thessaly, the present allocation is a blunder.   But, the Ophion myths are so plain, that search must be made into the writings of the early travellers, on the modern discovery of America, to see if they found any thing about the Alleghany mountains, that answers to Olympus.   The following facts are therefore transcribed, in short, from Picard's description of the religion of the Apalachian Indians, a race of red men, occupying a large area, in the South East portion of the United States, with the Alleghany Mountains themselves.

"The Apalachian Indians have no sacrifices, but they have temples, yet only for the purpose of burial.   They have a devil, one Toia, and they practise incision.   They have an idea of the deluge.   The sun stopped its course twenty-four hours.   The great lake Theoni overflowed the mountains, excepting only the Mountain Olaimy, one of the Alleghany mountains, which the sun preserved, because of a temple there, which the Apalachites consecrated, as a place of pilgrimage.   All who could get there avoided the deluge.   This led to the adoration of the Sun.   They salute the Sun with songs morning and evening.   Four times a year they offer sacrifices and perfumes on Mount Olaimy.   They shed no blood, as the Sun is the father of life: the giver of life would not be pleased with taking it away. They make presents to the priests with songs. The priests go to Olaimy in the evening before service, and light a fire on the mountain during night at the temple. Only Jouas or Jouans are permitted to enter. On sunrise, they sing and offer perfumes. The priests pour honey into a stone box, with maize and the pature of the bird Tonazulis, because it sings the praises of the Sun. At noon they set free six birds. They then descend the mountain with boughs and go to the temple. The pilgrims wash in sacred water. The temple is a spacious grotto, in the rock of the mountain, 200 feet long, with a vault 26 feet high."

This has to be compared with another account of a temple, at Cofaciqui, connected with the same people, given by Garcilasso. "The temple at Polemeco was the tomb of the chiefs, 100 paces long and 40 wide. It had shells on the roof, with festoons of pearls. At the door were twelve statues of giants, made of wood, and fierce. The Spaniards thought them worthy of Rome. There were guards, armed with clubs, hatches, &c. Round the temple were two rows of statues, one of men and one of women. The bucklers were pearled. The great hall was full of arms." There is a picture given of women dancing round. Then there is an account of the dance. "The Jouans,—painted, enter, with tambours, and they dance, and the assembly joins in the chorus. Then the priests run away to the woods to consult Toia. The people cut themselves. Next day, the Jouas return, and there are further dances. They fast three days, and then feast." Page 85. "In their colonies, they elevate a little Pyramid of stones."

This curious and unexpected discovery of a sacred mountain in the Alleghany range, bearing the name of the sacred mountain of the Greeks, demands careful notice—the more so, as the search for it has been made necessary, by the myths of the Ophiuchus. It turns up exactly where it ought to be, for the elucidation of those myths. One may be slow to believe that the celebrated mountain of Greece can have had its mythic antitype in the Mound cities of North America: but let the remarkable coincidences connected with the two mountains be studied. Not only is the name **Olaimy** the same as Olympus, but it is the sacred place of

Y

the Apalachian Indians,—carrying the name of the Greek
God Apollo. These Indians are worshippers of the Sun: but
Apollo is the Sun. The Jouans' temple is a Grotto—Grottoes
were erected on Olympus. In the temple there were twelve
statues—the Olympic Gods were twelve. At Olaimy were held
fasts and feasts and dances. At Olympus were the Olympic
games.

But this coincidence is insufficient of itself, because it does
not shew which mountain was the type, and which was the
antitype. That must be determined by mythology and the
localization of mythic personages. " The Olympic games are
said to have received their name, either from Olympia, where
they were observed, or from Jupiter Olympius, to whom they
were dedicated. They were, according to some, instituted by
Jupiter, after his victory over the Titans, or according to others,
by Hercules. Some attribute them to Pelops, but the more
received opinion is, that they were first established by Hercules
in honour of Jupiter Olympius, after a victory obtained over
Augias." In this passage, the Greeks do not claim the
establishment of the Olympic games as local to their country:
it is referred to their Gods, who may have lived anywhere.
The question must therefore be decided on the principle of
the present treatise—that of localization.

The three characters here mentioned are Hercules, the
Titans, and Jupiter Olympius. Hercules has been found to
be the embodiment of the northern region of the mound
cities. The Titans have been found in Mexico and Central
America. If therefore Hercules and the Titans were in
America, Jupiter Olympius must be there likewise. As to the
constellation Ophiuchus or Ophion, it overhangs the Mount
Olaimy itself. When, therefore, the Giant Ophion escapes from
the battle of Olympus, the mountain must have been in the
region he ruled. In other words, Olaimy must be the antitype
of the Greek Olympus, the original domicile of the Grecian
stemfathers. In this view, the name of the Apalachian demon,
acquires significance. It is Toia, a word bearing a curious
resemblance to Dia, a name of Jupiter. Dr. Movers shews that
Dia and Belus are the same. He quotes Berosus, by Syncellus,
who has it " Belus is interpreted Dia." Let it now be remem-

bered, that Ilus (Cronus) king of the mound cities, has three sons, Zeus, Belus, and Apollo.

This question of Olympus settled, the subject reverts to the mounds, but a material change has taken place, both in the locality of the Empire and the Emperor himself. Instead of the metropolis on the little Miami river, is Mount Olaimy on the Alleghany mountains; and instead of Saturn, is Jupiter Olympius, his son. But this change is in perfect accordance both with the myth of Saturn and the Cosmogony of Sanconiathon; and it shews what is meant by the concealment of Jupiter. It discloses later histories. The area of the myths shifts from Hercules and the northern mounds, to Zeus on those of the South. The Icelandic stories give way to Classical myths, and there opens up one of the most remarkable chapters in mythic history, the birth of the European deities in the Mound cities of America. Yet it is not to be inferred, that the mythology which reveals the birthplace of Zeus in the Earthworks, finds the Greek Colossus in a Red Indian. That were a mistake. The Pedigrees traced in this work, exhibit a pre-occupation of America by the white races, which, mingling their blood with the natives, have produced new modifications of Ethnology and the creation of a new order of Gods.

Although the Ophion myths have not exposed a Red God, they have revealed the original home of the Phœnicians. A nest of the Phœnix is found upon the Alleghany mountains. Like God, like people. If Belus were Emperor of the Southern mounds, the Phœnicians must have been his subjects. This can be proved by Classical myths and Phœnician mythology. The Greek family of Phœnix springs from Agenor and Telephassa. Agenor is son of Neptune, and brother to Belus. This might be beyond localization: but the moment it is found that Belus is at Mount Olaimy, it may be suspected that his brother Agenor is somewhere in the neighbourhood. But a lady God is sometimes more easily found than a gentleman God. It is so here. Telephassa has no parentage. All that is said of her is, that she is a nymph: but, as such, she must be American, and ought to be a river. This certainly is very curious, for any good map shews, that a river of that name actually has its spring in the Alleghany mountains. Tallapoosa is, to this day the name of the upper half of the river Alabama.

No one will deny, that this allocation of the Phœnix stem-fathers is a great breach of received opinions, and the theory certainly requires confirmation: but it can be conveniently studied by the myths of Cadmus, who is one of those fathers, being a brother of Phœnix and son of Agenor and Telephassa, and who ought therefore to stem from the river in question. Cœsius, who is an authority on such subjects, says that the history of Cadmus is tied to Ophiuchus, the constellation overhanging the Southern mound cities: so that there is a capital groundwork for this new enquiry.

It may be objected that Cadmus belongs to Phœnicia and Greece, but, in the Greek myth, he is changed into a Serpent, and a Serpent is his heraldic device. In the myth, "there is a dragon monster, that devours all his attendants, feeding on their flesh. He attacks the dragon and overcomes him by the aid of Minerva, and sows his teeth in a plain, and armed men spring up. He throws a stone among them and they kill one another. All perish, except five, who help him to build his city." This is sufficient to justify his localization in the Serpent land; but it does not bring him into the Southern mounds and their history. That is done in the Phœnician myth. In that myth, Cadmus is a cook, in the palace of the Phœnician Baalsamin, while Hermione his wife is a fifer. But that does not fix the locality of the palace. Dr. Movers supplies that desirable piece of evidence, when he quotes Martiana Capella, who says, that "it was at Mount Olympus, that the parties met." Now, it is certainly very curious, that this brings the Syrian and British Baalsamin, the heavenly Bel, into the same spot as the Greek Belus, and both of them at Mount Olaimy in the Alleghany mountains. This coincidence is very remarkable.

Yet this myth must not be interpreted in a literal and personal sense. Cadmus a cook and Hermione a fifer! These seemingly trifling tales have to be stretched into large histories: otherwise, they never would have been handed down by the ancients. Who is Cadmus? He looks like a Syrian, giving letters to Greece. But that is not the proper conception of Cadmus. The Oriental writers say, that Cadmus is Sammono-kodom, the Siamese Buddha, whose brother Thevatat was relegated to the lower regions. Cadmus is one of the names of the Ophiuchus. But who is Hermione? The following is her myth. "Hermione, a daughter of Mars and Venus, who married Cadmus. The Gods, except Juno, honoured her nuptials with their presence, and she received as a present a rich veil and a splendid necklace, which had been made by Vulcan. She was changed into a Serpent with her husband Cadmus, and placed in the Elysian fields."

Judging from these details, it may be inferred, without much fear of mistake, that the marriage of Cadmus and Hermione represents the junction of two branches of the Asiatic colonizations in America. This conclusion is justified by the remarkable presents given at the nuptials. A great deal of learning might be borrowed about these presents, but it is not necessary. On examination, the ring turns out to be the Serpentine ring, which is commonly seen in mythic pictures, encircling the Egg of the world, while the other is a Zodiac. They both belong to the mythology of the mound cities.

The marriage of Cadmus and Hermione loses none of its interest, when found to be a part of the history of the Phœnix stemfathers, in their original home. Nonnus gives the particulars, in the Dionusica. "Hermione, it is said, had been brought up in the palace of Electra." It will, afterwards, be found, that this palace is in Central America. There is a description of the palace. Cadmus himself arrives there. At the same time, comes Emathion, a son of Electra. Electra calls herself the 7th Atlantide, who will shine in heaven. Then arrives Mercury, from Zeus, to marry the happy couple.—A little further on is the deluge.

Let this be studied a little. Who is this guest Emathion? Stemfather of the Emathians, or early Macedonians. Who is Electra? Wife of Atlas the astronomer and mother of Dardanus, the founder of Troy. Where did the young clergyman come from? From Zeus, the Olympic Jupiter, sovereign of the Southern Mound cities. After that the deluge.

Now that the astonishment has passed, and the laugh subsided, on finding Olympus in the Mound cities of North America, it may be well to test the matter a little sharply. Much the best way of forming correct opinions on mythic histories, is to collate and compare the statements of the ancients, in relation to them. Let that be done in the present instance.

"Ophion, one of the oldest Titans, who with his wife Eurynome, daughter of Oceanus, ruled over Olympus, till they retreated before Chronus and Rhea, and both threw themselves into the flood of Ocean."

"Eurynome with Tethys drove Vulcan from Olympus." "Eurynome an Oceanide, spouse of Ophion, one of the five Giants that escaped from the battle of Olympus." Eurynome with Ophion, possessed the rule of the world, before Chronus." "The history of Cadmus is tied to the Ophiuchus." "The marriage of Cadmus was at Mount Olympus." In the myth of the Giants, it is said, "Some of them, as Cottus, Briareus and Gyges, had each 50 heads, and 100 arms and serpents instead of legs. The defeat of the Titans to whom they were nearly related, incensed them against Jupiter, and they all conspired to dethrone him. The God was alarmed and called all the deities to assist him against a powerful enemy, who made use of rocks, oaks, and burning wood for their weapons, and who had already heaped Mount Ossa upon Pelion, to scale with more facility the walls of heaven. At the sight of such dreadful adversaries, the Gods fled with the greatest consternation into Egypt, &c." "Styx, a nymph who dwelt at the entrance of Hades, a woman in black, with an Urn, in a lofty grotto, supported by silver columns. She was first of the immortals who took her children to Zeus, to assist him against the Titans, and in return her children were allowed for ever to live with Zeus." "Acheron, a mythic river, a river of Hades, into which the Pyriphlegethon and Cocytus flow. Acheron is called the son of Helios and Gaa, changed to a river of hell, because he had refreshed the Titans with drink, in their contest with Zeus." In the myth of Vulcan, it is said, "According to the more received opinions, Vulcan was educated with the rest of the Gods, in heaven, but his father (he was son of Jupiter and Juno), kicked him down from Olympus, when he attempted to deliver his mother, who had been fastened by a golden chain, for her insolence." In the myth of Saturn, it is said that "Titan was sometime after informed that Saturn had concealed his male children, therefore he made war against him, dethroned and imprisoned him, with Rhea and Jupiter, who was secretly educated in Crete." Most of the quotations have been given in former parts of this work : but it was necessary to place them here, in juxta-position, to enable the reader to form opinions. There is, however, no reason to argue on the matter. Every one will see at once, that neither the geography nor the dramatis personæ introduced by these passages, have any connection whatever with Greece. The only character that hangs on to Greece is Zeus himself, and he is a stranger. He is driven from some other land into Crete, where he is said to be educated.

On the other hand, all the places spoken of and the personages introduced, belong to the same location. What the location is, is plain enough. It is the region of the Earthworks of North America, round about the Alleghany mountains, the gulf of Texas (Styx), the Mississippi (Acheron), and Mount Olaimy, all within the large region delineated in the map by the figure of Ophiuchus.

The chief subject of the group of myths now under consideration, is the Wars of Olympus. It would seem, that Ophion and his wife Eurynome, possessed the rule of the world, that is to say, of the Southern Earthworks before Chronus. Ophion himself is not a native Indian. The serpents are the aborigines. Ophion is one of the oldest Titans, a race already discovered on the western shores of America. Eurynome also is an Oceanide. Then there are wars between Ophion, Emperor of the Southern Mounds, and Chronus, Emperor of the Northern Mounds. This battle must have taken place at Olympus, and Ophion with four other Giants escaped. But there must have been more battles than one, for Ophion and Eurynome retreat before Chronus and Rhea, and throw themselves into the flood of Ocean. They are driven out of the land altogether.

Then there is another war, from the west. Titan, who must here be taken for the Totonaque race of Mexico, is informed that Saturn had concealed his children,—probably by forming a new settlement at Olympus, and he makes war against him, dethrones him, and imprisons him with Rhea and Jupiter. Titan is assisted by the Giants, or savages from the Acheron,

the Mississippi. On the other hand, Jupiter is assisted by
Styx and her children, from the shores of the gulf of Texas.
Jupiter, alarmed, called all the Gods to assist him. But this
war must have been fatal to Jupiter, as he is driven out of the
country into Crete. But not before Vulcan had been kicked
out and fallen near the same island.

The wars, now described, constitute what may be called, the
birth of Europe's Gods. It must be so; as the characters
comprised in the myths now analysed, are not minor personages. They stand at the summit of the Hierarchy of European
deities. Chronus and Rhea, Jupiter and Juno, Zeus and Hera,
form in their several countries of the old continent, the chief
deities. This is an illustration of what is said in the myth of
Oceanus, that "he was the father of all the Gods."

Mythology teaches, that the races located in the Mound cities
of North America, must not only have been driven out by war,
but that, in various ways, they must have voluntarily forsaken
their Earthworks, and sent off colonies across the Atlantic
ocean into Europe, Africa, and Asia. The tale is told in many
different forms, and in the traditions of many nations. The
classics have it in a group of myths, headed by that of Europa,
who gives name to Europe. Jupiter retires to the sea coast,
and arrives safely in Crete. Cadmus and his brothers follow.
Another version of the story, is called the flight of Cadmus and
Hermione. Another is in the cosmogony of Sanconiathon,
where Cronus visits different regions of the habitable globe.
Some few details of this great historical event, will be developed
in later chapters of this work.

CHAPTER XVII.

The North American Indian from a modern Standpoint.

As the subject of the Mound cities and their inhabitants
is very interesting, in an Anthropological point of view, it may

be well to look at the questions raised in the last two chapters from a modern standpoint.

Mr. Schoolcraft enters largely into all the details concerning the North American Indians. He says, "At the close of the fifteenth century, the tribes of the present area of the United States were spread out, chiefly, in seven principal groups, or generic families of tribes, each of which consisted of numerous sub-tribes,—bands, or large totemic circles. Each of these spoke a language differing in some respect from the others. Each circle had some tribal peculiarities, in custom or manners. These groups were the Apalachian, Achalaque, Chichorean, Algonquin, Iroquois, Dacota and Shoshone."

This description of the modern area of the Earthworks compares well with the tracings of mythology. The Scandinavian tradition refers to Hela the dominion over nine regions. The Hindoo description of Patala divides the region into seven Patalas and designates them Hell Kingdoms. See the diagram at page 167, where the circles are called seven halls of purification, or Niriks, a word interpreted by Hells. As the seven modern tribes spoke a different language, it may be safely inferred that the modern tribal divisions were the outcome of totemic circles existing in the mythic ages.

The North American Indian of modern times, when first found in the vast woods and prairies, was a savage. He had no habitation except the meanest and the least substantial erection in which a family can live :—call it a lodge or wigwam. He was addicted to no mechanical arts, by which civilized life is distinguished. He spent his time in the hunting grounds, roaming through the wide expanse of hill and dale, in the track of wild animals. He was wholly uneducated. His pleasures consisted in the wild dances of the camp fire. He was habituated to the most cruel customs of torture,—receiving the lash and the gash with indomitable courage. The scalping knife, the tomahawk, and the war whoop were his pride and his delight.

Yet he had characteristics irreconcileable with savagery. He was a fine and noble specimen of a man. Intelligence sparkled in his eye. He was chaste, sober, honest, and religious. No warrior trained to the arts of civilized warfare, could plan or

z

execute a hostile attack upon a foe, with more adroitness than he. His skill in tracking the footprints of man or beast, seemed more than human. He dressed in habiliments gaudy and fantastic, it is true, but by no means destitute of picturesque effect. Thus attired, he stalked throughout the long vistas of his native woods,—a man.

This combination of good and bad qualities in the North American Indian is well illustrated by an anecdote told of a Virginian warrior chief. The writer says, " we commence the description of Indian customs with a piece of history, that serves to shew the greatness of soul of a people which we call savages. Oppechancanough, Emperor of Virginia, having had the misfortune to fall into the hands of the English, the Chevalier Berkley, governor of the colony, wished, one day, to let the public see him. The Virginian Prince, whose age had affected his eyes, so that he could not see without the assistance of one of his subjects, having many people round him suddenly had his eyes opened. The sight of the multitude threw him into a rage. He demanded fiercely, that the Governor should come—reproached him for the manner in which he had treated him, and said with disdain—'if fortune had let you fall into my hands, I would not have had the cowardice to expose you to the laughter of my people.'" Add to this what Mr. Catlin says, that "no Indian ever betrayed me—struck me a blow—or stole from me a shilling's worth of my property, that I am aware of."

The presence of such qualities as these in the red man, marks him out, not as the member of an aboriginal race, but as a deteriorated descendant of men of noble blood. He is not a savage—he is a degenerate gentleman. This is exactly his position in mythology. He is a Giant in strength, and a Mongolidan in courtesy. He is wound round by Serpents, but he strangles them. He is represented half-goat, half-man, to retain the remembrance of his ethnological position, as a junction of the two races, red and white.

Mr. Catlin gives some very interesting and curious traditions which seem to favour the supposition, that the modern Indians were the descendants of strangers who came from a distance. He gives the following Choctaw tradition. "The Choctaws, a great many winters ago, commenced moving from a place, where they then lived, which was a great distance to the west of the great river and the mountains of snow, and they were a great many years on their way. A great medicine man led them the whole way, by going before them, with a red pole, which he stuck in the ground every night, where they encamped. This pole was found every morning, leaning to the East. When the pole stood upright in their encampment, there the Great Spirit had directed, that they should live. At a place, which they named, Nak-ne-way-ye, the pole stood straight up. There they pitched their encampment, which was one mile square, with the men encamped on the outside, and the women and children in the centre, which is the centre of the Choctaw nation to this day."

Again, "The Great Spirit, at an ancient period, called the Indian natives together, and standing on the precipice of the red pipe stone track, broke from its wall a piece, and made a huge pipe by burning it in his hand, which he smoked over them to the north and south and east and west, and told them, that this stone was red, that it was their flesh, that they must use it for their pipes of peace, that it belonged to them all, and that the war club and scalping knife must not be raised upon its ground. At the last sniff of his pipe, his head went into a great cloud, and the whole surface of the rock for several miles, was melted and glazed. Two great ovens were opened beneath, and two women, guardian spirits of the place, entered them in a blaze of fire, and they disappeared."

It must be admitted, that these traditions harmonize in the highest degree with the histories and the classic myths which have been brought forward to elucidate the mysterious affairs of America. Uranus, the first king of the Atlantic Isle, does the very same thing as the medicine man referred to in the above tradition. He collects the people into confraternities and teaches them to build cities. To what extent he succeeded, must be estimated by the enormous multitude of earthworks, that lie scattered over the United States.

It would almost seem, from the Choctaw tradition, that the modern medicine man himself,—at once the physician and the priest of the tribe,—was a creation of this civilizing people.

In the imperfect conceptions of the Indians, he seems to be confounded with the Great Spirit himself. He leads the people. He fixes their abode. But it cannot escape notice, that this reformer is in possession of the noblest principles of religion and peace. He is averse to war, to the scalping knife and the tomahawk. It looks a great deal, as if this medicine man were the descendant of the Asiatic colonists, whose advent into America has been traced out, in the foregoing pages.

Under these circumstances, it is not at all surprising, that in the adaptation of the myths of the classics to the country, it should be found, that the civilizers of the people are called Gods, in distinction from the Giants, the aborigines of the land. In process of time, these Gods are found located in many favoured spots, such as the Alleghany mountains; mixing more or less with the natives in course of ages, they give rise to new races, half savage and half civilized, the deteriorated remains of which are the modern Indian.

In this native tradition, mention is made of a rod used by the guiding medicine man. This rod is discoverable in all traditionary histories. It is seen in the hand of the native Mexican figure, at page 158, and it is the rod that budded, laid up in the temple ark.

Among the perplexing questions which arise out of the last few chapters, there is perhaps none which is calculated to excite more astonishment than that which treats the Southern and South-Eastern states, as the original domicile of the Phœnicians. This hypothesis has arisen in two separate forms. It has arisen from the Cosmogony of Sanchoniathon, which is the cosmogony of Phœnicia. It arises also from the Greek myths of Phœnix and his brothers. It has been brought out prominently, to view, in the story of Cadmus, who is an eminent member of that distinguished race of men.

This teaching can be put to the test, by looking at it from a modern point of view. There is no better evidence of consanguinity, than resemblance between the religious habits and customs of people. In the great work entitled Aglio, to which valuable book frequent reference is made in this work, there is an important contribution to the elucidation of the present question. It consists of an account of the religious customs of the Chickasaw and Cherokee Indians. Mr. Adair who lived among those tribes, furnishes an account which may be conveniently epitomized.

The Indians of those tribes had the custom of tearing out the hair like the Jewish novitiate, priests and proselytes. They were divided into tribes with badges— families of eagles, panthers, tigers, &c. They had Cherubinical figures. They had the same regard for lineal descent as the Israelites. They call God Loak. Ishtohoolo—is great holy—great holy spirit of fire. They have the word Jehovah, which they pronounce Jehowah. They have no idol in any way. But he then says, that they have a wooden statue, which leads them in war. In their dances, they sing Hal-elu-yah Yo-he-wah. He says, that in the Synhedria, he has seen two painted Eagles, carved of poplar, with wings stretched out, and the Indians paint a chalky clay figure of a man, and it must be painted afresh at annual fruit offerings. Every warrior must make three wolfish campaigns, with the holy ark, before he can wear the buffalo horns on his head or have the tail behind him in the dance. They have the idea, that they are the peculiar and chosen people of God.

The Indian archimagus is dressed in a white ephod,—a waistcoat without sleeves. He has a breast-plate of white conch shells, and a wreath of swan feathers on his forehead. They have the daily lamb sacrifice. They have the same notions as the Israelites, in relation to clean and unclean beasts. Hogs are unclean. There are no eunuchs, nor have they the custom of circumcision. Blood for blood is a maxim among them. They have towns of refuge. They have an ark with sacred things deposited in it. In a note, it is said, that they have a tradition of leaving their native land, with a sanctified rod, and they came to the Mississippi.

Of course, any one is at liberty to judge, that these people must have been Jews, who had forsaken their home in the Holy Land, and had emigrated to America. But this conclusion is very difficult to believe, inasmuch as no Israelite would admit consanguinity in the absence of circumcision.

It is much easier to believe, that the early inhabitants of Phœnicia and Palestine were immigrants from the mound cities

of America. The cosmogony, by implication, does say so, when
it attributes to the Giants the naming of the Phœnician
mountains and towns.

There is still another question which has forced itself into
notice in working out the myths of the classics in their
relation to the South-Eastern portion of the Earthworks. It
is the birth of the Gods of Europe in that locality. Without
the localization of myths, such a thing looks chimerical. But
on study, it will be found, that the description given by early
European settlers in Virginia, concerning the customs of the
Indians in those parts of the country, creates a strong suspicion—to say the least of it—that mythology is only disclosing
the real origin of Europe's Gods when it brings them from
the mound cities of the United States. Let the following
account of the Virginian Gods be read.

A traveller says, "One day we fell upon the Quiocasan, or
temple, at an hour when every body was at a rendezvous.
Pleased with so good an occasion, we resolved to profit by it.
After having removed from the door twelve or fifteen bars
of wood, we entered and we at once perceived, that the walls
were bare, with fire in the midst. This house was eighteen feet
wide and thirty long, with an opening to give passage to the
smoke. The door of the temple was at one of the extremities.
Outside and at some distance from the building, there were
posts all round, of which the tops were painted, and represented the faces of men in relief. There was no window, nor
any place to let in the light, except the door and the opening
for the chimney. When we entered, we found towards the
middle of the enclosure, piles, upon the top of which, were
great planks. We drew out three boxes—one contained bows,
and another a tomahawk. Attached to one of the tomahawks
was an image of an Indian chief, painted red. The third
contained what we took for an Idol of the Indians."

"The Indians give divers names to this Idol. Some call it,
Okee; others, Quiocas or Kiwasa. Perhaps these names must
be regarded as epithets, which change according to fashion.
Others say, that this Idol is only a single being, and that
there are others of the same nature, besides the tutelary God.
They give to all these beings or Genii, the general name of

Quiocas; so that we designate particularly under the name of Kiwasa, the Idol of which we speak.

KIWASA.

"The artist has not represented here, the Idol Kiwasa in his temple. He places it in the open country, in a tent made of mats, upon a kind of seat or Altar, which the Virginians name Perowance. The people consecrate to their divinity, chapels and oratories, where one often sees several different representations of the Idol. They have them also in the interior of lodges. They consult them on occasions, and communicate to them their affairs. They serve them for tutelary Gods, and it is by their means, that blessings descend upon the family. They often represent Kiwasa with a pipe in his mouth, and real smoke, for the pipe is lighted."

"Kiwasa often manifests himself by oracles or by visions. They consult him for the chase and for objects of less importance. As among them, caprice is the effect of the inspiration of God, so in times that they go to the chase, he comes to them in the spirit of the chase. They terminate the chase because they believe that God orders it so. When it is necessary to invoke him, four priests go to the temple of the God, and conjure him, by the means of certain words unknown to the people. Then Kiwasa disguises himself under the form of a handsome man—ornaments the left side of his head with a tuft of hair, which descends to the heels, appearing in this state in the midst of the air. At first, he receives them with agitation, but calms himself the moment after, and calls eight other priests. The assembly being formed, he declares to them his will, after which he takes his way back again to heaven."

"The Virginians have symbolic figures. They often raise pyramids and columns, which they paint and ornament, according to taste. They elevate altars everywhere, where any thing remarkable happens. But there is one particular altar, which they honour above all the others. Before the arrival of the English, the great altar was in a place that the Virginians call Uttamasak. One sees there the principal temple of the country, and this place was the metropolitan seat of the priests. One sees there also three great houses, one of sixty feet long and full of images. They preserve the bodies of their kings, in their religious houses, for which the aborigines of the country have great respect. It was only permitted to kings and priests to enter. The people were not permitted and they dared not appear in their sanctuaries, without permission of the chief. The grand altar was a single crystal three or four inches square."

Compare this with Lucian's description of the Syrian Apollo. "Of the works of this Apollo, 1 could indeed say many things, but I will only mention the most remarkable, and first make mention of his oracle. By the Greeks and Egyptians were many oracles, but they were made known by priests and prophets. But this moved itself, and performed the business of soothsaying without the help of any one. The kind and way was the following; when he wishes to communicate an oracle, he first moves himself on his seat. Then the priests lift him on high; when they do not raise him, he lifts himself on high. If they carry him on the shoulders, he drives them round in a circle and springs from one to the other. Lastly, the high priest places himself opposite to him, and asks him concerning all. When he will not that any thing should be done, he goes backward. When he approves any thing, he drives those that carry him forwards as a leader."

It is impossible not to see that this description of the Syrian Apollo is the same as that of Kiwasa. Let it be remembered that Kiwasa is God of the Apalachian Indians, and that his temple is exactly at the same spot as has been tracked out by means of the Phœnician cosmogony itself, as the birth place of Zeus, Belus and Apollo.

It is now quite manifest that on the discovery of Virginia, the Indians of that part of North America were in possession of a religion, unlike that of the Indian tribes in general, but bearing a great resemblance to European Heathendom. There is no reason at all, why it should not be called the religion of Zeus, Belus, or Apollo. That being so, there is a very strong evidence of consanguinity between the two people, making allowance for degeneration on the one part, and the growth of civilization on the other. When, therefore, the localization of the dramatis personæ of European traditionary history leads to the vicinity of the Alleghany mountains, as the original domicile of Europe's Gods, there is no good reason why it should not be admitted.

Time and change work wonders in the revolutions of history. At the present day, Europe is giving to America—not gods—but population, intelligence, and wealth. Is it strange that, in earlier times, America should have given Gods?

According to Didorus Siculus, Stonehenge—the great and wonderful erection which stands on the plains of Salisbury—a puzzle to antiquarians and a mystery in the obscure history of Great Britain—was a temple of Apollo. It is quite manifest that Britain could not have received the religion of Apollo from Greece, for it is expressly said, that the Apollo of Greece came from the Isle of the Hyperboreans. Britain is the true Isle of the Hyperboreans, and Stonehenge, the high place of its God—Apollo. To find the birth of Apollo in the Mound cities of North America is to supply a natural and credible explanation of the mystery of Stonehenge. The Apalachian Indians are said to have erected altars, and to have massed heaps of stones wherever they founded colonies, and they must have carried with them the religion of their race.

In the great work of Picard, from which these extracts are taken, there is a picture of another Virginian Idol. A copy of it is here presented for study.

VIRGINIAN INDIAN GOD OF WINDS.

Unfortunately, there is nothing said respecting this figure. But verbal explanation of it is really unnecessary. It tells its own tale admirably. It is like opening the shutters of a dark room. If the Virginian Indians were found in possession of such an Idol as this, they must have had histories very different from those with which North American Indians are commonly credited. Looking at it, thoughtfully, one can hardly believe that the Virginian Indians worshipped such a God as this. Perhaps it is only a picture: but that makes no difference; where did they get it, and how?

Here is a black man, yet he has not Negro's features. He is well dressed. Then he holds in his hand a very fine specimen of a Negro's head, about which there can be no mistake. He is called God of the winds, and he holds in his hand the symbols of navigation. But who is he? From what harbour did he set sail? That question is easily answered, from his features and colour. He comes from Africa. But, is it possible that the Virginian Indians had intercourse, by navigation, with Africa, and that before the arrival of the European races! One is at liberty to hesitate before he reaches that conclusion. But why should he be called a God of the Virginian Indians?

On the whole, it is manifest, that the great hiatus of history, which has arisen out of the blunder of the sunken Island of the Atlantis, has to be filled up with incidents, histories, and navigation, of which the people of modern Europe have at present no reasonable conception.

The sudden appearance of this African navigator in the lodges of the Virginian Indians, acts as a stimulant of thought. Looking at the figure, it suggests the supposition that the route of Africa must have supplied the medium of communication between the inhabitants of the mounds and the shores of the old continent. The distance between the North-Eastern parts of South America and the coast of Africa is not greater than the length of the Mediterranean Sea. This suggestion agrees with the Classical myths. The course of research has now brought this enquiry to those events which must have opened up the passage of the Atlantic, and it will soon be found that the story hangs on to Africa, as being, at least, one of the earliest landing places of the Atlantic race, in their search for transmarine settlements.

Whatever opinions may be entertained by the learned concerning the method employed in this work to track out the mysterious histories of the mound cities of North America, it is undeniable, that the subject is one of the deepest interest, affecting as it does, the fidelity of all history.

CHAPTER XVIII.

CENTRAL AMERICA, No. 1. The MYSTERIOUS RUINS AND
HIDDEN HISTORIES OF CENTRAL AMERICA, STUDIED BY MEANS
OF THE SAGITARIUS AND OTHER SIGNS AS ZODIACAL POR-
TRAITURE OF THE COUNTRY.

THE SIGN OF THE SAGITARIUS AND ITS MYTHOLOGY.

MAP OF CENTRAL AMERICA.

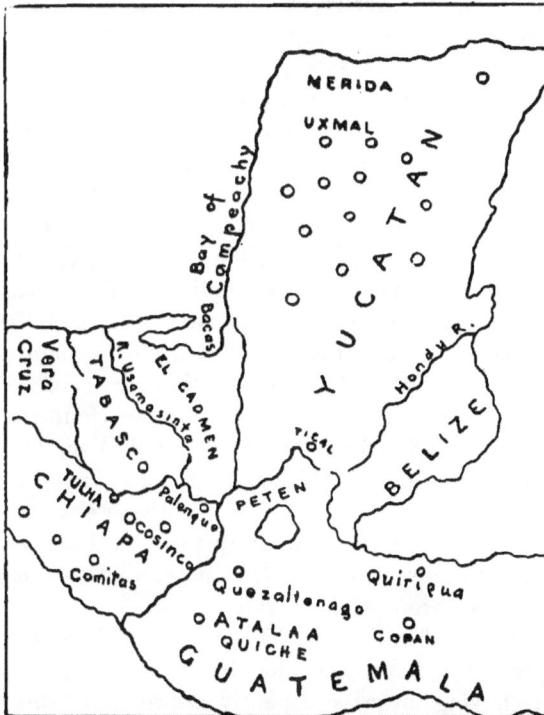

Central America proper, is the Isthmus which connects the
two Insular Continents of North and South America. The
conformation of the Isthmus is very remarkable, and it makes
a very noticeable feature in the Map of the world. Its position,
in modern times, may make it an impediment to the navigation
of large ships in the Great Oceans; but it must always have

been an inlet and outlet to both divisions of the hemisphere. It now becomes necessary to search the literature of the ancients, to discover if any light can be thrown upon its early histories.

The conquest of New Spain was soon followed up by priests and monks, who formed settlements throughout the acquired territory. To a resident clergy, the features of the surrounding countries and their condition, could not remain unknown; and in process of time, they became aware of the existence of ruined cities, in other possessions than those of Mexico and Peru. The first direct attempt to acquire a correct knowledge of the ruined cities of Central America, was made by the French; and an artist, both well qualified for the purpose, and supplied with a sufficient escort, was sent into the country. The result of this exploration was given to the world, in some volumes of extraordinary beauty and value. But it was reserved to Mr. Stephens, an American gentleman, to favour the reading public with an accessible volume on this subject.

Central America includes the provinces of Oaxaca, Tabasc, Chiapa, Guatamala, Yucatan, Honduras, Nicaragua, Costa Rica, and Panama. But the ruins and ancient remains are not discovered in all those provinces; they are spread over a much smaller area of country. They are found clustering around two centres—those of Quiche and Yucatan,—that is to say, they are found chiefly in the provinces of Tabasc, Chiapa, Guatamala, and Yucatan. In the work of Brasseur de Bourbourg, on the traditionary histories of Central America, it is made manifest, that the semi-civilization of Central America on a large scale, divided itself into three distinct parts,—first, the Empire of the Nahoas in Mexico, secondly, the Empire of Quiche, and thirdly, the Empire of Yucatan. The first having been sufficiently considered, the two last alone are embraced in the present study.

Central America, in the Ptolemaic Zodiac, is depicted by the Sagitarius. This sign is a compound-figure and a non-descript. It is a horse in its hinder parts and a human being in front, holding a bow and arrow. A few extracts from Poetical Astronomers are here necessary. "One makes him a son of Ocean. He beats the measure, when the Muses sing and dance. He loved navigation. He is seen not only by those who live on the land, but by those who go to sea. At his right hand rises the Ship Argo. Hyginus calls him the son of Pan and Eupheme."—Dupuis. In the Coptic Zodiac, there is the same figure, and it is supplemented by a human hand, holding an arrow, and called in both cases, Arueris or Regnum Arueris. The Hindoo Zodiac has the same figure, designated Dhanus the bow. In the Classics, it is Chiron the Centaur who is associated with the Sagitarius.

The following is the myth of Chiron. "Chiron, a Centaur, half-a-man and half-a-horse, son of Philyra and Saturn, who had changed himself into a horse, to escape the enquiries of his wife Rhea. Chiron was famous for his knowledge of music, medicine and shooting. He taught the use of plants and medicinal herbs to mankind, and he instructed, in all the politest arts, the greatest heroes of his age,—such as Achilles, Æsculapius, Hercules, &c. He was wounded in the knee by a poisoned arrow by Hercules, in his pursuit of the Centaurs. Hercules flew to his assistance, but as the wound was incurable, and the cause of the most excruciating pains, Chiron begged Jupiter to deprive him of immortality. His prayers were heard, and he was placed by the God among the constellations under the name of Sagitarius."

Montfaucon says that Xenophon makes Chiron to be the brother of Jupiter, but he was born of Nais, not Rhea. Nais is one of the Oceanides, mother of Chiron, or Glaucus, by Magnes. "The Naiades were certain inferior deities who presided over rivers, springs, wells, and fountains. The Naiades generally inhabited the country, and resorted to the woods or meadows, near the stream over which they presided. They are represented as young and beautiful virgins, often leaning upon an urn from which flows a stream of water. Ægle was the fairest of the Naiades, according to Virgil, &c." The Naiades were mothers of Priapus, God of gardens—Montfaucon. This curious character, Chiron, hardly has the lofty position in history which his tradition assigns to him. His monstrosity hides his dignity. When placed in Central America, as its impersonation, he recovers his consequence, as the brother of Jupiter. His parentage shews him to be the embodiment of the pre-occupants of North America, coming into the Paradisaical garden-land of Central America, from the woods and prairies of the red men. It is fair to suppose that he had something to do with the erection of the numerous cities which lie embedded in the luxurious foliage of his plants and flowers.

It is not possible to define his exact location His name is radically the same spelling as Charon, the boatman of the Styx, who must certainly be put upon the Mexican gulf. Wherever it was, Chiron must have had much to do with the civilization, education, and refinement of mankind. He was the teacher of the heroes and gods of the past world. His educational establishment was frequented by some of the most distinguished characters. Let them be mentioned. They must all have lived in the now forsaken ruins, at least for a time.

Hercules is among the scholars; so that it must be inferred that the inhabitants of the mound cities made settlements in Central America, and were put under a course of instruction, before they forsook the land in search of new homes. Esculapius was another of the scholars. This brings the Mexicans into the isthmus, before the serpent God became the God of Carthage, Epidaurus and Babylon.

It is curious to find Achilles in this school, yet it is consistent with the localization of his early mythic life. "Achilles, the son of Peleus and Thetis, was the bravest of all the Greeks, in the Trojan war. During his infancy, Thetis plunged him in the Styx and made every part of his body invulnerable, except the heel, by which she held him, &c." The very important personage called Æneas was likewise entrusted to Chiron the Centaur. This will be better studied in the chapter on the Inca of Peru.

It is certainly a surprise to find Jason under the training of Chiron, in the cities of Central America; but there is much to justify the allocation. It is said that "the Sagitarius loved navigation. At his right hand rises the Ship Argo." In the cosmogony of Sanconiathon, it is the Cabires who make the first perfect ship and put to sea. On the whole, it must be admitted that the mythology of Chiron, the Centaur, as exponent of the obscure histories of Central America and

its ruins, invests the land with great distinction and significance in the lost histories of America.

PAN AND CUPID.

Sagitarius is said to be the son of Pan and Eupheme.
As a father is earlier than a son, it may fairly be expected
that the study of Pan will carry back the histories of Central
America to an earlier date than Chiron.

THE GOD OF TABASC.

There can be no manner
of doubt that the present
tracing of the myth of
the Sagitarius is correct,
because Pan, the father
of the Centaur, was actu-
ally the God of Central
America on the dis-
covery of the Province,
in modern history. In
the work of Picard,
which treats of the re-
ligion of the country,
there is a picture entitled
the Gods of Tabasc and
Campeachy. "Tabasc is
one of the modern
provinces of Central
America, lying upon the
shores of the Mexican
gulf. It is described, by
travellers, as a marvel
of beauty, and such as
must have been one of the countries first civilized."

The present picture forms a part of the scene. It exhibits,
in a striking manner, the horrible practice of human sacrifice,
in the Mexican style. The priest after having opened the
breast of the victim, offers the heart to the Idol, and smears
its mouth with blood. In the original picture, on a hill, there
is another figure of small dimensions, holding a bow and arrows.
It does not require an expert to decide that this Tabasc Idol

is a Pan. It is so manifest as to require no argumentation. The figure is a Pan in the European form and dress, so that Pan, the father of the Sagitarius, must have been the God of Tabasc and Campeachy.

But not only is the Idol a Pan; the priest answers to Cupid. The symbol of Cupid is a bow and arrows. The Sagitarius holds in his hands the emblem of Cupid, and the figure of Cupid is on the hill behind the Idol. In a research into the dark history of this land, this circumstance requires notice. In European mythology, there is a curious connection between Pan and Cupid. In mythological monuments this connection is called the Struggle of Cupid and Pan. A picture is here given of that scene, where Cupid stands upon the recumbent person of Pan, and he holds the human heart in his hand, exactly in the same way as does the Tabasc priest. If he is not smearing the mouth of the God, he holds it very near to it. So complete is the identity of these two scenes, that it would be unreasonable to deny that the struggle of Cupid and Pan has its antitype in Tabasc Idolatry.

STRUGGLE OF CUPID AND PAN.

It is usual to consider Cupid as the God of Valentines and flowers, and it quite spoils the poetry to find him anything else; but this comparison of gods leads to the inevitable conclusion, that he is a sacrificial priest, instead. Time and change of place have so completely hidden the real historical antiquities of mankind, that even the bloody practice of human sacrifice has got metamorphosed into a valentine! But there hangs about the traditions and pictures of the ancient world so much of the original truth, as that, by research, it may be brought to light. That the character now assigned to Cupid is the true one, may be seen from the circumstance, that Kamadewa, the Hindoo Cupid, has the epithet of "Lord of punishments." He is an executioner. In Greek mythic history, there are two Cupids, Eros and Anteros. Anteros is a savage with a club.

But this subject can be carried further, and with historical conclusions that throw light upon the ruined cities of Central America. The picture of the struggle of Cupid and Pan has a counterpart in the Hindoo collection of historical pictures.

GARUDA AND HANUMAN.

There is no doubt about the identity of Pan and Cupid with Hanuman and Garuda. Garuda is the son of Vinata, just as Cupid is son of Venus. Hanuman is the son of Pavana. Garuda and Cupid are both men birds, the Harpies of the ancients. Pan is leader of the Pans and Satyrs, and Hanuman is the Monkey God of India, answering to the Pans and Satyrs. They play a great *rôle* in the story of the Ramayana.

The advantage of this comparison lies in the very plain nature and office of Garuda. He is the Vahan of Vishnu. He carries the Oceanides into India. He is a mystic ship, navigating between Central America and Hindostan.

One of the tablets discovered at Palenque is here given. It consists of a well dressed man, holding an ornamental staff.

NATIVE TABLET AT PALENQUE.   GARUDA AND HANUMAN.

On each side of him is a native flat headed Indian, sitting on his haunches, in attire quite original and unimproved. By the side of this group is another specimen of Garuda and Hanuman, still in company, but back to back.

Let the reader make a comparison of these pictures and their detailed features, and he will be sure to come to the conclusion, that the images of Garuda and Hanuman is a Hindoo reproduction of the Palenque tablet. Let the eye gradually pass down the head, bust, and arms of Garuda, comparing them with the Palenque figure. Then let Hanuman be compared with the two Indians. The monkey features are produced by the boards which formed the flat head.

Pan and Hanuman answer to the flat headed Indian, and Cupid and Garuda to the Atlas race, so that these two races must have formed the inhabitants of the land for ages.

ARUERIS.

In the Coptic Zodiac, the Sagitarius is designated Regnum Arueris. If there is one thing more important than another in Egyptology, it is the localization of the Egyptian Gods. It is by that means only, that it can be made available for the elucidation of history. In this case, the Copts assign to Arueris the province of Central America.

Aroeri, Aroeris, is the elder Horus, brother of Isis and Osiris. Aroeris was the son of Seb and Netpe, and at Philae he is represented under the form of a hierac-Sphinx. In a papyrus he is styled, "Haroeri, Lord of the Solar Spirits, the beneficent eye of the Sun."

It is highly confirmatory of the allocation of Arueris in Central America, to find him in the form of a Sphinx; for, in point of fact, the Sphinxes are Centaurs—they are half animals, half men. The Sagitarius may with propriety be called a Sphinx.

There is no very distinguishable difference between Aroeris, Horus, and Hor-Hat, Agathodemon. This is mentioned, because the travellers who have explored Central American ruins, found the peculiar emblem of Hor-Hat, the winged sun, over the doorway of a ruined house.

WINGED SUN AT OCOSINCO AND WINGED SUN OF HOR-HAT.

A copy of this fragment is here given, together with the emblem of Hor-Hat. The fragment was found at Ocosinco. Brasseur de Bourbourg describes the country about Ocosinco as a place of "the birth of civilization." He says, that "Tulha was the capital, where ruins are found near Ocosinco. It rivals Palenque. There is a curious tradition, that there was an underground communication between Tulha and Palenque." In Mr. Stephens' work, the travellers reach this place, where are ruins of pyramidal erections. "There is a door over which is an ornament like the Egyptian winged globe. There are no serpents."

The legend of Hor-Hat makes him "to have some connection with Horus. The winged Sun belongs to Hor-Hat, the Agathodemon. The device is over doorways. Sometimes he is a hawk, pouring life on kings. When drawn as a man, with a hawk's head, he seems to be the Agathodemon of the Phœnicians. Eusebius makes him to be Neph and a Serpent. The temple at Apollonopolis or Edfoo, was dedicated to him; so that he is a form of Apollo. He stands in a boat, and before him are Thoth, Isis, and Nephtys. Horus pierces Apophis with a spear."

But what is meant when it is said that Arueris was brother to Isis and Osiris, and son of Seb and Netpe? Turned into geography and history, it means that the inhabitants of Central America were colonists from China, Thibet, and Siberia. From this, it must be inferred, that the God or Gods to whom the temples of Apollonopolis and elsewhere in Egypt were dedicated, had been dwellers in the ruined cities of Quiche, Tabasc, and Yucatan. The capital of Tulha, Ocosinco, and Palenque, must have been the heavenly domicile of the Amenti Gods of Egypt.

There are many things about the ruins of Central America, that, of themselves, create a belief that the early Egyptians must have had something to do with the erection of the buildings. A few extracts from the work of Du Paix, entitled Antiquites Mexicans, will be sufficient to shew that the style of building is Egyptian. In the first Expedition, page 4, it is said, " At Tepayacan are the ruins of a Pyramid, 55-ft. square and 70-ft. high. The artist calls it Egyptian style. At

Quahnahuac, he found a stone with a Maltese cross sculptured on it." In the second Expedition, he comes into the country of the Zapotecs, where are numerous tumuli with underground chambers and figures of men very different from other places. He speaks of them as quite Egyptian. At page 87, he says, "No nation but Egypt was so careful of the dead as the Zapoteque." The author was convinced that an underground world could be found by digging. He also says, that "the Mexicans were not artists. They leaned upon the Zapoteque nation, who were artists." Add. to this, that a Basso relievo found at Chichen in Yucatan is drawn in a style so peculiar to Egypt, with Hieroglyphics on the sides, as to put it into the category of Egyptian designs.

The mysterious affinity between the Egyptians and the inhabitants of Central America can be elucidated by pursuing a little further the subject of the Gods of Apollonopolis. The Greeks saw in Arueris the elder Apollo. This must be interpreted to mean—not their own Pythian-Apollo, but some Apollo of earlier time. That earlier Apollo is found by comparative Idolatry to be Belus, or Bel, or Baal.

To the elucidation of this subject, nothing is wanted but the Greek myths of Belus and Ægyptus. "Belus, a celebrated deity, worshipped by the Assyrians, Babylonians, and Egyptians. This was one of the most ancient kings of Babylon, about 1800 years before the age of Semiramis. He was made a god after death, and was supposed to be the son of Osiris of the Egyptians, &c." "Ægyptus, a son of Belus and brother to Danaus, gave his fifty sons in marriage to the fifty daughters of his brother. Danaus, who had established himself at Argos, and was jealous of his brother, obliged all his daughters to murder their husbands, the first night of their nuptials. This was executed, and Hypermnestra alone spared her husband Lynceus. Even Ægyptus was killed by his niece Polyxeus."

DHANUS THE BOW.

In the Hindoo Zodiac, the name of the Sagitarius is Dhanus, the bow. It is a Centaur, shooting an arrow backwards. From this, it must be inferred, that Dhanus was the Hindoo name for the inhabitants of Central America, if not the country itself. This Dhanus corresponds with Danaus the brother of

Ægyptus; so that both the sons of Belus must have been local in the ruined cities in former ages.

"Danaus was the son of Belus and Anchinoe." The myth is not needed, as it refers to the movements which must have belonged to the settlements of the Oceanides in Egypt and Greece. It makes capital mythology to be obliged to transfer these two mythic stemfathers from the Mediterranean Sea to the gulf of Texas, as it is a very ugly, unnatural, and impossible story as it stands. Shifted, it takes the two races of Egyptians and Danaids from Central America to Egypt and Greece.

The subject of Bel and Belus, as a God in close affinity to Esculapius, has been referred to before. It makes a very conspicuous part of the mythology of Phœnicia, Babylonia, and Africa. Dr. Movers has a great many Bels, Bel-Itan, Bel-Saturn, Bel-Chomeus, Bel-Moloch, and others. He seems to treat them as if they belonged to Phœnicia. But that theory will not bear examination. Transferred to America, they acquire historical importance.

Demonology has four Bels. Baël, first king of Hell, has three heads. Balan, great and terrible king of Hell, has forty legions. Belphegor, demon of inventions, and Belzebub Prince of demons.

It is in America that these four Bels have an historical and ethnological existence. In the traditionary histories of Mexico and Central America they are stemfathers of great races of men.

Brasseur de Bourbourg, in his account of Yucatan, says, that "the Quiches have a tradition of four brothers called Balam— Balam Quitze, Balam Agab, Balam Mahucutah, and Igi Balam. They are each at the head of tribes to date the epoch, most remote, of their departure from the land of darkness, Camuhibal, till their definite installation in the mountains of Quiche. They are called masters of holocausts. They came from Tulan Zugwa, Wucub Pek, Wucub Ciman, from the East a long way. They came with the families of Tamub and Itocab. They had been forced to quit their country by tyranny."

CHAPTER XIX.

CENTRAL AMERICA, No. 2.   THE DESCRIPTION OF THE
CENTRAL PART OF THE ATLANTIC ISLE, BY PLATO, IN CRITIAS,
COMPARED WITH THE MODERN ACCOUNT OF CENTRAL AMERICA.

In the fourth chapter of this work, as a part of the evidence
that America was known to the Ancients, the writings of Plato,
in Timæus, were transcribed.   It is there given as Egyptian,
because the facts were related by an Egyptian priest.   That
account of the Atlantic Island is limited.   It relates, chiefly,
to the irruption of warlike nations into the old continent, from
beyond the pillars of Hercules.   It gives an account of the
existence of the Atlantic Isle, and then describes its sub-
mergence in the Ocean.

Plato returns to the subject, in his writings entitled Critias,
and he gives a much more extended account of the Island—
entering a little into its histories, and describing at great length
the practices of the inhabitants, giving a particular account of
the temple of Poseidon.   From the details of the statement,
it can be safely judged, that Plato is really giving a description
of what specially belongs to Central America.   On that account,
the quotation has been reserved for the present place, and it
is now given with the view to throw it into juxta-position
with the modern state of the province and its histories.   It
is hardly necessary to advert to what some say of the passage,
that it is spurious; as the invention of the narrative is less
credible, than the facts narrated.   It is shortened.

"First of all, let us recollect, that it is about 9,000 years,
since war was proclaimed between those dwelling outside
the pillars of Hercules and all those within them.   Of the
latter party, then, this city was the leader, and of the
former, the Kings of the Atlantic Island.   To the Gods
were once locally allotted the whole Earth, different Gods
having received, by lot, different regions, proceeded to
cultivate them.   But Hephœstus and Athena, having a
common nature, from having the same father, arranged the
order of government. Page 420.   In the distribution of the
Earth, Poseidon got, as his lot, the Atlantic Island, begot

children by a mortal woman, and settled in some such spot of the Island, as we are about to describe. Towards the sea, but in the centre of the whole Island, was a plain. On this plain dwelt one of those men, named Evenor, with his wife Leucippe, and they had an only daughter Clito. He begat and brought up five twin male children, and bestowed allotments on them. To the eldest, who was the King, he gave the name of Atlas, from whom the Island and Sea were named Atlantic. The others were Eumolus, Amphres, Euamon, Musæus, Antochthon, Elasippus, Mestor, Azaes, and Diaprepes. All these and their descendants dwelt, for many ages, in the Sea of Islands, and extended their empire as far as Egypt and Tyrrhenia. By far the most distinguished was the race of Atlas. The temple of Poseidon himself, was a stadium in length, having something of a barbaric appearance. All the outside of the temple they lined with silver, but the pinnacles with gold: and as to the interior, the roof was formed wholly of ivory, variegated with gold and wichalcham. They also placed in it golden statues: the God himself, as standing in a chariot, holding the reins of six winged horses, of such size as to touch the roof with his head, and round him were 100 Nereids, with dolphins. Round the outside of the temple were likewise golden images placed, of all men and women that were descended from the ten kings, and many other large statues, both of kings and private people, both from the city itself and of the foreign countries, over which they had dominion."

After a description of the land and its practices, it is said, "Of the ten Kings, each individually, in his own district and over his own city, ruled supreme over the people and the laws, constraining and punishing whomsoever he pleased, and the government and the commonwealth in each was regulated by the injunctions of Poseidon, as the law handed them down and inscriptions were made, by the first (Kings) on a column of wichalcham, which was deposited in the centre of the Island, in the temple of Poseidon, where they assembled every fifth year. And when they were about to judge, they gave pledges. As there were many bulls grazing in the temple of Poseidon, ten men went to hunt, and whichsoever bull they took they slaughtered. They then filled a goblet with clots of blood and threw the rest into the fire, and after this, dipping out of the goblet with golden cups, they poured libations down on the fire and swore to do justice. They then dressed in beautiful dark blue robes, and sitting on the ground mutually judged each other — assigning the Empire to the Atlantic race. Zeus collected all the Gods into their own most ancient habitation, situated in the centre of the whole world, said,"

In Mr. Stephens' valuable work, there is an interesting account of the Empire of Quiche. It appears, that the mountains of Quiche occupy the centre of the provinces in question, and on one of them was the town of Utatlan, the capital of a great and rich Empire, arising out of the Nahaos race. Mr. Stephens says, that the kings of Quiche were descended from the Toltec Indians. They came under the guidance of Tunab. They had passed from one continent to the other, to a place called the Seven Caverns. From him descended the kings of Tula and Quiche. Balam Acan was the next king of Quiche." In Brasseur de Bourbourg's Work, vol. 3, 43: it seems that "this Balam or Baali, was sent by the Zapoteque King, with troops. They attacked the mountain, and victory led to the Zapoteque grandeur. A temple and a fortress were erected on the mountain. After death, he was held in great veneration." Mr. Stephens describes the palace. It was 876 feet by 728 paces deep. It was of hewn stones of various colours. There was lodgement for troops and archers. In a saloon stood the throne, under four canopies of feathers. In the palace there was a treasury—tribunals for judges—menageries, &c. The chief ruin of the palace was a place of sacrifice 70 feet square and 33 feet high, with steps." This Empire of Quiche seems to embrace a large part of the ruined cities, now under consideration, among which are Copan and Palenque, the founder of which latter place is said to have been one Votan. Before him, the characters are mythological,— Imos, the first, then Ik or Igh—then Votan.

The quotation from Plato is remarkable, as describing in ancient times, the identical palace and temple, or one similar to it, which is described by Mr. Stephens. The temple is called by Plato, a temple of Poseidon, and it is especially referred to Atlas and his descendants.   It must have been a most magnificent building, with 100 Nereids.   The God stands in a vast chariot, with six winged horses, so gigantic, as to touch the roof.   The palace described by Mr. Stephens must have been an immense edifice, made of hewn stone, of various colours. In a saloon, stood the throne under four canopies of feathers.

It will naturally recur to the reader, that this curious temple or palace, must be the same as that which stands for frontispiece to the present work.   More properly speaking, the picture of the throne of Neptune must be a representation of the Quiche palace, but with such features of difference, as to shew that time and forgetfulness had produced a scene, somewhat altered.   It has been already pointed out, that the throne of Neptune is the dragon throne, so that the picture ought to be the throne of Poseidon, in the Atlantic Isle.   At Quiche it is found.

This comparison between the writings of Plato and the modern description of Central America is singularly valuable in forming conclusions concerning the ruined cities, their probable history, and the manner of their abandonment. Let the chief points in the case be considered.   Plato puts into the country, one Evenor, with his wife Leucippe and a family.   The descendants of these people dwell for ages in the sea of Islands,—a capital description of the Isthmus and the Caribean Sea, and then they go to Egypt and Tyrrhenia.   They forsake the land and migrate to the old continent.   Then, in the description of the buildings, they are not only great, but decorated with images of kings and private people, both of their own race and of others, subdued by them. It is fair to suppose that the numerous bassos relievos and carvings, now found in the forsaken cities, are the actual images mentioned.

Then Plato goes on to say, that there were ten kings in the land, each of whom had despotic sway over his subjects. After mentioning customs and laws, many of which are omitted in this transcription, for want of space, mention is made of a column, deposited in the temple of Poseidon, on which were inscriptions.   These inscriptions may be the hieroglyphics, which abound in the land: but which have baffled the skill of residents and visitors to the spot till the present day.

The document then comes to an abrupt termination. The account says, that "the people, dressed in beautiful dark blue attire, assigned the Empire to the Atlantic race," that is to say, to Atlas, the son of Japetus,—the ancestor of the Zapoteque sovereign. At last, Zeus collected all the Gods into their own most ancient habitation and made a speech to them. What he said, or what he intended to say, must remain an eternal enigma!

The latter part of this interesting document, accords exactly with what is said in the traditionary histories of Central America.

In those histories it is said, speaking of the races to whom tradition assigned the dominion, that "they were ultimately installed in the mountains of Quiche," the beautiful region in which the ruined cities are discovered. When the statement of Plato, that Zeus assembled the Gods into this particular spot, is compared with the tradition, that they were ultimately installed in the mountains of Quiche, the conclusion cannot be avoided, that the ruins were the cities of the Titan race, which, after a residence for ages, they were either compelled to leave, or which they voluntarily forsook.

CHAPTER XX.

CENTRAL AMERICA, No. 3. ATLAS AND THE ATLANTIDES.

The extract now transcribed from Plato's Critias differs in nothing, except the details, from the writings of Diodorus and Philo. The three together form a very complete history of the Atlantic Isle.

As to Atlas himself, he is found in all of them, and he is located in the centre of the Island.

To understand Atlas, in his identification with the Aztlan race, the reader should reperuse the Third Chapter of this work, where he will see that the history of astronomy proves the identity of the race of Atlas with that of the Aztlans.

There is a curious native picture in the collection of Mexican antiquities, which gives a pictorial description of the movements of the Aztlan race. It is called "a place of magpies, where the Mexicans were first called Aztlanechi." It is much too large for insertion in this place. It shews that the Aztlans were not the aborigines of the country, and it so far justifies the European mythology of Atlas.

It is fair to raise the question, whether there is anything in Central America to justify the belief that Atlas and the Atlantides ever had any existence in that country. The myth of Atlas is as follows, "Atlas, one of the Titans, son of Japetus and Clymene, one of the Oceanides,—His mother's name according to Apollodorus, was Asia. He married Pleione, daughter of Oceanus, or Hesperus, according to others, by whom he had seven daughters called Atlantides. He was king of Mauritania and master of one thousand flocks of every kind, as also of beautiful gardens, abounding in every species of fruit, which he had entrusted to the care of a dragon. Perseus, after the conquest of the Gorgons, passed by the palace of Atlas and demanded hospitality. The king, who was informed by an oracle of Themis that he should be dethroned by one of the descendants of Jupiter, refused to receive him, and even offered him violence. Perseus, who was unequal in strength, shewed him Medusa's head, and Atlas was instantly changed into a large mountain. This mountain, which ran across the deserts of Africa east to west, is so high, that the ancients have imagined that the heavens rested on its top and that Atlas supported the world on his shoulders. Hyginus says that Atlas assisted the giants in the wars against the Gods, &c."

The only part of this myth which puts Atlas in Africa is that in which he is turned into the mountain, a thing that is impossible. All the rest of the myth belongs to the Atlantic Isle. His parentage—the beautiful gardens—the dragon and the wars of the Gods and Giants, are all Atlantic.

There is an abundance of evidence in the ethnology and topography of modern Central America, to prove that it was the domicile of Atlas and his race. Utatlan, the capital of Quiche, described as "the large and rich capital—court of the native kings of Quiche and the most sumptuous found by the

Spaniards," carries his name to this day. The Castle of Atalaya which defended Utatlan, the ruins of which are the most striking feature of the place, and which forms a round tower, carries his name in a form still nearer. The plain of Quiche is said to be "on the charming river of Atolam." The capital of the Zapoteques was Teatzapo-Atlan. Mention is made of the conquest of the mother of the Sun, in the mountain chain of Teut-itlan. Then there is the lake Amatitlan and another called Atilan.   In addition to these facts, the Professor Raffinesque, in his enumeration of the Indian races of America, puts at the head of them the tribe of Atalam or Otolam, which he glosses by Cutan, and locates in Central America.

Among the interesting tablets which were discovered on the ruined buildings of Palenque, there is one which may have been the likeness of Atlas himself. It is here given, if not for an argument, at least for a curiosity.

NATIVE TABLET.

In the tablet itself, there is a man kneeling before the present figure. He appears as if in deep admiration of the man. It will be observed that the figure carries behind him an object which looks very much like some astronomical instrument, such as the Aztlan astronomers must necessarily have used. On his head he carries the head and tusks of an elephant. In the description of the Palace of Quiche, mention is made of ivory, in large quantities. Ivory shews intercourse with Africa, and the myth of Atlas makes it manifest that Atlas and his race must early have crossed the Atlantic into Mauritania. That must be what is meant by his being turned into the mountain. That being so, the present figure may have been the portraiture of Atlas, or one of his astronomical disciples.

"The Atlantides were the daughters of Atlas. They were seven in number, Maia, Electra, Taygete, Asterope, Merope, Alcyone, and Celœno. They married some of the Gods and most illustrious heroes, and their children were founders of many nations and cities. They were called Nymphs, &c."

On the common interpretation of mythic traditions, these Atlantides ought to be provinces or places in Central America. They ought, in fact, to be the inhabitants of the numerous and extensive ruined cities which are scattered over the province. There is, however, a passage in the mythological Lexicon which throws doubt on that allocation, by representing the Atlantides as a people of Africa near Mount Atlas. That is where the mistake lies, and it is that which creates such confusion in history. The learned, both in ancient and comparatively modern times, seem to have found it difficult to believe in the existence of a great land beyond the Atlantic Ocean. It is only when that mistake is corrected, that history becomes consistent.

There is a speech in Nonnus' Dionusica which shews where the Atlantides ought to be placed before their arrival in Africa. Electra, in a conversation with Cadmus, says, " I am Queen and have been one of the Pleiades. I have lived so far from my eternal home,—who shall never again see one of my seven sisters, Sterope, Maia, and Celœno,—who shall never press to my bosom Lacedemon, son of my sister Taygete, to whom is refused to enter the house of Alcyone, or to have sweet conversation with Merope. Ah! what I regret most, Dardanus, my son, leaving his country to pass to the plains of Ida. Of his side, my father Atlas in his old age, and in the enclosure of the seven Zones, still bends his shoulders at the bottom of Libya. I hope to exchange the sojourn of the earth for the sojourn of the Atlantic sphere and to shine among the Stars."

In this beautiful and touching speech, Electra shews, in the most convincing manner, where was her celestial domicile and that of her sisters. It was in the Atlantic sphere, not in Africa. The term Seven Zones is an expression,—if judged of by the Ophite Gnostic map, at page 80, that must be synonymous with the seven provinces of Central America. If judged of in the light of the Hindoo diagram of Patala, at page 167, it must be considered as one of the seven divisions of North America.

The only Atlantide that can be discovered as Ethnological, in Central America, is Maia; but that is very important in this research, as the Mayas form, at this day, a very large part of the population, both of the peninsula of Yucatan and the Islands of the Caribean Sea. The province of Yucatan is full of ruined cities, and it is expected by modern travellers that any diligent search and the use of the pickaxe may lead to discoveries of the highest possible interest.

The account of the Empire of Yucatan is in the work of Brasseur de Bourbourg. The author shews, that "the traditionary histories of the country make four brothers to enter Yucatan. They are called Tutul Xius. They have a priestess of fire. They conquer Chichen—Itza, and form an alliance with the kings of Mayapan. Cukulcan is at the head of this state. It is a state of great wealth and has fine roads, &c." It is then said that these four Tutul Xius are the same as the four Balams of the Empire of Quiche, and the four Mexican personages of Nahutl. They had a temple to the Sun at Izamal. They had a God of music and poetry. Cukulcan is described as the sage governor of Yucatan. He introduced confession and interdicted human sacrifices." This is the kingdom of Mayas.

This extract is suggestive. It shews that the ruined cities of Yucatan must have been a great and civilized kingdom. Its religion is described. It was that known in history as the Sun worship, with fire rites. It was religious—it had confessions, and it was free from the crying evil of human sacrifices,—a custom prevalent in the adjoining province of Tabasc and Campeachy, at the time of modern discovery. These religious peculiarities are in accordance with the buildings themselves. They had monasteries and nunneries, and no temples nor idols seem yet to have been found.

As to the race itself, what is said is conclusive. It was the same as the Zapoteque race of Quiche, and the Nahoas of Mexico—the civilizers of those lands. In that case, the kingdom of Mayas must have been a branch of the great Titan race, and one of the Atlantides. It is confirmatory of this teaching, that the pictorial map-makers have delineated the region as the Corona Australis. Both in the Atlantis of Diodorus and the Cosmogony of Phœnicia, the race is made to spread abroad over the length and breadth of the Atlantic Isle. Time and migration must have shifted the location of the people, but they still have the Crown as their Heraldry.

It would seem from all that can be gathered from native sources and European traditions, that the mountains of Quiche must have been the spot where were assembled in the later ages of the pre-occupation of America, the remnants of the descendants of the colonists from all parts of the hemisphere. Wars and dissensions appear to have driven them together. There must have been many from Mexico, as the presence of the Zapoteques shews. There must have been people from the Mississippi, as the presence of flat-headed Indians proves. The Apalachian Indians,—their medicine men and Gods must have been there, because the Carib Indians, whom Mr. Stephens found at Palenque, are said to have been Apalachian Indians from Florida, and later studies will shew that there must have been many from the western shores of South America. It is then said that it was Zeus who assembled them in the centre of the Island.

This mingling of races is seen in the mythology of Electra. Apollodorus makes Electra to be "a daughter of Atlas, by Pleione. She was changed into a constellation." Ovid makes her to be "one of the Oceanides, wife of Atlas, and mother of Dardanus, by Jupiter." If this has any real significance, it exhibits a mixture of races among the Atlantic kingdoms.

The sudden appearance of Dardanus in this short myth introduces one of the most important and interesting chapters in this story, or call it drama, for the *dénouement* is at hand.

When the Antiquities of Europe and Asia come to be studied in the light of the Zodiac, it will be found that

2 D

the traditionary histories of Europe are almost as dark and as disarranged as those of America itself. The mythic life of Dardanus needs readjustment. As has just been seen, he is an Atlantide, son of Electra, "queen," as she says, and "one of the Pleides." In the myth of Boreas, it is said, that "Boreas changed himself into a horse to unite himself with the mares of Dardanus, by which he had twelve mares, so swift, that they ran or rather flew over the sea, without hardly wetting their feet."

Who was Boreas and where did he reside? He is commonly put on the Thracian mountains,—"Thracia was the residence of Boreas." When that mistake is corrected, it will be found that "the Isle of the Hyperboreans is Britain,—a very suitable place for his mares.

Dardanus and Boreas marry and have twelve flying mares. That can mean nothing else, than, that the inhabitants of Palenque and Yucatan had ships, in conjunction with the inhabitants of Britain; and that creates a regular navigation, between the two hemispheres.

This is one of the innumerable instances in which the tracing of myths introduces a personage just at the moment he is wanted. The history of the northern part of the Atlantic Isle has been traced with great care, and it is now brought to the eventful moment when the Gods and Kings are about to forsake their country and to marshal their troops for that great warlike invasion, in which they conquered all Libya and Western Europe. Or, in other words, that great dispersion is about to take place, by which the inhabitants of the Oceanic hemisphere mingled their blood and fortune with the people of the old continent. At this moment two characters appear whom mythic history represents as the navigators of the Atlantic Ocean. But not only do they appear at the right moment: they shew themselves at the proper place. Quiche, Palenque, and Yucatan form the convenient spot for this great maritime adventure. But before the flight of the Gods is introduced, it is necessary to protract the story a little, to examine the tablets and sculpture which have been discovered in the ruins and entangled foliage of the great woods of the land.

CHAPTER XXI.

CENTRAL AMERICA, No. 4. THE BASSOS RELIEVOS, SCULPTURE AND GRAVED STONES, FOUND IN THE RUINED CITIES OF CENTRAL AMERICA, COMPARED WITH THE MYTHOLOGICAL MONUMENTS AND DESIGNS OF THE OLD CONTINENT.

The great Hierarchies of Idolatry, which have constituted the religions of the ancient world, have left traces of their nature and practices in the images, temples and pictures, handed down to posterity. The history and ethnology of mankind lie hidden in the pictures of the Gods. When a people has been compelled to change its place of abode, or to migrate into transmarine lands, its primary care has been to carry with it the images of its Gods. It results from such a custom, that there are scattered over the whole globe the same images, with but slight variations. Where there are confraternities of nations, there must be a resemblance of divinities.

The Bassos relievos and sculpture discovered in the ruined cities of Central America, are an illustration of these remarks. Although they are silent themselves, any expert in European mythology and pictures can readily detect a great many of them. The Bassos relievos and sculptures of antiquity are not to be regarded as one would inspect a picture gallery of modern art. Before the discovery of letters, the ancients had no effectual mode of handing down their histories, or of preserving the memory of their kings, heroes and gods, but by sculptures and gravings on the wall. Mythological monuments must be taken as a sort of writing. They are pictorial writing. An extended acquaintance with ancient figures will convince any one, that they faithfully represent the personal appearance of former generations, even in costume, heraldic devices and tribal signs. On this account, it is not impossible to form a credible estimate of the images of Central America.

The first figure to be introduced is one that was found in the ruins of Copan. In the work of Mr. Stephens, a large number of similar stones are exhibited. They were hidden and covered with vegetation; but the artist succeeded in copying them. They all have the figure of a human being graven on the face of the stone, surrounded by numerous heads and minute carvings. It appears that, originally, they were coloured red.

STONE AT COPAN.   PUZZA.

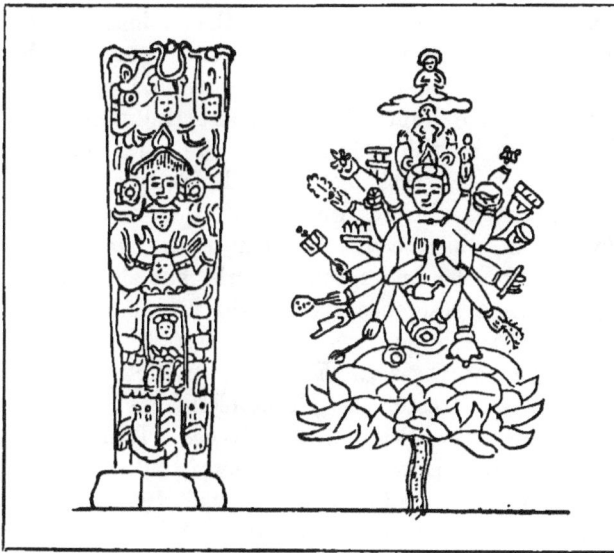

There can be no mistake made in putting these figures into their proper category. They are, evidently, what may be called Chinese Puzzas or Japanese Quanwons, which answer to them. One of these Asiatic Idols is here given for comparison. Puzza, in the Chinese Hierarchy, is the mother of the Gods with varied forms of representation. The present form has a precise resemblance to the Japanese Quanwon; but the latter is surrounded with what is called a seething pot crown, which is decorated with images of small angels. The Chinese Puzza has a tradition connected with it, which is as follows:—"Ten ages since, three nymphs came from Heaven to bathe. Their names were Angela, Changela, and Fæcula. Fæcula swallowed a lotus and had a son. The other two went back to Heaven, but Fæcula's son was brought up by a fisherman, and afterwards ruled all the nations of that great state."

On comparison, it must be acknowledged that the Copan

image bears a great resemblance to the Chinese and Japanese Idols. The central figure is not only very similar, but the hands are held up in a like attitude, while the faces and head-dresses are alike. The numerous arms, heads, and objects in the Asiatic figure have their counterpart in the numerous heads and irregular carvings of the Copan image. It is not quite safe to determine which of these two figures is the type and which the antitype,—which the original and which the copy; but, judged in the light of the Chinese tradition, the Copan figure ought to be the original. All the three females come from Heaven in the first instance. To determine a point so difficult, the myth of Ceres, given in a former chapter, ought to be adduced in illustration. In that myth Ceres appears to descend, first to the underground world, but she returns back again, and has a residence six months in one hemisphere and six months in the other.

In the light of Classical European mythology, the Copan figures must be treated as Hecatonkeiri. There are three Hecatonkeiri, Cottus, Briareus, and Gyges. There is no myth of Cottus. That of Briareus is as follows. "Briareus, a famous Giant, son of Cœlus and Terra. He had 100 hands and 50 heads, and was called, by men, Ægeon. When Juno, Neptune, and Minerva conspired to dethrone Jupiter, Briareus ascended heaven and sat himself down next to him, and so terrified the conspirators by his fierce and threatening looks, that they desisted. He assisted the Giants in their war against the Gods, and was thrown under Mount Ætna, according to some accounts." The myth of Gyges is as follows:—" Gyges, a son of Cœlus and Terra, represented as having 100 hands. He, with his brothers, made war against the Gods and was afterwards punished in Tartary."

These myths must be located, in the ordinary way employed in this work. This cannot be done by a Zodiacal sign.

The parentage of the Hecatonkeiri does not locate them with any precision. Briareus is called by men Ægean, another spelling for Ocean. But what is said of them ties them to the vicinity of the gulf of Texas. They engage in the wars of the Gods and Giants. The graved stones of Copan may fairly be considered to put them in the ruined cities of Central America.

There they must have remained till the general dispersion. This is taught in the myths. They are driven to the East and West. "Gyges is punished in Tartary," and Briareus is "thrown under Mount Ætna" in Sicily.

NATIVE FIGURE.   EUROPEAN SILVAIN.

Among the native pictures relating to Central America, is one that, may be pronounced a Silvain. It not only exhibits a characteristic specimen of the Sylvan deity; but it carries the pine, and the curious head dresses are alike. The following is his myth.

"Silvanus, a rural deity, son of an Italian shepherd, by a Goat. According to Virgil, he was the son of Picus; or, as others report, of Mars; or according to Plutarch, of Valeria Tusculania. The worship of Silvanus was established only in

Italy, where, as some authors have imagined, he reigned, in the age of Evander. This deity was sometimes represented holding a cypress in his hand, because he became enamoured of a beautiful youth called Cyparissus, who was changed into a tree of the same name. Silvanus presided over gardens and limits, and he is often confounded with the Faunes, Satyrs, and Silvains." •

This is one of many instances which shew how completely the Romans of Virgil's time had forgotten the history of their own divinities, while, at the same time, their literature contained in it their true origin. In this myth, Silvanus is the son of a goat, and is confounded with the Faunes and Satyrs and Silvains, all personages represented by the Romans as half-man—half-goat. When a capital specimen of this deity is found among the ruins of Central America, one sees, at once, that Tabasc and the vicinity is the original domicile of Silvain, for the country suits him to perfection. Tabasc is the garden of the world, and it has been seen that Pan, in his European form, as half-man, half-goat, was the native deity of the country.

In some mythological collections, there is a picture of a pavement found at Lyons, where Silvanus, Pan and Cupid, are found in company. All these characters belong to Central America; so that it is not at all surprising that the God Silvanus is found among the native designs of the land. At the same time, it is a strong confirmation of the present system of the discovery of obscure histories by tracking the pedigrees of the Gods, upon the basis of a map.

It is at Palenque, that the best specimens of Bassos relievos and images are found. Palenque appears to have been a very important town in Central America, as may be inferred from the extent of the ruins. It is situated in a recess of the mountains and near a river which connects the place with the gulf of Mexico, and so gives access to the Caribean Sea and the Atlantic Ocean. It is in the province of Tzendales, between Tabasc and Yucatan. The native Indians are Caribs. The figures of the Bassos relievos have Indian features; but Mr. Stephens thinks that the heads were flattened by boards. This flat-headed Indian race does not now exist in the neighbourhood, but Mr. Stephens met an Indian with the exact kind of face seen in the tablets. These figures are in a style very different from those at Copan, and much more diversified, exhibiting marks of greater antiquity. The hieroglyphics are the same as those seen at Copan.

SCULPTURE AT PALENQUE.   DIANA OF EPHESUS.

The only complete sculpture found at Palenque is one that is here given. By comparison with the European mythological image that stands at its side, it can readily be detected as a Diana of the Ephesians. This is proved by its general resemblance to that remarkable Idol—by the extraordinary and unusual head dress they both carry, and especially by the mural crown, which is a symbolic object too peculiar to be mistaken.

Diana is a triple goddess. She has three different forms. The first is that in which she here appears: the second is that of Hecate, the underground Diana, who, again, is a threefold image, holding the infernal key: the third is that of a huntress. These three forms exhibit her race, whatever it was, as having three different domiciles.

Towards the explication of the present figure, it would be useless to transcribe the entire myth of Diana. It would be misleading. She is said to "represent the moon, and to be the same as Isis." If she be the same as Isis, she coalesces with Puzza, the Goddess of China, who has been already identified with the figures of Copan, and whose legend has been transcribed.

Diana of Ephesus stands out prominently as the progenitor of the human race, by her mammal attributes. When she is found in Central America, she must be considered as the Goddess of races that came originally from Asia—from the great country of Isis and the Issedones—from the vast and ancient Empires which have retained to the present day, the being, characteristics, and religion of a world too ancient for research—in short, from the stem-mother of the white races.

The Palenque image now before the reader, must have been the earliest type of Diana of the Ephesians. This is proved by the simplicity of the sculpture, and by the absence of numerous emblems always drawn on the Ephesian goddess. In this simple form, it can be traced across the Atlantic Ocean, into Western Europe. The German Hertha is the same figure. Perhaps it may be a question, whether the German Hertha cannot claim primogeniture for the Idol. It may have been carried into the Atlantic Isle. If otherwise, it must have been carried from Central America into Germany.

But the Palenque image must have gone round the world. It must have been carried into Africa. At Ephesus the image was black, or, at least, the tint of ebony, and it was covered with Zoomorphic attributes. Wild beasts hang about it. Ephesus was built by the Amazons, who worshipped Diana of the Ephesians as the mother of the Gods. Diodorus Siculus puts the Amazons in Africa before they settled in Asia Minor; so that the Image must have travelled, picking

2 E

up fresh attributes and changing its colour, till at Ephesus, the city of the Amazons, it became a compound figure, crowded with indications of a world-wide history.

Under these circumstances, it is interesting to turn to Acts xix. 35, to see what the town clerk of Ephesus said, on the occasion of the tumult created by the preaching of the Apostle Paul: "Ye men of Ephesus, what man is there that knoweth not, how that the city of the Ephesians is a worshipper of the Great Goddess Diana, and of the image which fell down from Jupiter?" In the Greek, this is "'Αρτέμιδος καὶ τοῦ Διοπετοῦς." This can be well understood, from a quotation from Parkhurst's Lexicon.

ΔΙΟΠΕΤΕΣ. An image which fell down from Jupiter; αγαλμα being understood. So Numa persuaded the Romans, that a certain shield fell from heaven, to which Plutarch applies the same word Διοπετες, as he also does to the famous Trojan palladium, or image of Pallas, which protected Troy and was supposed to have fallen from heaven: and Euripides speaking of the image of Diana Taurica, says,

"And th' image of the Goddess take, which fell
"They say, from heaven, into this holy fane."

He afterwards calls it ΔΙΟΠΕΤΕΣ ΑΓΑΛΜΑ, the image which fell from Jupiter. So Herodian calls the image of the mother of the Gods, αγαλμα Διοπετες.

It may be thought by some to be straining the inferences that arise from the comparison of pictures; but it is very hard to look thoughtfully at this subject, without coming to the conclusion, that the image which fell from Jupiter must be this Palenque image. In the extract just given, the Palladium has the same history as the present image. Pallas is the husband of Styx, who is described as a Nymph who dwelt at the entrance of Hades, which will presently be found to be in the Caribean Sea. So, again, Dardanus, who founded Troy, and who must be supposed to have taken the Palladium there, locates in Central America. He is a son of Electra, the wife or child of Atlas, and he has twice made his appearance in these histories, and both times in the palace of Electra, which has been shown to be at Utatlan, the capital of Quiche.

It goes far to confirm the present strange theory, that there are other instances of a similar kind in ancient legends, especially in regard to what are called "the stones of Baal." Mr. Squires, in his work called the Serpent Emblem, says that "Baal's image was a black stone fallen from heaven into the Estuary of Hamath (Emessa) or the mouth of the Orontes, on the coast of Syria." There is a similar legend in Ireland. In the Chronicle of Eri, it is said, that "long before the Celts left Spain, the God Baal had sent the blessed stone, the Laic feal, to their ancestors." This last tradition shews what is meant by the saying "fallen from heaven." These stones, shields and images, must have been brought into Europe and Asia, from across the Atlantic Ocean, in those great migrations and warlike expeditions, of which Plato speaks in the Timæus.

CROSS AT PALENQUE.

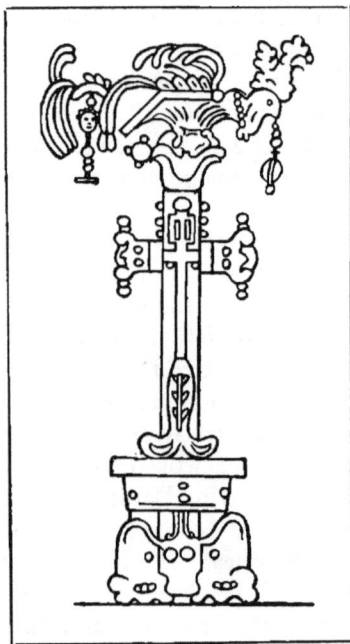

Another image found in the ruins of Palenque is that of a cross. This cross has given name to what, in Church Architecture, is called the Palenque Cross. It must be taken as indicative of the presence of Asiatic monks, or hermits, and this is confirmed by the nature of the buildings where the cross was found. They were monasteries. In the Ptolemaic Zodiac there is a cross with a bird on it and called the Cross of Antinous. That double constellation is so similar to the present cross, with a bird on it, as to raise a question as to the localization of the sign. In some copies of the spheres, the two objects are severed, and in the Etruscan sphere the sign is placed more westerly. Who Antinous was, is uncertain, and a question arises whether it is Anchinoe, the wife of Belus. On the whole it is safest to consider the constellation as belonging to Italy; but it makes good mythology to bring the sign originally from Palenque to the Mediterranean Sea as the Maltese Cross.

TABLET AT PALENQUE.

The next Basso relievo at Palenque that calls for notice must be pronounced a Bacchus, and it is a beautiful specimen of that mythic personage. Not only is he seated upon his tub but he has beneath him the peculiar non-descripts, which, in European mythology, are called Panthers. This tablet is remarkable as being surrounded with hieroglyphics, placed precisely as they are in Egyptian portraits of Gods. These Hieroglyphics have baffled interpretation; but two of them are deserving of notice. One at the right hand has an oval, enclosing a cuneiform letter, such as are found in Assyria. How it could form a part of a Central American alphabet is left to the learned to determine. Another on the same side is a man blowing a pan-pipe, constructed exactly like a common street pan-pipe in Europe. This fact becomes significant, when it is discovered in the land of Pan, where he was the native God of the country. In the picture of the struggle of Cupid and Pan at page 201, a similar pan-pipe is observable.

Bacchus, by name, has not hitherto presented himself in this history; but when his mythology is studied, Central America is the spot where he ought to be found. A few extracts from his tradition may here be transcribed, and they will give rise to some comments.

"Bacchus, son of Jupiter and Semele, the daughter of Cadmus. After she had enjoyed the company of Jupiter, Semele was deceived and punished by the artifice of Juno.— Bacchus is the Osiris of the Egyptians—Bacchus assisted the Gods in their wars against the Giants and was cut to pieces.— Bacchus is represented as accompanied by Pans and Satyrs."

These extracts belong to Bacchus in the present locality. The remaining part of his myth relates to later histories, in the old hemisphere. Bacchus, at Palenque, is in the exact place for what is called his birth,—inasmuch as some myths which were transcribed at the end of the 16th chapter made Hermione to have been brought up in the palace of Electra, which has since been discovered at Quiche, not far from Palenque itself.

But the expression "birth of Bacchus" is one that demands consideration. What can be meant by it, in an historical and ethnological sense? This question is best answered by shifting the Latin name of Bacchus into its Greek equivalent—Dionusus. It is no play upon words: it is the result of the tracing of history to see in the word Dionusus—the God Nahoas. He is the race of Nahoas or Toltecs of Mexico and Central America deified. He is the mythic embodiment of the mingled races of Asiatics and natives of the Atlantic Isle, whose joint history has been traced in the preceding pages. When this race leaves the Oceanic hemisphere and spreads itself over Europe, Africa, and Asia, it is deified as Bacchus or Dionusus. He is a new God—a strange and wild god—god of wine and leader of the Pans, Satyrs, and Centaurs. That is his birth.

But the same explanation applies to the saying, "cut into pieces." The new race branches off by separate migrations, East and West, till it is found in all lands. "It is cut into pieces." At Nysa, at the sources of the Nile, he is an Ethiopian. In Egypt he is Osiris. This is not a fancy. The Græco-Egyptians recognized that identity. In Greece, he is Dionusus, with numerous and surprising festivals called the Dionusica. In Italy, he is Bacchus. In Phœnicia, he is Adonis. In Hindoostan he is Chrishna. In these facts lie, what are called "the mysteries of the ancients." This is the explication of those mysteries and of the fasts and feasts which were everywhere held to commemorate them—fasts to mourn over the loss of people, who, in the early ages, had migrated from Asia into America, across the Pacific Ocean, and feasts to commemorate their return, in later ages, across the Atlantic.

TABLET AT PALENQUE.

Another Basso relievo, in the ruins of Palenque, courts special attention. It is very curious. Of course, the interpretation here put upon these tablets is open to challenge; but to the eye of a mythologist, here is Bacchus again. He is still seated on his panthers, but he is in the boat which bears him from the shores of the Atlantic Isle, in that great dispersion of the Atlantides, by which he became the God of the old continent in later ages.

In this tablet, the true and hidden character of Bacchus is betrayed. He is Neptune himself, to whom the Atlantic Isle had been originally allotted. This is seen by the circumstance, that he carries on his head the European emblem of Neptune—the dolphin. This emblem is too well defined, in the symbolism of the Gods, to be mistaken. This is the ancient Neptune of the Pacific Ocean, who, in earlier ages, had taken Ceres upon his back and landed her in the Oceanic hemisphere. After a mystic residence in that hemisphere, for untold ages, in which must have been enacted those great histories which have been faintly traced in these pages, he is, like all the other Gods, born again. Seated in his boat, he is seen habilitated in all the fantastic paraphernalia of his Island domicile.

Seated opposite to him is his lovely wife Amphitrite, who has considerately provided for her husband and herself an ample stock of provisions for their long and perilous voyage. Her myth is as follows: "Amphitrite, daughter of Oceanus and Tethys, married Neptune, though she had made a vow of perpetual celibacy. She had by him Triton, one of the sea deities. She had a statue at Corinth, in the temple of Neptune. She is sometimes called Salatia, and is often taken for the sea itself."

This myth is one of a thousand which come in exactly at the proper time and place for the localization of mythic personages. She is a daughter of Oceanus and Tethys; so that she must have been the Atlantic wife of the Sea God. She has a statue in her husband's temple at Corinth, of which city the Dolphin is Zodiacal portraiture. She has a son, Triton, who locates in Northern Africa on the Tritonian lake. These localizations point out the route which the boat must have taken. It must have crossed the Atlantic to the North of Africa. Neptune there takes another wife. He marries Libya, and becomes the God of Mauritania.

CHAPTER XXII.

The Evacuation of the Cities of Central America, and the flight of the Gods.

The Sign of Cerberus and its Mythology.

Neptune is in his boat. He is about to forsake the Atlantic Isle that had been assigned to him, and to seek for new territories on the shores of the Mediterranean Sea; but there is danger ahead. Mythology teaches that the entrance to the underground world was guarded by a monstrous dog. The following is the classic myth of Cerberus. " Cerberus, a dog of Pluto, the fruit of Echidna's union with Typhon. He had fifty heads, according to Hesiod, and three according to other mythologists. He was stationed at the entrance of hell, as a watchful keeper, to prevent the living from entering the infernal regions and the dead from escaping from their confinement. It was usual for those heroes who, in their lifetime, visited Pluto's kingdom, to appease the barking mouths of Cerberus with a cake. Orpheus lulled him to sleep with his lyre, and Hercules dragged him from hell when he went to redeem Alceste."

The constellation of Cerberus answers very well to the Caribean Sea. That sea is at the entrance of the gulf of Texas, and consequently of all America. The word Cerberus clangs both with the Caribean Sea and with the Carib Indians, who inhabit the West India Islands. One of those islands, now called St. Domingo, carries the native name of Haiti, a word that clangs as well with Hades as Cerberus does with Caribs.

This very good identification is much strengthened by the

description given by Picard of the religious customs of the Carib Indians in the Island of Hayti.

In that book, there is a very characteristic picture of a place of worship of the Carib Indians. The temple is a sort of grotto, and there is a procession of priests and people dancing and playing on musical instruments. The grotto is guarded by a couple of demoniacal figures of a terrific aspect. The Idol, as seen in the present picture, has five heads and he holds a pitchfork. So close is this identification, that it can scarcely be doubted that Xemes is the Idol that gives rise to the Greek and Egyptian conception of Cerberus.

Closely allied to Cerberus, is Charon. His myth is as follows: "Charon, a god of hell, son of Erebus and Nox. He conducted the souls of the dead over the rivers Styx and Acheron, to the infernal regions for an obolus. Such as had not been honoured with a funeral, were not permitted to enter his boat, without previously wandering on the shore for one hundred years. If any living person presented himself to cross the Stygian lake, he could not be admitted before he shewed Charon a golden bough, which he had received from the Sybil. Charon was imprisoned for one year, because he had ferried over, against his own will, Hercules without this passport. Charon is represented as an old robust man, with a hideous countenance, long white beard and piercing eyes, &c."

But Charon could not have been the only boatman on the Gulf of Texas and the Mississippi; it is the Stygian birds, which, in a mythic sense, exhibit the boats and navigation

XEMES, GOD OF HAYTI.

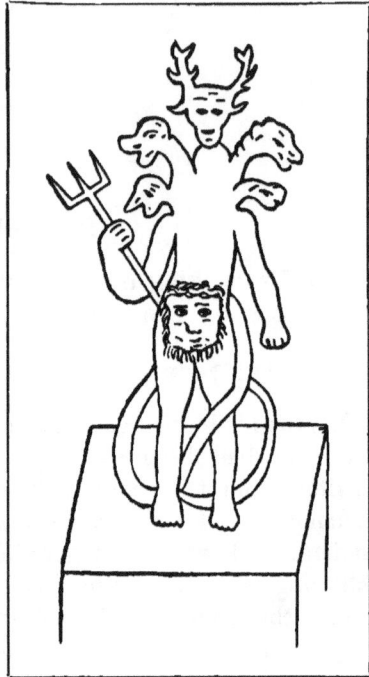

2 F

of the Atlantic Isle. In the tracing of myths, Atlas is distinguished as the father of the Harpies, or Stygian birds. His wife or daughter, Electra, is the mother of the Harpies. This puts the domicile of the Harpies in Utatlan, the capital of the Empire of Quiche. The Atlantides of Quiche and Yucatan must, therefore, have been shipbuilders.

It has been already shown, that Dardanus, the son of Electra, by Jupiter, had a fleet of twelve flying horses, between Central America and Britain. It must now be added, that Iris, his sister, who is also the daughter of Electra, must have had a fleet of flying men. In the next chapter, it will be shown, that Iris is the mother of the Irish. The British Isles are, in the Zodiac, delineated by a Harpy. It thus appears that there must have been two lines of packets between Quiche and Britain,—a line of flying mares and a competing line of flying men.

It would appear from the myths relating to the Atlantic Isle, that in process of time, there must have been some sudden consternation among the Gods, and they all took to flight. Dressed in their purple robes, and in enjoyment of their music and perfumes, the ten kings were assembled, and Jupiter was about to make a speech to them, when that horrible spit-fire Typhon suddenly burst in upon them, and there came on an ignominious scamper. The frightened Gods seem to have lost their divine courage:—" they fled away and assumed different shapes." Some of the cowards turned themselves into rams, swans, cows, goats, cats, and fishes. At length, the king of the gods plucked up a little, and with his thunderbolts, crushed the spit-fire under Mount Ætna.

Judging of the transformations contained in the myth, in the light of Poetical Astronomy, the rams must have gone into the Orient, the swans must have swam to Gaul and Germany, the cows to Spain, and the goats to Egypt, where the Mendesian goat was made God. The cats may have accompanied the goats, as, in the Egyptian Hall, in the British Museum, there is a grand row of black cat gods or gods of the order of *felis*, seated in colossal state. The fishes must have swam to Carthage, Phœnicia, and the Islands of the Mediterranean Sea.

Judging from the pictures which the ancients have given of this maritime dispersion, there must have been many different modes adopted for the passage of the Atlantic. As to the gods that took tickets by the flying mares, they must have got across in first class style. Some must have done it by express. They caught a Stygian bird and mounted on his back, as Ulysses says, "ingloriously;" they speedily came to dry land. As to the boys and girls, it was fine fun. Their divine fathers had bought them each a penny trumpet, and they are blowing away lustily. One lady, painfully short of travelling rugs, had caught a dolphin and standing erect on its head, she made a breezy passage. The young ladies seem to have had the best of it. The jolly old jack-tars with fishes' tails accommodated them in their arms; so that they got across "without even wetting their feet!" On the whole it must have been a sight!

The case is put very differently by Plato. Divested of the simplicity of story-telling, and free from the concealment of mysticism and fancy, his account of the occurrence takes the form of a great historical event. He makes the Kings of the Atlantic Isle bring great warlike hosts from beyond the pillars of Hercules. It is pretty plain, that no flying mares nor dolphins could have brought that class of people across the turbulent Atlantic. Instead of a hasty and disgraceful flight, in fear of Typhon, those great warlike hosts are made to conquer all the western parts of Europe and Africa. A warlike invasion of that magnitude must have been the downfall of kingdoms and the production of new and mighty states. It must have revolutionized the world.

In any case, the flight of the Gods from the shores of Quiche and Yucatan must have led to the evacuation of the cities which composed those states. Perhaps it may have left them in the pitiful condition in which they were found on the discovery of the provinces, in modern times. If it cannot be supposed that the flight of the Gods had left the cities without inhabitants, it may be inferred, that the remnant left, had in lapse of ages so degenerated, as to suffer the long forsaken erections to fall into ultimate decay.

It would be quite worth while to follow these scampering

divinities, in their flight from the palace of Atlas, were it not that it would take a volume instead of a chapter. Yet the story of this great historical event would be incomplete, without at least following Atlas himself and the father of the Gods, whose speech was so unhappily cut short, on the assembling of the kings of the Atlantic Isle.

The myth of Atlas has been already transcribed at page 213. There can be no doubt about the spot in the old continent to which this distinguished character migrated, on his removal from the Island which bore his name. The myth expressly says, that he was turned into a mountain at the western part of Africa. If so, he must have gone from Central America into the country now called Morocco. To suppose that the original home of Atlas was in Africa, it must be concluded that Astronomy had its rise in Morocco. But Morocco puts forth no claim for astronomical discovery, and one would look to almost any country upon earth, rather than to Morocco, for Gods. Besides, how could Atlas have given name to the Atlantic Isle, if he resided originally in Africa? Nothing can be plainer, than that Atlas, and in him, the Aztlan race of Central America—the inventors of astronomy, must have migrated across the Atlantic Ocean and settled in Mauritania.

The Atlantides or daughters of Atlas must have been among the flying gods, as it is said that "they married some of the Gods, and most illustrious heroes, and their children were founders of many nations and cities." The Atlantides are said to have become the Pleiades—stars that form a part of the constellation of Taurus the Bull, a constellation that delineates Assyria in the Ptolemaic Zodiac.

Closely allied to the Atlantides were the Hesperides, who, also, must have been a part of the population of the evacuated cities. Their myth explains their migration.

" Hesperides, three celebrated Nymphs, daughters of Hesperus. Apollodorus mentions four, Ægle, Erythia, Vesta, and Arethusa, and Diodorus confounds them with the Atlantides, and supposes that they were the same number. They were appointed to guard the golden apples which Juno gave to Jupiter on the day of their nuptials, and the place of their residence, placed beyond the Ocean, by Hesiod, is universally believed to be near Mount Atlas, in Africa, according to Apollodorus. This celebrated place or garden abounding with fruits of the most delicious kind, was carefully guarded by a dreadful dragon, which never slept, &c."

The double localization of the Hesperides seems to be justified. Being, like Atlas, children of Japetus, they must have been a portion of the Zapotec race of Central America. But the name of the Hesperii is geographical on the west coast of Africa, where it is placed in the classical maps. When this curious myth comes to be studied, it will be found that the golden apples are the produce of the golden sands of Africa, so that the Hesperides must have crossed the Atlantic Ocean to the gold coast of Africa.

By far the most important personage concerned in the evacuation of the now ruined cities of Central America is Jupiter himself. This distinguished God has been traced to the southern mound cities of North America. According both to the native traditions and the statement of Plato, there must have been a general gathering of the Gods in Quiche and Yucatan, and Jupiter himself was among them. He seems to have led the great warlike hosts to Europe. The story of his own passage to Europe is told in the myth of the swimming bull. The following is the tale.

"Europa, daughter of Agenor, king of Phœnicia, and Telephassa. Jupiter became enamoured of her and assumed the shape of a bull. Europa caressed the animal, and mounted him. The bull crossed the sea with Europa on his back and arrived safe in Crete. Here he assumed his original shape and declared his love. The nymph consented, though she had once made vows of perpetual celibacy, and she became mother of Minos, Sarpedon, and Rhadamanthus. After this distinguished amour with Jupiter, she married Asterius, king of Crete, &c."

At first sight, this tradition appears to be contradictory of the theory educed by the tracing of the myths of the Atlantic Isle, as Europa is a daughter of a king of Phœnicia; but this seeming contradiction arises from the want of localization in the interpretation of mythic history, and the need of readjustment of the several clauses of the myth, in accordance with that localization. This will be best shown by a short paraphrase of the myth.

Europa, daughter of Agenor, [who was afterwards] king of Phœnicia and Telephassa. Jupiter became enamoured of her. She became mother of Minos, [who was Judge of the infernal regions in South America, and Sarpedon and Rhadamanthus, in other parts of those regions]. Jupiter assumed the shape of a Bull. Europa caressed the animal and mounted him. The Bull crossed the sea with Europa on his back and arrived safe in Crete, &c.

To understand the transformation to a bull, it is necessary to have recourse to Poetical Astronomy and the Sidereal heraldry of ancient nations. In the Zodiacs, there are three bulls. The first is the bull of Eastern Asia, standing for China and Japan. This bull rips up the egg of the world. See page 85.

The second is Taurus Major, which gives portraiture to Assyria, and the third is Taurus Minor, which delineates Spain. As Spain is in Europe, of course this is the Bull of Europe. Jupiter assumes the shape of a bull, by crossing the Atlantic Ocean and landing in Spain, situated at "the Gate of the Gods." There, Europa, as the first or the most important arrival of the Phœnix family, gives name to Europe.

This transformation into the Bull of Europe is comprised in what has been called in this work the master myth of antiquity. It is entitled to that character, partly from the extreme clever-ness of the couplet,—partly from the deep mystery involved in the transformation, and chiefly from the vastness of the histories lying hidden in the transformation.

" *Taurus genuit draconem et Taurum, Draco.*"
" *The Bull begat the Dragon and the Dragon the Bull.*"

The present transformation is the complement of the couplet. When the Bull of Asia crossed the Pacific Ocean, and gave population and influence to the Atlantic Isle, he transformed himself into a dragon. When the Dragon race left the eastern shores of the Oceanic hemisphere, and landed in Hispania, the land of Bulls and Bull-fights, it was transformed into a Bull.

The flight of the Gods into the Old Continent, constitutes one of the grandest features in human history. The vast temples and pyramids of Mexico and Peru,—the 1500 mounds, scattered over the area of the United States, and the evacuated cities of Tulha, Quiche, and Yucatan, stand as imperishable attestations of the power and civilizing influences of races, which, mingling their blood with the physical strength and ingenuity of a clever people, created a new world. Forsaking their Oceanic domicile, or, impelled by war and the lust of gold, they land upon regions, which, from the absence of aboriginal traditions, must have been absorbed in somnolence and inactivity, giving birth to that revival of national life science and religion, which characterize the modern world.

CHAPTER XXIII.

THE SCULPTURED EDIFICES, CYCLOPEAN BUILDINGS, AND OTHER REMAINS, IN WESTERN EUROPE, ATTEST THE PRESENCE OF AMERICAN RACES, IN CONFORMITY WITH THE CONCLUSIONS REACHED IN THE FOREGOING PAGES.

With some antiquarians, ancient structures and sculptures are more regarded than the traditions which belong to them. Yet it ought not to be so. Antiquarianism, as it busies itself with old stones and implements of art, is an interesting study; but it leads to no useful conclusions. It is only when ancient edifices, bridges and towers are made to tell the tale of their early builders and the histories connected with them, that they serve the purpose of practical enlightenment.

There is a remarkable group of myths in the classics, relating to Sardinia, which, as they throw more light upon the connection of America with Western Europe, and are more local than other myths, are worthy of attention. In this study, the works of La Marmora de Ferrara and of Mr. J. W. Tyndale, can be used with advantage.

"The Island of Sardinia is said to have received its name from Sardus, a son of Hercules, who settled there, with a colony, which he had brought with him from Libya. Other colonies came, under Aristæus, Norax, aud Jolaus. A family called the Thespiades, or children of Thespius, also went to Sardinia, with Jolaus, the friend of their father, whose fifty daughters were married to Hercules."—*Lempriere*.

In the works referred to, considerable notice is taken of what are called Sarde Idols, a number of small metal images, and of certain towers, called Noraghe and the Sepulchres of the Giants. The Noraghe, of which there are said to be as many as 3000, are "towers, in the form of a truncated cone, from 30 to 60 feet in height and from 100 to 300 feet in circumference, at the base. They are built upon natural or artificial mounds and are inclosed by a low wall. The ascent is from the interior, and it is supposed that they must originally have had a platform on the top."

These towers are referred to by several ancient authors. Aristotle says, that "in Sardinia are edifices of the ancients erected after the Greek manner, and many other beautiful buildings (domes) finished in excellent proportions," and he refers them to Jolaus, the son of Iphicles with the Thespiades. Diodorus Siculus says the same thing, but makes Jolaus send to Dœdalus out of Sicily, to build them. Jolaus builds public schools and temples of the Gods, and everything for the benefit of mankind.

Mr. Tyndale reasons on the possibility of the erection of the Noraghe by the Phœnicians, but comes to the conclusion, that "there is nothing like them, except in the Balearic Isles, where they are called Talayots," which word, ·he says, "is a diminutive of Atalaya, meaning the Giant's burrow. These are more Cyclopean than the Noraghe, and have but one principal chamber. Many of them are surrounded by circles of stones, and what are supposed to have been altars."

To understand these Noraghe, their builders and the hidden histories which must be connected with them, the myths, pedigrees and names of places mentioned in the above extracts, from Greek authors, are necessary.

The myth of Norax himself, whose name the towers· bear,

is as follows. "Norax, a son of Mercury and Erythæa, who led a colony of Iberians into Sardinia." Now, Norax is a son of Mercury. It has been amply shown in the foregoing pages, that Mercury is the Quetzalcoatl of Mexico. He, by crossing the Atlantic into Western Europe, becomes the God of Gaul. As Erythæa, the mother, is an Island between Gades and Spain, it follows, that this son of Mercury must have landed at the gate of the Gods and become an Iberian. He it is that passes into Sardinia and builds the towers.

In another myth, already given, Sardus the son of Hercules gives name to Sardinia. Now, Hercules is the constellation overhanging the lands of the red men in North America. It is in those lands, that the mound cities are found. It follows that Sardinia must have been colonized from the mound cities.

Both Aristotle and Diodorus Siculus refer the Noraghe to Jolaus, the son of Iphicles. Iphicles is another name for the constellation Ophiuchus, which overhangs the mound cities of the Southern States of America. He is a brother of Hercules. Jolaus, the son of Iphicles, is traceable across the Atlantic Ocean into Northern Africa, where he becomes God of the Mauritanians.

There is no actual inconsistency in these myths. They shew that the Noraghe were built by races who came from beyond the Atlantic. There is nothing in the myths mentioned that gives the exact spot from which the actual builders came: but that desirable link in the evidence is supplied by what is said of the corresponding towers in the Balearic Islands. It is Atalaya. They are towers of Atalaya, which word by use shortens itself to Talayots. Atalaya is the name of the tower of Quiche in Central America. The reader will remember that Atalaya was the capital of the Empire of Quiche under Balam its sovereign.

In an American work by Squier, called the Serpent Emblem, there is a picture of a tower at Tescuco, near the ruins of Quiche, the city now referred to. It differs from the Noraghe of Sardinia, in only one circumstance, and that is, that the ascent is from the outside.

In addition to the towers, in the work referred to, by Mr. Tyndale, much is said of the Sarde Idols. "Some of these figures have heads of animals, such as Apes, Antelopes, &c.

2 G

Most of them have tails." It is said that similar Idols
have not been found in any other
country. The figure, now presented, is
one of the Sardinian Idols. If the
reader will take the trouble to turn
to the end of the 21st chapter, he will
there find a picture of Xemes, the God
of Hayti, one of the West Indian Islands,
and there identified as Cerberus. On a
comparison of the two images, it is
hardly possible to deny, that they are
one and the same.

SARDINIAN IDOL.

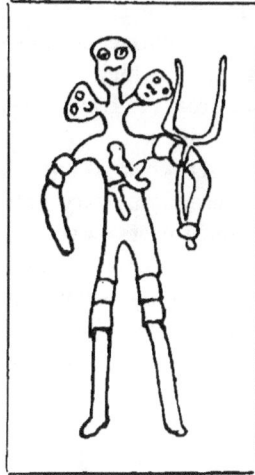

Now the constellation of Cerberus
overhangs the West Indies, and it
follows that the Sarde Idols must
have been brought by Hercules or his
son Sardus, from Hayti. This is the
very thing said to have been done by
Hercules. "He brought away Cerberus, when he went to
redeem Alceste."

The classical mythology of Ireland hangs upon Iris. "Iris,
a daughter of Thaumas and Electra, one of the Oceanides: she
was the messenger of the Gods and more particularly of Juno.
She is the same as the rainbow, and represented with all the
variegated and beautiful colours of the rainbow."

Iris is identical with Ireland in name and nature. Great
Britain and Ireland are depicted in the Zodiac as a bird,
or bird harper, holding a harp. This latter object is the
Heraldry of Ireland, and Iris herself is a woman bird. This
identity of Iris with the Irish is confirmed by the myth
of Orpheus. The Lyre is his. He passes backwards and
forwards to the under world.

The symbolism is slightly varied, when Iris is made a
Rainbow, over which, as a bridge she becomes "a messenger
of the gods" to the green and emerald Isle. The American
localizations have been noticed before. Iris is the child of
Electra, the wife of Atlas, locating in Quiche, in Central America
Thaumas, her father, is a son of Neptune, standing for the
Naohas race. Thus the Aztlans and the Naohas are parents

of the Harpies, and they fly across the Atlantic Ocean, and settle in the first land they come to, that is to say, in Ireland.

This theory is novel, but it challenges criticism. Let it be put to the severest test. There is a valuable and costly work by Mr. Marcus Keane, entitled "Towers and temples of ancient Ireland," which can be utilized for this purpose. Nearly 200 pictures of Irish erections and sculptures adorn this work. It forms a complete picture gallery of Irish antiquities.

This work shews that Ireland is remarkable for numerous old erections, very unlike European buildings. Among them are round towers—cyclopean walls and crosses, adorned with curious and complicated sculptures. On the sculptures are symbolic figures that belong to classical mythology and the Zodiacs.

There are beautiful specimens of doorways adorned with what is called Ashlar enrichments. These remains have their most remarkable exemplification in the renowned Chapel attached to Cashel Cathedral.

The author proves that these things belong to a period reaching back to times anterior to all modern history and architecture. The Celts, from Spain, could not have erected them; they did not build in stone. The English could not have built them; they conquered Ireland only in 1172, A.D. The Irish Saints could not have built them; as the sculptures are not of the Christian type. The Normans could not have built them, as they never went to the West of Ireland, where the buildings are chiefly found. Besides, the Norman arch is a simple arch, destitute of the rich Ashlar ornamentation of the Irish doorways.

Without entering largely into this question, it is sufficient here, to point out that in the light of the localization of mythic personages practised in this work, it is not difficult to understand the Irish question. The architectural remains and the symbolism sculptured on them, accord minutely with the mythology of Iris. They, of themselves, point out their historical origin.

One of the most significant objects found on the Irish sculptures, is that of the Sagitarius. This compound figure is over the doorway of the Cormac temple. It will be remembered, that the Sagitarius is the Zodiacal portraiture of

Central America; so that it ties Ireland to that land, quite as well as the myth of Iris.

It has been shown in its proper place, that the Sagitarius is the son of Pan. It may be asked, what significance can Pan have in Ireland. The answer is, that in the Book of Lecain, where the question is put—"whence the origin of the Gaed-hael—what was the land in which they lived—Lordly men of Fene?": the Fenians carry the name of the father of the Sagitarius.

Another emblematical object found on the Irish sculptures is that of the human hand. "The red hand of Erin," as it is called, is sculptured on the cross of Kells, within a circle. It is also on the cross of Monastabois. It will be remembered that in the Zodiacal portraiture of Central America the human hand is one of the Coptic figures, called Arueris. In Mr. Stephens' Incidents of Travel, it is said, that "prints of the red hand are found on all the ruined buildings of Yucatan." Here the colour is material. "The red hand of Yucatan" is reproduced in "the red hand of Erin." Now the word Erin is only a different form of the Harpy Iris.

One of the most noticeable features in the architecture of the Irish remains, is the Ashlar ornamentation. It is exceedingly rich, and forms a most elaborate and splendid exhibition of enrichment. This particular form of ornamentation has been found extensively in the ruins of Yucatan. It must be a mistake to call the Ashlar Norman. It is found in Europe where the Normans never went. It corrects a mistake to bring it from Central America.

It is much the same with the Irish crosses. The crucifixion scenes which characterise the Irish crosses are not Christian. The form of the figure suspended, differs from that of a Crucifix. The picture of the Palenque cross has been given at page 227, and discovered as it was in Monastic Buildings, it may safely be considered as the Antitype of the Irish Cross.

But it is the round towers of Ireland which form the most conspicuous part of these remains. The origin and the uses of the round tower have been a great mystery. The veil of mystery is suddenly removed, when mythology reveals the real origin of the tower. It is at Atalaya and other places in Central America that the antitype of the round tower is found. In the treatment of the Noraghe of Sardinia, in a former part of this chapter, the question of the Irish tower receives its elucidation.

Mr. Keane has a theory. He finds in the legends of Ireland, and in the histories of the Tuatha de Danans, the race of the Cushites. The Tuatha de Danans are, with him, the last Cushite colony that settled in Ireland, 1900, B.C. But who were the Cushites ? On the tracings of mythology the Cushites are the Atlantides. This is seen in the native name of the Indians of Central America and Yucatan. Atalan is glossed by Cutan. Yucatan is Yu-cutan. The Danans of Ireland have been found at page 206 in Central America, as the Hindoo Dhanus and the Greek Danaus. Tuatha is the leader of that race into Ireland, as Teutates is into Gaul, and Thoth into Egypt. It is said that " King Alfred was educated in Ireland at the college of Baal in Mayo. All of his time came to Ireland for education." It would seem, from the map of Mayo, that the Mayas of Yucutan, in crossing into Ireland, must have settled in Mayo, and have given their own name to the land, for the county is full of the name of the God Baal, Balla, Ballyglass, Ballymote, and others.

Passing from Ireland and its myths to the other parts of the British Islands, it may be noticed, that one of the most observable subjects, which the British Antiquarians have been accustomed to study, is that of the heaps of stones which are discoverable on the summits of hills, in England and Wales. In England, they are called Barrows, and in Wales Cairns. In the account of the Apalachian Indians, transcribed at page 177, it is said, that that race of Indians were accustomed to observe this particular practice : they erected heaps of stones in all their colonies. From the position of the Apalachian Indians, they must necessarily have been among the earliest arrivals of the Oceanides in Europe.

Again, the hill forts of Wales and England are faithful reproductions of those of Mexico. It is the same with the Cyclopean bridges. The hill fort called the Castle of Tintagel is a famous specimen of the one, and the Cyclopean bridge at Longbridge, near Trevena, on the west coast of Cornwall, is a good specimen of the other. In the work of Du Paix on Mexican Antiquities, there is a picture of a bridge at

Tlascalla which might have been the model for this bridge, so exact is the resemblance of the two bridges. There is also a picture of a hill fort exactly like the Castle of Tintagel.

It has been seen that Herodotus makes Hercules to be the father of Agathirsus, Gelonus, and Scytha. If so, there must have been vast numbers of the inhabitants of the Mound Cities of North America in Britain. The existence of circular mounds of a similar character to the American Earthworks, is an ocular demonstration of the correctness of Herodotus. The dimensions of the British mounds are usually small, as if built by small numbers of men; but the great earthwork at Abury, exhibits a great city, similar to that described on the Miami river Ohio.

But the most remarkable remains discoverable on the west coast of Europe are the Cromlechs or Dolmens. These extend from Sweden, where they are seen in their most complete form, at the summit of artificial mounds, all down the west of Europe. The mounds bear the nearest possible resemblance to the pyramidal mounds of North America.

The mounds in Sweden and other northern lands have all a Cromlech at the summit. In all probability such Cromlechs must have been used as stones of sacrifice. The mounds with the altars look as if they had been cast up by immigrants from Mexico, in imitation of the Mexican temples and teccallises. This is corroborated by the circumstance that in Arnkiel's work on the Cimbrish Religion, there is a picture of a human sacrifice in the Mexican form.

The coast of western France and Brittany is full of ancient stones, of a Celtic character. The same may be said of the Land's End in England. Wales is covered with Cromlechs, Dinas, and collections of stones. It is observable of these stones that they are all upon the western shores. Even the Cromlechs of Hindoostan are in the west. This circumstance points to the erection of them by some extraneous race or races, from the west, who were not powerful enough to penetrate beyond the coast.

The most remarkable ruined edifice in Western Europe is Stonehenge. This has been referred to before, at page 193. It is necessary now to refer to it again. The passage from Diodorus may be transcribed with advantage. "Hecateus and some others say, that in the Ocean there is an Island over against Gaul, as big as Sicily, where the Hyperboreans under the Arctic Pole inhabit. They say that Latona was born here, and therefore they worship Apollo above all the Gods. There is a stately grove and a circular temple with rich gifts. There is a city whose citizens are most of them Harpers, chanting to Apollo. They have a language of their own. They have a special kindness for the Greeks. From them Abaris travelled into Greece. The sovereignty of the Island belongs to the Boreades, the posterity of Boreas."

If the reader will take the trouble to reperuse the close of the chapter referred to, he will find an argument to prove that the religion of the European Apollo must have had its rise in the Southern mound cities of the United States. There is an extract from Lucian to shew that the religion of the Syrian Apollo must have gone from the country of the Apalachian Indians into Syria. There is no difference between the Syrian Apollo and the oracular Apollo of Delphi, and the extract now given draws the Greek Apollo from the Isle of the Hyperboreans, that is to say, from Britain. Abaris—an impersonation of Abury, carries it there. That is confirmed when Orpheus, who, according to Archbishop Potter taught religion to Greece, is himself one of the Harpers of Britain.

The extract now given makes Stonehenge to be the high place of the Apollo worship. Stonehenge is half-way between the mythic Olympus and Greece. It must therefore be inferred that the Apalachian Indians with their priests and medicine men must have been the builders of Stonehenge. That grand and marvellous erection, therefore, attests the truthfulness of Plato, when he brings into Western Europe a great conquering people from beyond the pillars of Hercules.

The remainder of the work will be occupied with researches into the South American histories.

PART OF THE PTOLEMAIC ZODIAC AS A MAP OF SOUTH
AMERICA IN THE MYTHIC AGES.

PART OF THE COPTIC ZODIAC, AS A MAP OF SOUTH
AMERICA, IN THE MYTHIC AGES.

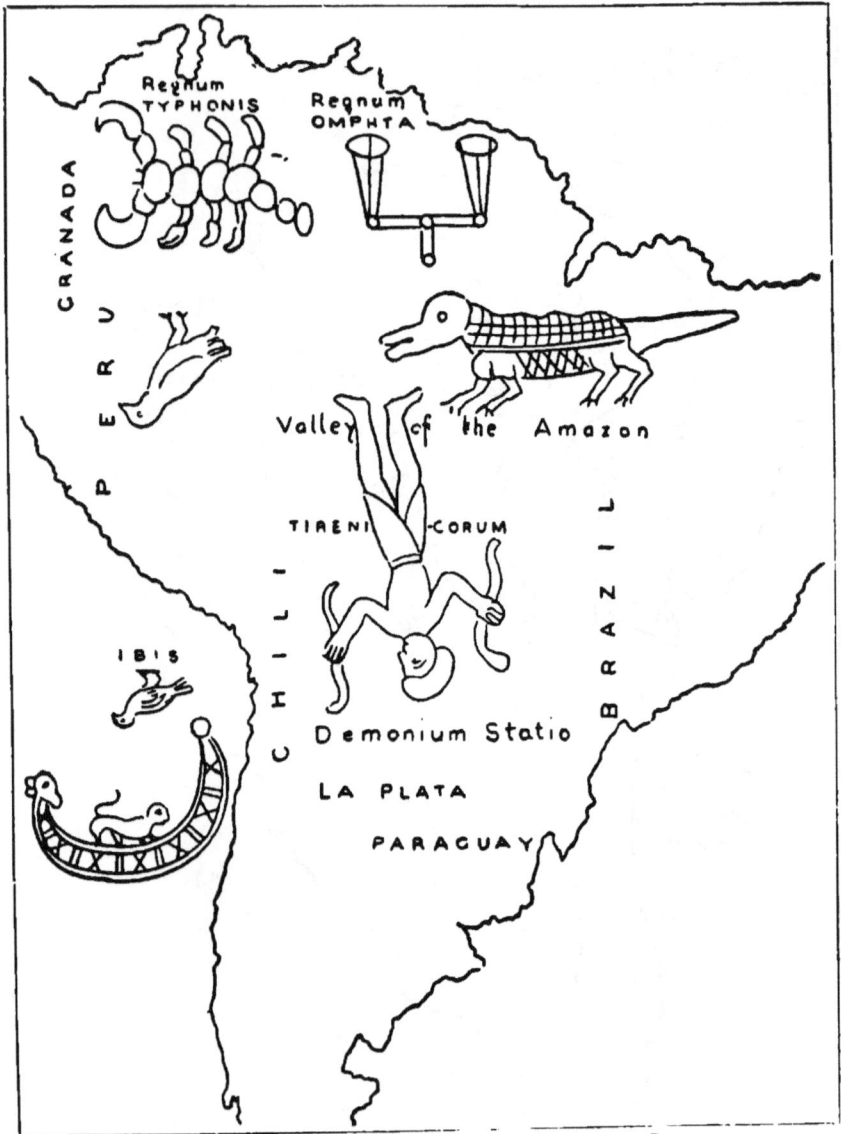

CHAPTER XXIV.

GENERAL VIEW OF THE FIGURES OF THE ZODIACS WHICH
SERVE AS DELINEATION OF SOUTH AMERICA.

The obscurity which hangs over the historical antiquities of
North America, is intensified when South America becomes
the subject of research. That vast insular continent, watered
by some of the greatest rivers on the face of the earth—
teeming with tropical vegetation—and in possession of mines
of the choicest metals that are coveted by man, is a blank
in history. In that circumstance it differs nothing from North
America: but that portion of the hemisphere has had its
annals told by, at least, three creditable historians—obscure
and fragmentary, it may be, but not beyond the penetration
of study. Unfortunately, no similar documents can be produced
for the elucidation of South American history. It is left wholly
to the inferential teaching of allegorical literature. Yet that
literature is full of suggestiveness, and it creates a suspicion, that
South America has, in ages past, been known to the Ancients.

Two mystic maps are now introduced. The Ptolemaic Zodiac
has the Scales with the name of Libra. The great region of
the Amazon and the Orinoco has the significant figure of the
Scorpio. Two imposing figures occupy the region of Peru
and Chili—the Wolf and the Centaur, supplemented by the
Building Tools. Ara the Altar, with a fire on the top of it,
is in the group of signs, and the Crux is under the legs of
the Centaur. A bird called Apus is located with some
uncertainty, south of the Centaur; and Musca the bee completes
the signs.

The Coptic Zodiac has the Scales, designated Regnum
Omphta, but its localization is dubious. The Scorpion re-
appears with the description Regnum Typhonis. The great
valley of the Amazon has a monstrous crocodile without a name.
The region of Peru is represented by a Bird, also without a
name. In the centre of the whole Insular continent is a
standing man, holding in each hand what must be supposed
to be a serpent. He has the name Tirenicorum, with the
description Demonium Statio. A Bird called Ibis, and a Boat,
appear in positions open to doubt as to their correctness.

It cannot fail to be noticed that there is great uncertainty in the localization of the figures. It must be remembered that the modern Zodiac is drawn in a spherical form, differing from the dish-like form of old maps. This difference of form creates uncertainty in all cases, and the position of the signs has to be fixed by the mythology connected with them. In this case, they nearly all seem to cluster round the upper waters of the Amazon, and this agrees with what is now known concerning the country.

It is certainly remarkable to notice, that in a part of the world supposed to have been destitute of history, and to have been shut off from the rest of the world through all known time, the building tools and the Altar are found. One would hardly have expected to find the building tools in South America: but by travellers it is said, that the slopes of the Andes and the parts adjacent have great works, excelled by none and equalled by few, · in the known world. It is more curious still, to look for religion in South America. One thing may safely be inferred from it, that the insular continent must have had histories which have greatly affected the other quarters of the globe, although unwritten on the page of European literature.

The same reflection arises from the observation of a ship among the signs, and it has a rudder. A rudder is indicative of some advance in navigation. In one of the works concerning Peru, there is a picture of a Peruvian raft which has a rudder of the same construction and placed in the same position. When compared with specimens of ancient boats on the tombs of Egypt, there is found a resemblance between them that leads to the suspicion that South America must have been comprised in the countries visited by the navigators of the old world.

Among the present group of signs is Libra the scales, and it is found in all Zodiacs. In the Ptolemaic, it has the type of modern commercial scales. In the Coptic and the Hindoo it is the same. The Hindoo carries the name of Tula, a man holding the scales.

The localization of the scales is equivocal. Like the Crown in the North, it is moveable. It is said that " formerly the scales were in the hands of Virgo," a sign that designates Siam, Cambodia, and South China. "Sometimes they have an independent existence, and sometimes they hang on to the folds of Scorpio." The scales would suit China very well, as that country has scales. The same may be said of Peru, as the Peruvians had balances of the kind drawn in the Zodiacs. The Mexicans had none.

One thing seems to fix the Scales to the western shores of South America, as the Poetical Astronomers describe the Balances, "as the sign under which begins the reign of the Devil." This is very material to the localization of the Sign. as the Coptic map makes the continent to be "the Statio Demonium." This strange identification gains countenance from the Coptic name of the Scales—Omphta. In the Egyptian legends, Ombte is the Evil Spirit.

On the whole, it may be concluded, that the Libra is correctly located when it is put in New Granada, or thereabouts. It seems to belong, in the first instance, to Eastern Asia. It then passes into the underground hemisphere and becomes demoniacal. This explains what is meant by Poetical Astronomers, when they say, that "the Libra is a sort of flying bridge." It unites the two hemispheres in the Southern Sea, as the Crown does in the northern, in a sort of mystic navigation.

CHAPTER XXV.

The vast region of the Amazon and the Orinoco is represented in the Zodiacal Maps by the Scorpion and the Crocodile, and ascribed to the Typhonian race as its inhabitants.

The Sign of the Scorpio and its Mythology.

The position of the Scorpio, in the Ptolemaic Zodiac, is very well defined in its use as an ancient map. It overhangs the vast region of the Orinoco and the Amazon, called by its present inhabitants the Maranon. The Empire of Brazil is admirably represented by the Southern Cross. In the Coptic Zodiac a crocodile lies along the great valley of the Amazon. It will be acknowledged, at once, that all these Zodiacal Signs are admirably adapted to the tropical countries and rivers which lie beneath them. If any one wants to enlarge his knowledge of the natural history of caymen, boa-constrictors, and scorpions, he naturally has recourse to books relating to the region now under consideration.

It will be found, in the study of South America, in the light of mythology, that the ancients have regarded it as the domain of monsters and demons. It is not at all improbable that this conception has arisen, in part at least, from the great reptiles and wild animals that abound in the continent. The Spaniards, on the conquest of the countries, appear to have imbibed the like idea of the Idols they found in the land. They are described as specially demoniacal, and pourtrayed in the most vivid forms of horror. In short, they seem to have been so frightful, that the Spaniards destroyed them ruthlessly.

This description of the northern parts of South America as monstrous and demoniacal, is curiously countenanced by that great and philosophic traveller, the Baron Von Humboldt. He gives a description of his visit to the Grotto of Caripe, which he calls the Tartarus of the Greeks, and he gives a graphic account of the Guarcharas, uttering plaintive cries that reminded him of the Stygian birds. This is the more remarkable, as in Chapter V., it will be remembered, that Styx was identified with the Gulf of Mexico, not far from the Cave of Caripe; and the Harpies, to which birds he alludes, are stated in Greek books to be located on the Styx.

In the Coptic Zodiac, the region of the Scorpion is called the Regnum Typhonis, and as the principle of the present work requires, peremptorily, that the gods and demons mentioned, should be placed where the pictorial maps put them, Typhon must be considered as appertaining to the present region. It is true that the same Zodiac makes him descriptive of Mexico and the Serpent land: but it may be remembered, that in the quotations transcribed for the purpose of forming opinions on the matter, it is said of Typhon, that "his seat is in the

Scorpion, over which sign he triumphs." It may fairly be inferred, from this statement, that the Typhonian race settled in Mexico, must have spread itself into the region of the Scorpion, as they must also have done into the whole of North America, judging from the extended territory appropriated to Typhon.

If Typhon is to be sought in South America, there is no difficulty whatever, in finding him there; inasmuch, as the whole region of the Amazon and the Empire of Brazil is inhabited by the Tupy Indians. The race of Tupy appears from the accounts given of it, not to have been the native race; and that fact leads to the fair supposition, that it may be the descendants of some intrusive people, who have, in times of high antiquity, mingled with the Guarany race, which is called the Aboriginal race, and which occupies the greater part of South America. This is made more probable from the circumstance, that the word Tupa is the name of God, both in the Tupy and in the Guarany languages. It looks as if he had been, not only the stemfather of the Tupy Indians, but as if the larger and older race had considered Tupy as a God. But it is made still more probable, from the additional fact, that, even in the Quichua language of modern Peru, the word is still used in the same sense, as in the form of prayer, " O Tupa Dios," Oh, Lord God.

Mr. Brinton, in his myths of the red men, says, that " the myth of Tupa makes him to be the highest God, who gave name to the race. He was the first man of Brazil. He taught agriculture, gave them fire, and now, he is a bird, that sweeps the heavens. He was depicted with horns. He is one of four brothers, whom he drove from the field, after a desperate struggle. In his worship, the priests place pebbles in a dry gourd, and deck it with feathers and arrows. Then, rattling them, they reproduce the tremendous drama of the storm."

This character is found in Demonology, a study which, though somewhat repulsive, must be called in aid in treating of South America, as it is the region of monsters and demons. Among the demons of the Sabbat, which is the assembly of demons, and which includes, by far, the most important of these grim gentry, is Tap or Gaap.   " He is the grand President, and grand prince of Enfer. He commands the four principal kings of the place. He is as powerful as Byleth. He formerly had necromancers, who offered him libations and holocausts. They invoke him, by means of magic arts. He serves himself by Byleth and has a book, which is appreciated by mathematicians. He has empire over Amaymon. He transports men into different countries."

In view of the tradition of the God Tupa, it is not going too far to say, that Typhon is alive at the present day, in the persons of the Tupy Indians, his descendants.

TUPY INDIANS OF BRAZIL.

A picture is here given of the Indians. It will be admitted that they exhibit a very favourable specimen of Indian human nature. They have nothing of the spitfire about them. If the mythology of Typhon makes them to be descendants of some race of men who were preoccupants of the tropical region of Brazil, their general appearance is such as to do honour to their descent. The man has a fine martial front. He carries splendid banners, ornamented with Heraldic symbols. He is habited in a dress not at all unlike that of an ancient Roman soldier, who, likewise carried a flag. This resemblance is the more remarkable, as, in the Egyptian pictures, in the Typhoniums of Africa, a specimen is given where Typhon is dressed like a Roman soldier.

But the woman is more remarkable than the man. In the Ptolemaic Zodiac the Centaur pierces the wolf, just as the Tupy Indian woman is here represented as spearing some monster not easy to recognize. This coincidence is noticeable. It looks as if the people of the land were acquainted with traditions of some preoccupation of the country. This preoccupation is foreshadowed in the local myth of the God Tupa. It likewise appears in the statements of Poetical Astronomers, already mentioned, that Typhon conquered the Scorpio, "over which region he triumphed." This preoccupation of South America corresponds with the preoccupation of North America. The conquering race must have been the same.

There are other indications of this preoccupation of Brazil and La Plata, from native sources. In Picard's work on the religion of all nations, it is said that the people of Brazil fear the demon whom they call Agnian, but without worshipping him. A stranger came and destroyed them by a deluge. In the centre of Brazil they have ceremonies like the Catholics. They have a Hierarchy with confession, absolution, chaplets, &c. The Boies or priests interpret dreams in accord with Agnian. In La Plata they have priests. Some adore the sun and moon. They admit an Universal Spirit penetrating matter.

In the Egyptian mythology, it is said that "there is a connection between Typho and Mars, of both of whom the hippopotamus is an emblem, and there seems to be an analogy between Hercules and the Typhonium figures. In buildings called Typhoniums are hideous figures."

In the same system, Typhon is called Tipo, and he is represented not as a man but as a female. Pictures are given of Tipo, in which she has the form of a hippopotamus or bear, or crocodile, with the hands and breast of a woman. Sometimes she stands on a crocodile.

In the light of the present system of tracing history, these Zoomorphic forms of Typhon possess historical significance. They justify the saying that "Typhon triumphed over the sign of the Scorpio." They exhibit the Tupy Indians as the ancient occupants of the great valleys of the Amazon and the Orinoco, and they shew that the northern parts of South America have been, at some time or other, under the civilizing influences of the same Titan race as has been seen in the Northern half of the Oceanic hemisphere.

This conclusion is strongly countenanced by the accounts given of the races which, in modern times, have been found located on the upper waters of the Amazon and its tributaries. One very large province situated in this region is called Mainas. In Adelung's Mithridates, there is a description of the language spoken by this race of men, from which it must be inferred that they were the descendants of some intrusive race that belonged to the old continent. These people call Father, Papa. One of the dialects of the Mainas is called Roaminas. A neighbouring race arrests attention. It is that of the Aissuaris, situated on the river Issa. On observing these names, one involuntarily thinks of Osiris and Isis, especially as Isis is sometimes called "Queen of the Manes." In their language, they call Father, Papa, and Mother, Mama. Man they call Mena. Hand is Pua (paw) and Foot is Pucta.

There are not wanting authors on Ethnological Philology, who have noticed these remarkable instances of linguistic affinity with Latin and Greek. Without entering upon that question, it may safely be concluded, that the important words Papa and Mama, must be referred to the ancient country of China, as their source. It is manifest that the words Papa and Mama, wherever they are found, are the Chinese words Pou and Mou doubled.

The existence of a large province on the upper waters of the Amazon, which bears marks of the former presence of the monastic races of North Eastern Asia, is most material for the elucidation of the very obscure histories of South America.

The mythological monuments which belong to Egypt and Ethiopia, and the Typhoniums of Africa, have upon them mysterious pictures, which can meet with their historical solution only in the great tropical and equatorial region now the subject of research.

Among these African monuments is the present figure. It is found in a form slightly different, in works on Egypt.

ABRAXAS GEM—SERAPIS.

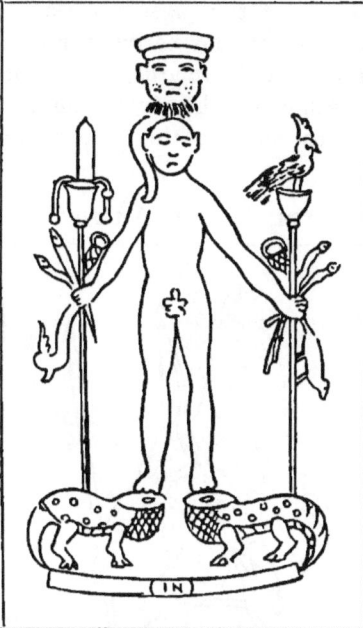

The present specimen is an enlarged Abraxas gem. It is full of significance. The emblems, as well as the inscriptions, serve to fix the localization of the scene. It is a human figure, with two heads, standing on two crocodiles, and grasping in his hands serpents, birds, and other animals. It is called Osiris or Serapis, and is inscribed, Phren, Abraxas, Iao. To make this subject intelligible the legend of Serapis, is required.

"Serapis is a modified form of Osiris. Serapis answers to Osiris, after he had changed his nature, in Amenti. The figure is azure in colour, approaching to black. Serapis was recognized as Pluto,—some thought him to be Esculapius—others Jupiter."

This remarkable picture exhibits the race of Osiris in his underground form as Serapis, dominating the crocodiles and other reptiles. This must be interpreted to mean, that the race had spread itself into the region of the crocodiles, which in the Coptic Zodiac, lies along the valley of the Amazon. This is explained by the legend of Serapis. "It is Osiris, after he had changed his nature." The figure has two heads— one old and one young. This is an allegorical method of exhibiting an old race, taking a new form,—resuscitating itself, or, as it is often said, "being born again in the west." It is now not at all surprising that travellers in Central South America and La Plata, have met with Indians in possession of monastic practices. Lastly this character is called Pluto. This must be studied in the next chapter.

In the Heraldry of the ancients, the Scorpio is the banner of the Queen of the Amazons. This brings the Amazons rightly or wrongly, within the range of the present research. It is said that the word Amazon is not the native name of the great river. It was given by the Spaniards, but it is probable, that the Spaniards so designated the river, from the resemblance that the native Indians bore to the pictures of the ancient Amazons.

ANCIENT AMAZON.   MODERN INDIAN OF THE AMAZON.

In a splendid French work containing the costumes of all nations, the present two figures are given with an evident design of shewing the identity of the races. Without presuming to pass judgment on that debated point, it may be

observed, that what has just been said concerning the Tupy
Indians of Brazil, lends countenance to the opinion of the
French artist. It cannot but have been noticed that it is the
female Tupy Indian that holds the spear and pierces the
monster—not the man. Again, the Egyptians have represented Tipo (Typhon) as a woman and not a man. This
ascription of martial prowess to the female, is the peculiar
characteristic of the ancient Amazons.

The localization of the ancient Amazons is beyond research,
simply because they have no pedigrees. Mythic pedigrees,
constituting the ethnology of the early ages, the absence
of a pedigree is fatal to the formation of opinions concerning
the migrations of the mythic period. Diodorus Siculus,
however, says that in Africa there was a nation of Amazons,
before they appear in Asia Minor. Under those circumstances,
it makes very good mythology to bring them from the
southern portion of the Atlantic Isle, as the South American
Indians. In that case, they would be, as Diodorus observes,
"neighbours of the Gorgons."

<hr>

CHAPTER XXVI.

South America as the Land of Demons.

In the Coptic Zodiac, in the centre of that portion which
must be allotted to South America, there is a human being,
with the designation "Tirenicorum" and the description
"Demonium statio." From this it must be inferred, that the
ancient Egyptians have considered the continent as the land
of Demons.

In the European system of mythic history, it is Pluto that
answers to the Prince of demons. "Pluto was the son of Saturn
and Ops. He received as his lot the kingdom of hell, and
whatever lies under the earth, and as such he became the god
in the infernal regions, of death and funerals, &c."

In the fragment of Marcellus, transcribed at page 33, after mention is made of Islands sacred to Persephone, it is said that "there were three others of an immense magnitude, one of which was consecrated to Pluto, another to Ammon, and that which was situated between them, to Poseidon."

This quotation locates Pluto in South America. It is very lucid. The Atlantic Island is divided into three parts. Ammon has North America, Poseidon Central America, and Pluto South America. It has been abundantly proved, that Ammon, who is the outcome of Pan, represents the North American Indians. It has likewise been shown, that Poseidon had Central America. It is a natural sequence that South America was consecrated to Pluto.

This coincidence is very strong, because it locates Pluto exactly where the Copts locate the land of demons. But the coincidence is stronger still, when it is noticed, that it brings Pluto into the great province of La Plata, a word in which his name is exactly discovered. It may fairly be supposed that the modern province of La Plata derives its name from the river Plata, and it is the rivers of the earth which longest retain the old nomenclature of countries.

It would seem that the Spaniards, on the discovery of Peru, were impressed with the demoniacal aspect of the Idols which they found in the land. It gives a lively idea of what they were, to read the description of one of them. This image was found at Hilavi. " It was a statue 18 feet high, made of stone. There were two monsters at its side. On both were serpents, twined round them from head to foot. About the feet were reptiles like toads." In pious horror, the Spanish priests appear to have destroyed them ruthlessly.

Nevertheless it is necessary to observe, that the word Demon, like many others which have been used for ages in relation to religion, has lost its original signification. It is used for something horrible and fiendish; but its real meaning expresses the idea of divinity. By the Greek poets, it is used for god. It is the frightful sculptures and pictures of the dark ages, which have changed its ideal conception. To acquire for the word demon, as employed in the Coptic Zodiac, its true signification, it must recover its

original meaning.   At page 86 will be found a picture of
Japanese navigation compared with a Hindoo picture of the
same navigation, in the Kurma Avatara of Vishnu.   In those
pictures the gods and the demons join in navigation.   From
this, it must be inferred, that the demons of the Coptic map
were not aboriginal savages, but civilizers of the land, in the
possession of ships.   They were a junction of the races of
Asia and America.

This teaching is supported by the details of the last chapter,
where Serapis, the Egyptian Pluto, is none other than the
divine Osiris, after he had changed his nature.

In works on Peruvian Antiquities, the Idols of Peru are
exhibited in caves.   One of these caves is here presented for
examination.   The cave is occupied by a row of figures, most
of which are small.   For want of space, some are here omitted.
The chief Idol stands erect in the centre of the company,
supported by two other images.

PERUVIAN CAVE IDOLS.

The figures in this cave are unnamed. Nevertheless, it is not impossible to detect their real character. A nobleman is known by his crest, as easily as by his name. The gigantic personage in the centre of the group carries upon his head the well-known emblem of the demon god of Europe,—Serapis. It is the vase of Serapis or Pluto. Both those gods are known by it in European mythological monuments. An instance of it appears in the picture of Serapis, given in the last chapter, at page 258. In that gem, the vase is on the head of the old man, before he assumes his new and younger form as god of the underground world, in the old continent in Africa and Europe. It would seem from this image, that the ancient Peruvians must have deified the race of men that had produced their civilization, and they give their representative the highest possible honour, by making him the greatest among their native divinities.

The two chief images which support the God of the infernal regions can be also recognised. The one on the left can be pronounced a Peruvian Canopa, which, in a future chapter, will be found to be the antitype of several gods in the old continent. That, on the right, holds in his hands the well-known emblem of both Serapis and Osiris.

The myths of Pluto and Serapis have been already given; but it may be well to read the legend of Pluto, in Demonology. " Pluto, a king of the infernal regions, according to Pagans, archdevil, governor, general of inflammable countries, and superintendent of forced labour in the dark Empire." This legend adapts itself well to the present localization. Perhaps South America is the most inflammable country on the face of the earth, and the great public works existing in Peru, are such as could not have been constructed without forced labour.

At page 80 of the present work has been given a Gnostic diagram. It is somewhat altered, to adapt it to the size of the page. It is there treated as a mystic map of ancient America. On inspection, it will be seen that the great oval which represents South America is called Behemoth, a word which the learned Bochart takes to be the hippopotamus, or river horse. It will be observed, that the diagram has the same demoniacal character as the Coptic Zodiac gives to the continent. Yet the names affixed to some of the circles, are Rabbinical names for angels. In this circumstance the diagram accords well with the present treatment of the demons.

It is noticeable, that the Gnostic Ophite map denominates one of the lowest circles of Behemoth, Thauthabaoth. It is said by one author (Musters) that the Patagonians call God Settaboth. As the two words are literally the same, it must be concluded, that the diagram really is an imperfect map of America. It has been said by many travellers, that the Patagonians are men of a gigantic stature. Turner, in his work on Thibet, says that "in a country which lies East of Bootan, are men of gigantic stature, being not less than eight feet high." This is mentioned, because in the study of comparative religions, the word Thauthaboath points to Thibet and Tartary for its origin.

If this be admitted, the Patagonians ought to be descendants of that gigantic race of men, who in the former parts of this work, have been traced from Asia into the Atlantic Isle, taking with them the religion of the Grand Lama. But this subject will have to be resumed, under the constellation of Ibis or Apus.

It is interesting to notice what the ancients have said concerning the Demons, to judge whether the vast works, temples and roads, found about the Andes, ought to be attributed to them. The legends of Demonology, certainly ascribe to the demons the inventive arts, though under the name of magic; and they make them to be teachers, with knowledge of the past, present, and future. Sabasius, himself the leader of the Sabbat, is a Gnome, a building and mining dwarf, so that the demons must be credited with much of the civilization which the Spaniards found in South America.

CHAPTER XXVII.

PERU IN ITS MOST ANCIENT FORM.

THE SIGN OF LUPUS AND ITS MYTHOLOGY.

Peru is a puzzle. When the Spaniards found Peru, and published an account of it, they threw upon the tables of the learned one of the most perplexing historical problems they ever had to solve. To find a country on the west coast of South America, in possession of social and political institutions resembling in great measure the choicest models of European nations, and in some things excelling them, presented to the philosopher and statesman a very curious subject of thought. It seemed impossible to believe that civilization so refined, could exist out of Europe. Yet why should it be thought incredible that great centres of civilizing influences should shift their place? Are not the British people, at the present time, engaged in laying the foundations of great nationalities, at their very antipodes? Why should it be thought that the present distribution of busy, thriving, commercial communities should necessarily be the same as that which existed in the vast past of the world's being?

The practice of the pictorial map-makers of antiquity, in requiring that the name of the figure should clang with the Ethnology of the country, makes it proper, in all cases, to search into the nomenclature of the lands pourtrayed. In the present instance, there is nothing to shew what was the ancient name of Peru. The enquiry, therefore, fixes itself upon the races which have been discovered in the province.

Peru, on a large scale, is inhabited, at the present time, by the Quichua race. About the lake Titicaca is a large nation, called Aymara, which includes Canchis, Canas, and other provinces. The Lupacas are said to be the chief race. The Mobinish and the Itonamish, (Adelung's spelling), are also mentioned. The Latin word for Wolf is Lupus, and that word is employed in the Zodiac. Here it is observable that the word Lupacas, the chief race in the land, clangs well with Lupus.

The first mythic personage that must be put under the constellation of Lupus the wolf is Osiris. Plutarch says that

2 K

"Osiris took the form of a Wolf." This brings him into Peru ; and it is remarkable, that an image of him has just been seen in the Peruvian Cave. The first time that Osiris made his appearance in the tracing of myths in these pages, was when he was a passenger in the boat of Phre. See page 92. He is now found turned into a Wolf.

In his legend Osiris is "Judge of the dead, and rules over the kingdom where the souls of good men were admitted to eternal felicity. Horus, his son, introduces the deceased into his presence, bringing with him the tablet of Thoth. Horus is assisted by Anubis, the dog-headed God, brother to Macedo the wolf."

But what is meant by Osiris? This question is answered by Clemens Alexandrina, when he says, "Sciaka is the germ of Osiris." Sciaka is the Thibetan Buddha, so that Osiris is the embodiment of the Grand Lama. He and his sons are missionaries all round the world, planting hermitages and building Lamasaries everywhere.

The next character that comes under the Wolf is Macedo. "Macedo was a son of Osiris. He had a share in the divine honours which were paid to his father. He was represented clothed in a wolf's skin."

This is one of the curious things that disclose themselves in the localization of the Gods. Macedo gives name to the Macedonians. It will be remembered, that in the 4th chapter, page 33, an account is given of the discovery of a stone in Brazil, shewing that the Macedonians had been there in the time of Alexander, son of Philip, 63rd Olymp. The banner of the Macedonians was a wolf.

According to the principle of this treatise, Romulus and Remus must be put in this location, as they were brought up by a she-wolf.

The story of Remus and Romulus as men, is quite unintelligible. The mistake is corrected by Zodiacal localization.

Demonology corrects the mistake when it makes "Romulus" to be "a child of the Devil and Grand Magician. Mars, in fact, who was his father, was but a demon. After being established in his kingdom, in the presence of his army, there was a great whirlwind, and the devil carried him to another kingdom."

In the Classical mythology, "Romulus was a son of Mars and Ilia, grandson of Numitor, king of Alba. He was born at the same birth with Remus. These two children were thrown into the Tiber, by order of Amulius, who usurped the crown of his brother Numitor, but they were preserved, and according to Florus, the river stopped its course, and a she-wolf came and fed them with her milk, till they were found by Faustulus, one of the king's shepherds." After a description of the building of the city, and the histories connected with it, the laws of Romulus are mentioned as follows :— "Romulus divided the lands he conquered, one part was preserved for religious uses,—to erect temples and to consecrate altars: the other was appropriated to the expences of the state, and the third part was equally distributed among his subjects, who were divided into three classes or tribes.—Romulus was ranked by the Romans among the twelve great Gods." ·

The mythology which compels the allocation of Remus and Romulus in Peru, before their removal to Italy, looks at first sight problematical, but there is much to justify it. Already it has been seen that the Tupy Indians bear a resemblance to the Roman Soldiers. The Roamainas were a race of men in the region, with language analogous to Latin. In the next chapter, the Inca of Peru will be identified with Æneas, whom the critic Niebuhr shews to have been the grandfather of Remus and Romulus. Then, the institutions of Romulus in Italy, as transcribed above, were precisely the same as those of the Inca of Peru, although dissimilar to those of all other nations.

It is remarkable, that Mr. Hawkes, in his Peruvian antiquities, describes an Idol in Peru of a name bearing a great resemblance to Remus. He says that "at Lima is a Huaca"—a sort of god "called Rimac. It is a human figure. It is in a magnificent temple. It has oracles by priests. The nation of Yuncas, who occupy the valley, worshipped it." In a note, it is said that "there is a tradition of a celebrated temple of the Idol Rimac, in the Valley of Huatica, contiguous to Lima-tamba, now Magdelene. There are many Huacas still" As the valley of Magdelene is in the Northern part of South America with access to the Caribean Sea, the area of the worship of Rimac must have been very extended.

In the Hindoo mythic system, the demon wolf is Yama: he has "a wolf-like belly." "Yama is judge of departed souls. He is in the infernal regions, south. He is called Vaivaswata, offspring of the sun, and Dherma, king of Justice, and Pitripati, lord of the Pitris. He is Mrita or death. He lives in the infernal adode called Yamapur. His steward is Kasmala, who brings the righteous on self-moving cars to the Judge. Yama is lord of Patala. He has a servant Kashmala, who drags the wicked into hell."

This myth, like many of the Hindoo myths, is more geographical than those of Europe. Yama is in the infernal regions, south. This puts him in South America. In Adelung's Mithridates, there is a province of this name, Yamea. In the description of the language, it is put with the Mainas and the Omagua and Aissuaries, before mentioned. Thus Yama not only coalesces with Serapis and Pluto in nature, but in Ethnology and Geography. It will be observed, also, that he is a navigator. He has self-moving cars or ships, and there is maritime intercourse with other lands. The Japanese have the like god of hell, with the like name Jemma. He has two assistants. One writes the crimes of men: the other reads them. This is in a Pagoda near Miaco much frequented.

The most circumstantial account of the demon wolves is in the Scandinavian mythology. M. Bergman gives the details in his work, La fascination de Gulfe. "There are two wolves—the one called Sköll and the other Hati. They dwell in a wood to the eastward of Midgard, called Jarnvid, which is the abode of a race of witches, called Jarnvidjur. This old hag is the mother of many gigantic sons, who are all of them shaped like wolves. The most formidable of all is called Managarm: he will be filled with the life blood of men who draw near their end." Again, Sol is pursued by Sköll, but has to avoid Hati, the enemy of Mani, page 208. The Jotnes are Zoomorphic. The sun and moon were considered the Bull and the Cow, or the Celestial horse. The demons or enemies of these divinities were wolves. They had the name of Thurses and Jotnes. The name Itan-thurses means great Wolf. The demons are Giants, wicked. These demons were the primitive race of the world, and anterior to the race of the Gods. They had great wisdom of antiquity, but it was magic, page 209. They have females, daughters of the wolf Kokuo, derived from Gug. These are friends of the Thurses. In Sclavic, the issue of the wolf is Volchava. In Russian it is Volchor, page 240. These Giants are shut up beyond the sea north and east. One of these Wolf Giants is mother of the most famous of the wolves—Mana.

This mythology is very curious, to say the least of it. But, there are many things in it which countenance the theory, that it is a mythic description of ancient races, in the region now under consideration. It is observable that the principle of the Zodiacal signs, as Geographical, is recognised in the extracts. These wolf Giants are beyond the sea, east. It must have been beyond the Pacific, as there is no other sea. The wolves are called Itans, the name of a race still in the region. The great wolf, Mana, has its identification in the province of the Mainas, the very large district on the upper waters of the Amazon.

The mythology of the Wolf in the second Edda is very complete. It will be remembered that the Wolf is one of the three children of Loki, by Angurbodi, a Giantess of Jotunheim. "The wolf Fenrir was bred up among the Gods, but Tyr alone had the daring to go and feed him. The Gods determined to make an iron fetter for him; but Fenrir burst the chain. They then made a stronger chain, which he burst. Alfather then sent Skirner to the dark Elves to engage certain dwarfs to make the fetter Gleipner. It was made of the noise of a cat's footfall—the beards of women—the roots of stones—the sinews of bears—the breath of fish, and the spittle of birds. The Gods then took the wolf to the Island Lyngvi, in the lake Amsvartner. The wolf stipulated that a God should put his hand into his mouth, when bound. The chain of the fetter was drawn through a large rock named Gjöll, and fastened to a stone called Thviti. The wolf made violent attempts to break loose, when the Gods thrust a sword into his mouth. The blood formed the river Von."

Two things are wanted here, the locality of the wolf and its father. Take the locality first. The Lupacas are the chief race of the Aymaras and they are placed about the lake Titicaca. It is in that neighbourhood, that the most ancient ruins of Peru were discovered. On the principle of localization, here adopted, the wolf locates himself at this lake. There is a passage in Markham's Travels in Peru, which shews that this identification is correct. It is at page 113, "a rock, called Titicaca, gave name to the lake and island. Titi, in Aymara, is Cat, and Caca is rock. Capacalana is a peninsula, in the lake. The Idol of Capacalana was made of a beautiful blue stone. It had an ugly human head and a fish's body, and it was adored as God of the Lake." In the myth, it is said that they fastened the fetter to a stone called Thviti, in an island in the lake. Now under the wolf, there is no lake except Titicaca, so that that must have been the locality of the myths.

Now take Loki. To see the Ethnological position of Loki, as father of the wolf, as well as the Midgard Serpent and Hela, a few extracts are required. "Loak was the name of the stem-father of the Cherokee Indians." Picard says that "Louque was the first man among the Caribs." The Caribs are a very extended race in America. They are not only found in the Caribean Sea, which carries their name, but they are spread over a great part of South America. Adelung says, that they consider themselves to be strangers there, and they say, that all other people are their slaves. Tradition brings them from Florida, as the Apalachian Indians. Thus the Indians of North America and the Caribs of South America are, in point of fact, children of Loki, according to the myth.

The Scandinavian myth of the wolf Fenrir is particularly instructive, in its application to the present subject. It contains in it the exact points that are wanted to be known, as to the early settlements of Asiatic races on the western shores of South America. It is very explicit. It makes the wolf Fenrir to have been bred up among the Gods. Then, the Gods determine to fetter him: he had become too unruly. Then Alfather sends to do it. Then Tyr had the daring to go and feed him.

From these details, it is easy to see, that the settlements in South America were well known to the Asiatic people,—that they had become a source of alarm and fear to the nations of the East, and that there was a general desire to interpose and restrain the colonists. But such was the violence of the demoniacal race, that none could be found daring enough to cross the Pacific Ocean to grapple with the demons. In their difficulty, the Gods send to the dark Elves, whoever they may have been.

But the grand point, in the present enquiry, is to find out, who Tyr was. His tradition is as follows—Gangler interrogates Har, who replies, " Ay, there is Tyr, who is the most daring and intrepid of all the Gods. 'Tis he who dispenses valour in war, hence warriors do well to invoke him. It has become proverbial, to say of a man who surpasses all others in valour, that he is Tyr strong, or, valiant as Tyr. A man noted for his wisdom is also said to be wise as Tyr." The myth then gives the story of the wolf as transcribed above.

It would seem that there must be real history comprised in this myth, for in the Coptic Zodiac the wolf is substituted by a human being holding in his hands what may be supposed to be snakes, and designated Tirenicorum. The figure carries the name of Tyr himself, and is contiguous to the Lake Titicaca and the ruins of ancient Peru.

CHAPTER XXVIII.

THE INCA OF PERU.

In ordinary books relating to Peru, as discovered by the Spaniards, the Inca is simply the sovereign of a country, suddenly disentombed from the oblivion of ages. No mortal in the old hemisphere, had ever heard of such a person. In the traditions of the country, he seems to have been the outcome of some seven or eight generations. In another estimate, the dynasty widens out to three or four thousand years. But the Inca of Peru, in the light of mythic histories, is one of the most ancient and well known characters, in the antiquities of the writing nations of the world. It may be said of the Inca, as of the Gods. that when he is examined

and pulled about to discover who or what he was, he tumbles
into a name, but when the name is looked at closely, it swells
and swells, till it becomes a history of gigantic proportions.

In the endeavour to find out who the Inca of Peru was, by
ancient writings, two of the curious mythic pedigrees of China
must be, in part, transcribed. This can be conveniently done,
from the great work of Anderson on National Pedigrees.

No. 1.   CHINA.

		Yrs.
1	VITEY, a Giant famous for Architecture.	
	he reigned...	100
	He had 25 sons, whose offspring had 116 kings. they reigned...	2257
118	TZINTZOM. Last of Vitey's offspring. He built the wall of China	40
119	ANCHOSAU. Root of a new race	12
120	TUTEY, &c., &c.	

No. 2.   CHINA.

		Yrs.
1	FOHI. Son of heaven. Inventor of Hieroglyphics. reigned...	65
2	XINNUNG. Invented Agriculture.	
3	HOANGT. Lord of all the world. First Emperor. The Chinese say he never died, but was carried up from the mountains of XINSIANS.	

A classic scholar is very likely to observe, in the first of
these Pedigrees, that after a race of Giants, there appears
one Anchosau, root of a new race. It is natural for the scholar
to ask: how is this? What can Anchises have to do with
China? This makes it necessary to study his myth and
relationships. "Anchises, son of Capys, by Themis, daughter
of Ilus. He was of such a beautiful complexion, that Venus
came down from heaven on Mount Ida, to enjoy his company.
The child which Venus brought forth, was called Æneas. He

was educated, as soon as born, by the nymphs of Ida, and when of proper age was entrusted to the care of Chiron the Centaur. Virgil, in the 6th book of the Æneid, introduces him in the Elysian fields, relating to his son, the fates that attended him and the fortune of his descendants, the Romans."

On the principle of localization adopted in this work, both Anchises and Æneas must have been of Asiatic origin. Anchises is the son of Themis, one of the names of the Virgo, the asterism that overhangs the Celestial Empire. Æneas is the son of the Goddess Venus, stem-parent of the Northern regions of Asia. The Scythians and the Chinese produce two mythic Emperors.

Again, when Æneas is entrusted to Chiron the Centaur, the same principle of localization makes him to cross the Pacific Ocean, and settle on the west coast of South America, because the Centaur Chiron is embodied in the Sagitarius, and the Centaur overhangs Peru. That this is the true interpretation of the myth is proved by the fact, that Virgil puts both Anchises and Æneas in the Elysian fields. The Inca of Peru, therefore, must have been the mythic Æneas, in his own name. Divested of the mysticism which hangs about the history, it makes the Inca to be the outcome of a Chinese and Scythian occupation of Peru.

The myth of Anchises has to be compared with the native traditions of the land. The Inca is called "the son of the sun." In national heraldry Japan is the rising sun. This native account of the origin of the Inca differs little from the classic myth. If there is any difference, it makes the Japanese, rather than the Chinese, to have created the race of Incas.

Again, in works upon this subject, great mention is made of one Viracocha. Mr. Hawkes, in his valuable work, entitled "Peruvian Antiquities," says of him, "The chief person, and one intimately connected with Peruvian history, was Viracocha, an apparition, who appeared to an Inca, calling himself the son of the Sun." There was a grand temple to him. He was a man with a large beard, dressed in garments long and wide, with a tunic down to his feet. He held in his hand an image of an unknown animal, with lion's claws." Mr. Prescott says, that "the name of Viracocha is interpreted as "the foam of the sea." Again, it is said, that the last Inca was told by his father, that the Viracochas,—white men, would come from their father the sun, and subject them."

This, again, has to be compared with the tradition of Anchises. If the word Viracocha means, "the foam of the sea," the inference is very remarkable, if not conclusive. Every scholar will notice that the expression "foam of the sea" is the European origin of the Marine Venus. In the classic mythology, Urania, the Celestial Venus, is transformed into the Marine Venus. In other myths, she is transformed into a Serpent. Now Æneas is the son of Venus by Anchises. If the mythic Æneas is the Inca, according to the combination set forth at the commencement of the present chapter, then the Inca is of the race of Viracocha, just as Æneas is the son of Venus. In that case, the native tradition accords exactly with the myth of Anchises.

There is yet another native tradition, and it is one that is worthy of some attention. Mr. Brinton says, that "the myth of the Muyscas has a hero—Bochica or Nemquataba, or Sua, the white one; an appellation which they give to the Europeans. He taught them the art of building, &c. When he disappeared, he left four chiefs and laid down rules. Some mention a distinction between Bochica and Sua." This tradition is also referred to in Adelung's Mithridates. In the description of the language of Darien and the surrounding tribes, "Tradition makes a bearded man come to them,—one Bochica, a civilizer."

This tradition cannot be compared with the myth of Anchises, in a direct form; but it shews that there must have been more than one civilizer in the north-west of South America.

There is yet another claimant for this honour. Brasseur de Bourbourg, treating of Bards and Chroniclers, says, quoting Las Casas, "In all the Republics in these countries, there were those that performed the functions of chroniclers and historians. They had knowledge of the origin of all things, touching religion and founders of cities. They kept account of months and days and years. Though they had no writing, they had figures and characters, and thus had great books, so ingenious, that our letters are not more useful. I have seen a great part of the doctrine of Christianity in figures and images. These Chroniclers passed from father to son, and they were attached to kings and princes and priests."

The following quotation will shew that this practice existed in Peru, and it relates to the subject in hand. "Ovallo, a traveller in the neighbourhood of Quito, in the year 1646, after describing the Quippos, and speaking of the excellent memories of the people, says, that Father Diego, Torres Bollo, in a place where. four ways met, saw an Indian, who, to the sound of a drum, was singing a great many things, all alone, in his own tongue. The Father called one in his company, who understood it, and asked him, what the Indian meant by that action. He told the father, that the Indian was, as it were, the Registrar of that country, who, to keep up the memory of what had passed in it, from the deluge to that time, was bound every holiday to repeat it, by the sound of a drum, and sing, as he was then doing. He was, moreover, obliged to instruct others, in the same way, that there might be a succession of men, to do the same thing after he was gone: and that which he at this time is singing, is that in such a year, there had been there, a white man, called Thomas, who did great wonders, preaching a new law, which, in time, was lost and forgotten."

It is now quite manifest, that this ancient country had been visited by some individual or some race, that had instructed the people in religion and laws. It may be a curious question, who Thomas was. It is most likely that some may jump to the conclusion, that the Apostle of Christianity had been in Peru and New Granada. There is no real difficulty in supposing that he had so done: but Thomas, the apostle, is quite historical, and can in no way explain a very ancient myth. This story has also to be compared with the tradition of Anchises. Now Anchises was the son of Capys, by Themis, the daughter of Ilus. Here is the very name itself. But who is Themis?

"Themis, a daughter of Cœlus and Terra, who married Jupiter against her own inclination. She became mother of Dice, Irene, Eunomia, the Parcœ, &c. She was the first to whom the inhabitants of the earth raised temples. Her oracle was famous in Attica, in the age of Deucalion, who consulted it with great solemnity, and was instructed how to repair the loss of mankind. She was generally attended by the seasons. Among

the moderns, she was represented as holding a sword in one
hand, and a pair of scales in the other." Poetical Astronomers
call the Virgo, Themis, who also holds the scales. In this
myth Themis answers to Thomas in name and nature.

It may fairly be objected, that this comparison of the myth
of Anchises with the native traditions of the Peruvians concerning the civilizer of the land, gives to the Inca much
greater antiquity than that assigned to him by the Spanish
writers. But traditions have no chronology. They can be
trusted for facts, but not for the time of their occurrence.
The Inca and his institutions may have been unknown in
Asia and Europe, from Plato to Columbus; but there is
ocular demonstration, from the monuments of antiquity, that
the Inca and his customs were known in ancient Ethiopia
and Babylonia.

Here are two pictures. The first is that of the Inca, at his
devotions. He is seen making an offering to the Sun of a

INCA BEFORE THE SUN.

golden vase, probably filled with wine, according to the
practices of the Peruvian Court, described by travellers. The

second is taken from Sir G. Wilkinson's valuable work on Egypt. It is called Atin Re, or the Sun Atin. It was found in the grotto of Tel-el-Amarna. It is exhibited for comparison with the Peruvian scene. A casual inspection is enough to establish the identity of the two pictures. But it is manifest, that the Ethiopian picture is taken from the Peruvian scene,

ATIN RE IN ETHIOPIA.

on the rule that decides such questions. The Peruvian picture is a simple, natural scene. It is the Inca in his temple, before the sun, while in the Ethiopian design, there are ghosts bringing offerings to him. It must have been drawn by artists who had copied some historical picture; but they had no real knowledge of what it was intended to represent. The historical inference to be deduced from this comparison of pictures is inevitable and plain. There must have been intercourse between the countries, and that at a time so ancient, as to have been forgotten.

But there is a similar thing found among the Babylonians. One of the Babylonian cylinders, among the pictures given in works relating to Babylonian subjects, has the same Peruvian scene; but on a smaller scale and less perfect. Yet the evidence furnished by it leads to the same conclusion, and proves that the Inca must have been visited by the Babylonians, and that at times of great antiquity, the Inca was established in the land.

CHAPTER XXIX.

PERU IN ITS MORE RECENT FORM.

THE SIGN OF CENTAURUS AND ITS MYTHOLOGY.

The Centaur is one of the grandest objects in mythological pictures. It abounds to an immense extent in the collection of the monuments of pictorial art, practised in the Pagan and Monkish ages of the world. Chariots drawn by Centaurs, and accompanied by the accessories incident to such designs, make the most imposing scenes in the great works of Montfaucon and other authors, who have preserved the remembrance of the mythic ages. They also abound on the Etruscan Vases, and by their vivid and elegant forms, they grace the finest specimens of the pottery art.

. Such magnificent pictures as are classed among this sort of designs, are, in all probability, the work of artists, who have lived in times comparatively modern. The elaboration apparent in them, and the artistic grouping of the fantastic animals, betray a lofty state of pictorial art. It cannot be supposed that these splendid designs appertain to the original country which gave birth to the conception of the compound figure. The Centaur of the vase and the painting, must be considered to owe its character to the great nations of the Orient of Assyria and Babylonia, and to the chariot and the charioteer of the rich and luxurious monarchs, that appear upon the walls of the subterranean palaces. Even the Sphinx of Egypt must be looked upon as a kind of Centaur. Wherever an animal winged and endowed with a human head is found, it must be classed in this category.

But the first idea of a Centaur must be ascribed to the lands of Peru and Chili, because the Centaur has been employed as portraiture for those countries. The creature itself, is confessedly a nondescript,—a monster; but to understand it, it must be dissected. It is compounded of a figure half man and half horse. All the compound figures of the mythic ages indicate the mingling of races. The Centaur is no exception to the rule, and the figure ought to represent two races of men.

It is said that neither horses nor bulls were native to South America. There are not wanting those who disbelieve the Spaniards when they deny the existence of horses on the Pampas, on the discovery of America. One traveller says, plainly, that the wonderful horsemanship on the Pampas is an indication, that horse riding must always have existed there. But one is not driven to the necessity of proving the existence of horses in South America. The slightest study of this subject reveals the fact, that a Centaur, a horse-man, is not the ancient figure of the constellation.

In the Coptic Zodiac, it is a bird instead of a horse; and it will be seen that the bird is the real Centaur. It is the result of artistic liberties and mistakes of copyists, that it is turned into a man-horse. Pictures have histories, as well as occurrences. The earliest form of a Centaur is an upright man, holding by the legs an upright lion. The next form is a human figure, with the lower members of a lion, that is to say, a man-lion. A horse-man is its latest change.

The word Centaur has no meaning, in any language, and cannot be dissected. Montfaucon gives the true Centaur, when he exhibits a man-bird, and the nature of the figure is pictorially explained, when he shews a sculptor in the act of chiselling a huge pair of wings, for the Centaur. It is a curious circumstance, and one strongly confirmatory of the applicability of the Centaur to Peru, that it is in the description of Peruvian customs, that an explanation of this obscure

subject is obtained. In the feast of Ramey, there was a great
procession to the Inca's palace, in which a large number of
the people were dressed in the wings of a great bird. In
explanation of this custom, it is said, that "those who appear
in the wings of the Cuntur, do it to shew that they drew
their origin from these birds." This sentence has the French
name of the bird. In English, it is the Condor, a bird peculiar
to the Andes, with wings extending to the length of 15 feet.
This is the Centaur.

The Zodiacs differ in their symbolic representation of the
region of the Centaur. The Coptic Zodiac has the bird, and
the Ptolemaic has the man-horse. It will be necessary,
therefore, to treat the subject in conformity with that difference.
Let the bird be considered first.

It might be difficult to discover the nationality indicated
by wings without the Zodiac. It is the Virgo that is dressed
with wings. As the Virgo is portraiture for Southern China,
Cambodia, and Siam, it may be inferred that the winged men
in the Peruvian processions to the temple of the Sun preserved
in the Peruvian mind, the remembrance of former enrichments
of population, of a beneficent character, from those lands.

It cannot be expected that the classical myths will throw
light upon the subject of the winged men: recourse must
therefore be had to Oriental and Rabbinical literature. If the
reader will take the trouble, once more, to turn to the Ophite
Gnostic map, at page 80, he will see their names. The upper
circles, which seem to belong to the northern parts of South
America, there mystically called Behemoth, have the names
affixed to them of Suriel, Gabriel, Erathoth, Michael, and
Raphael.

It is in the book of Enoch, a curious Ethiopic book, written
in the Amaric letter, that this subject has to be studied.
The book is far too mystical for use in the present treatise:
nevertheless there can be no doubt at all that if its mysterious
contents could be made contributory to the elucidation of the
histories of the Atlantic Isle, it would illuminate many dark
pages in the antiquities of the human race.

It is not within the design of the present work to employ
the Scriptures as elucidatory matter. Otherwise it could easily

be made apparent, that the winged men were the missionaries of other days—sent "to preach to the Spirits in prison," what by the Oriental writers is always called, "the Unity of God and righteousness." What effect the labours of the winged men had, is traceable in the religious tenets both of Mexico and Peru. But the subject is too long for the present volume.

The first of the winged men enumerated in the mystic diagram, links Rabbinical knowledge to profane mythology, and serves to bring back the present research to its legitimate medium of study. Suriel or Uriel is discoverable in Euryale. "Euryale is one of the Gorgons, who was immortal." "Euryale was a daughter of Minos, mother of Orion by Neptune."

The latter part of this pedigree belongs to another chapter. Here it is necessary to fix attention on Minos, as to all appearances, the classical equivalent for the winged men. The myth of Minos is as follows:

"Minos, a king of Crete, son of Jupiter and Europa. He flourished about 1432 years before the Christian Era. He gave laws to his subjects, which still remained in full force in the age of the philosophic Plato, about 1000 years after the death of the legislator. His justice and moderation procured him the appellation of the favorite of the Gods,—the confidant of Jupiter,—the wise legislator, in every city of Greece, and according to the poets, he was rewarded for his equity, after death, with the office of supreme and absolute judge in the infernal regions. In this capacity he is represented, sitting in the middle of the shades, and holding a sceptre in his hand. The dead plead their several causes before him, and the impartial Judge shakes the fatal Urn which is filled with the destinies of mankind. He married Ithona, by whom he had Lycastes, who was the father of Minos the Second."

This myth is one of a class which may be called semi-mythic. It is real history, so far as belongs to Crete; but it contains mythic histories that belong to the ancestors of Minos the Second, in high antiquity and at the antipodes. The Greeks were in possession of traditions of the whole world, and wonderfully complete; but, for the want of localization they are confused. They require readjustment only, to bring out of them reliable history.

2 M

To understand the mythic Minos, the grandfather, as Judge in the infernal regions, he must be put into comparison with the Egyptian Osiris, in Amenti. "His principal office was Judge of the dead, and to rule over that kingdom where the souls of good men were admitted to eternal felicity. Seated on his throne, accompanied by Isis and Nephtys, with the four Genii of Amenti, who stand on a lotus growing from the waters, in the centre of the divine abode, he receives the account of the actions of the deceased, recorded by Thoth. Horus, his son, introduces the deceased into his presence bringing with him the tablet of Thoth, after his actions have been weighed in the scales of truth. To Anubis, who is styled director of the weights, belongs this duty, and assisted by Horus, he places in one scale the feather or the figure of Thmei, the goddess of truth, and in the other a vase, emblematical of the virtuous actions of the judged. A cynocephalus, emblem of the Ibis headed God, sits on the upper part of the balance, and Cerberus the guardian of the palace of Osiris is present."

If the winged men taught to the ancient Peruvians "the Unity of God," the people must have imbibed that divine sentiment. Mr. Hawkes says, that "before the time of the Inca, the supreme being was called Con. He is described as an immaterial spirit, created and happy, till the advent of crime. Being angry, Con converted the race into black cats, &c., leaving the earth uncultivated till Pachacamac the son of Con, recreated what his father had destroyed, Gratitude to Pachacamac led them to erect temples to him and to worship him, with the use of sacrificial altars and pilgrimages; but they raised no temple to Con, judging him to be a spirit."

In this extract mention is made of Altars. It is remarkable, that in the Ptolemaic Zodiac, the altar is one of the constellations beneath the Centaur. The religion of the Inca's court was Astral. The Sun itself, in the open air,—and a great golden Orb, in the temple of the sun, constituted the object of worship. Before the golden Sun was an altar, at which the Inca kneeled, see page 276. In the presence of his family, he offered to the Sun, a Vase, full of wine. It was in the processions to this grand temple, that the winged men took a part.

The religion of the Inca's court embraced two of the most remarkable forms of worship practised in ancient Asia and Europe. One was that of the fire rites, with the everlasting fire and Vestal Virgins—similar to the fire rites practised both in Persia and Rome. The other was that of Monasteries, with buildings and cloisters like those of the old continent. In connection with these religions, there were four feasts, vast and splendid, during which were Lamb offerings and great feasting.

Dr. Robertson observes that "the most singular and striking circumstance in the ancient Peruvian government, is the influence of religion upon its genius and laws. The whole system of civil policy was founded upon religion. The Inca appeared not only as a legislator, but as the messenger of heaven. Hence it followed, that his authority, in the most extensive sense, was unlimited and absolute, and to this circumstance it was also owing, that all crimes were punished capitally, because they were not considered as transgressions of human laws, but as insults offered to the Deity."

If the winged men succeeded in their sacred mission to preach "to the spirits in prison" the sublime religion of "the Unity of the Deity," it is quite manifest that the Judges of the infernal regions,—that is to say, the lands at the antipodes,—succeeded also in inculcating on them the principles of "righteousness." All authors who have written upon the subject commend the social and political institutions of the Inca's government. They may be termed model laws. Witness the following extract,—from Rees' Cyclopædia.

"All the lands capable of cultivation, were distributed into three shares: one share was consecrated to the sun, and its product was applied to the support of religious rites: the second belonged to the Incas, and was devoted to the support of government, and the third, being the largest share, was reserved for the maintenance of the people. No person had a right of exclusive property in the portions allotted to him: he possessed it only for a year, at the expiration of which, a new distribution was made, according to the rank, number and exigences of each family. All these lands were cultivated by the joint industry of the community, and the people were summoned by the proper officer to the fields and performed their common task, while songs and musical instruments cheered them to their labour. In consequence of this mode of distribution, selfish principles were restrained and extinguished, and each individual felt his connection with those around him, and the state thus constituted might be considered as one great family, in which the union of the members was so complete and the exchange of good offices so perceptible, as to create stronger attachment than subsisted under any form of society established in America." It need only be added, that if the laws of Minos and Phoroneus were based upon institutions such as these, there is no wonder that ancient books have referred to them with commendation.

In the Ptolemaic Zodiac, the modern provinces of Peru and Chili are delineated by the Centaur, a very large figure, corresponding with the wide domains of the ancient Inca—said to have extended 1500 miles. The Centaur is a horse with a human head. In the Classical Lexicon, there are many myths of this nondescript. The shortest is as follows: "Centaurus, a ship in the fleet of Æneas, which had the figure of a Centaur." As this is taken from the Æneid, it may refer to the Mediterranean Sea; but it would suit the Ship Argo, exactly, as that vessel stands off the coast in both the Zodiacs. The ship Argo with its figure head and numerous oars makes a fine stalking Centaur, carrying the Oceanides on his back, to all parts of the world.

The Centaur hangs upon the myths of Menalippe and Ixion. Take Menalippe first—" Menalippe, a daughter of the Centaur Chiron, beloved and ravished by Æolus, son of Hellen. She retired into the woods to hide her disgrace from the eyes of her father, and when she had brought forth, she entreated the gods to remove her totally from the pursuits of Chiron. She was changed into a mare and called Ocyroe. Some suppose that she assumed the name of Menalippe, and lost that of Ocyroe. She became a constellation, after death, called the horse. Some authors call her Hippe or Evippe."

Admitting the correctness of the present allocation of this myth, there is something about it that must be pronounced very remarkable. It is said that on the discovery of Peru by the Spaniards, they were told that the natives attributed their civilization to one Oello, whom they called the son of the Sun. Now in the present myth, Menalippe is loved by Æolus. This resemblance of names may be accidental, but Euripides says that " Jove's nephew had a son from Aelo ; to avoid detection, he was changed to a horse and put in the stars." This looks as if the Greeks had preserved the name of the Peruvian civilizer in their national traditions, and it makes that civilizer to be the Centaur himself. Æolus is here called the son of Hellen. In another myth, he is king of storms and winds—presumably a navigator. Hellen, again, is the son of Deucalion, who is a son both of Prometheus and Minos.

Menalippe is the daughter of Chiron the Centaur, who has been found embodied in the Sagitarius, portraiture for Central America. He was the instructor of Æneas himself. If so, the first Incas of Peru must have been in Central America, before they created a dynasty in South America. Chiron was the son of Saturn, one of the most eminent of the Titan race; so that the Centaurs must have formed with the Nahoas or Toltecs, one great and beneficent family.

In the Classics, the parentage of Centaurus is also referred to Ixion. The following is his myth, slightly curtailed. " Ixion, a king of Thessaly, son of Phlegias, or Leontes, or Antion.—He married Dia, daughter of Eioneus or Deioneus. He promised his father-in-law a present, and being unwilling to fulfil his promise, he invited Deioneus to a feast and murdered him, and he was shunned and despised by all mankind. Jupiter had compassion on him and carried him to heaven, where, by Juno, in the form of a cloud, he became the father of the Centaurs." Afterwards he was tied to an everlasting wheel, in hell.

On this myth, it may be observed, that in the localization of myths, it is necessary to keep in mind, that the Greeks have misplaced the order of events, in their collection of national traditions. Forgetting the migrations of their ancestors, but finding that the Muses of history have made heaven and hell the domicile of their ancestors, they have reversed the order of the history, and put them in the unseen world, after death. That mistake corrected, real history is the result. In this myth, the parentage of the Centaurs is referred to

Jupiter and Juno, ancient Gods that have no existence in Greece.

In their splendid collection of world-wide traditions, the Greeks have a great many Centaurs, Philyra, Pholus, Nessus, and others. It will not be necessary to trouble the reader with them.

The myth of Centaurus himself is as follows:

"Centaurii, a people of Thessaly, half-men and half-horses. They were the offspring of Centaurus, son of Apollo, by Stilbia, daughter of the Peneus. According to some, the Centaurs were the fruit of Ixion's adventure with the cloud, in the shape of Juno, or as others assert, of the union of Centaurus with the mares of Magnesia. The battle of the Centaurs with the Lapithæ is famous in history. It was represented in the temple of Jupiter at Olympia, and also at Athens, by Phidias and Parrhasius. The origin of this battle was a quarrel at the marriage of Hippodamia with Pirithous, where the Centaurs intoxicated with wine, behaved with rudeness, and even offered violence to the women that were present. Such an insult irritated Hercules, Theseus and the rest of the Lapithæ, who defended the women, wounded and defeated the Centaurs and obliged them to leave their country and retire to Arcadia, &c."

This myth brings the study of the Centaurs, in relation to the constellation, to a sudden termination. If the Centaurs formed a part of the population of Thessaly, and if the map makers have rightly placed the sign of the horseman, the Centaurs must have travelled to the extremity of the earth, as the Anglo-Saxon race have done in modern times. Yet this is the teaching of the pictorial map. One half of a horse overhangs Thessaly, Thrace, and Arcadia, and the other half overhangs Peru. The same teaching arises from the Ship Argo. The Argonautic Expedition is the central point of ancient history. The classic myths exhibit the ship in European waters; but in the Zodiacs it is put in the Erythrean Sea, if not in the Pacific. It is impossible to reconcile the traditions of the ancient world, except upon the admission of some great maritime movements, by which the inhabitants of the two hemispheres mingled their blood and histories. Not only must the Oceanides of North America and Central America have crossed the Atlantic Ocean and conquered Libya and Europe, as has been shown in earlier parts of this work; but the people of South America and the Inca's court must, likewise, have crossed the Pacific Ocean, and coming up the Eythrean sea, have spread themselves over Asia, Africa, and Europe.

CHAPTER XXX.

The Manaos and Canopas of Ancient Peru considered in the position they occupy in the Idolatries of many Nations of the World.

It is somewhat unfavourable to the argumentation of the present treatise, that it is based, to a very large extent, on the interpretation and localization of myths. There is a natural and unavoidable prejudice against that class of reasoning. It cannot be denied, that the traditions hang together, with an amount of consistency that deprives them of a fabulous character, and that entitles them to respectful consideration. Still it requires long study, extended research, and persevering thought, to classify and arrange the legends, so as to secure for them a thorough belief. In the present chapter, that class of argumentation can be dispensed with.

The remains of ancient art, even in the rudest forms connected with semi-civilized races, stand upon a very different basis to the concealed histories of people who had two modes of writing, one for themselves and another for the general public. Art cannot well be turned into allegory. It is an argument to the eye and not to the reasoning faculty. It is a poor evidence, by itself, and leads to the most uncertain conclusions. But when there are histories of any sort, even those of an Esoteric character, art carries with it what may be justly called ocular demonstration.

In the study of Peruvian antiquities, the vase forms a most

material factor in every question. It has already been found to be the special emblem of the demon Gods. It forms the main feature in the curious Japanese tradition of Maurigasima, where the Peruvian vases, with their short necks, can be easily detected as the produce of the sunken Island of the Pacific Ocean.

It would seem, that the art of pottery is native to South America. The celebrated traveller, the Baron von Humboldt, has given an interesting and instructive account of the practices of the South American Indians, with regard to painted pottery. He says, Vol. II., 308.—"The Indians of Maypure often painted, before our eyes, the same ornaments we had seen in the cavern of Ataripe, on the vases containing human bones. They were figures of crocodiles and monkeys, &c. I might hazard the hypothesis, that the type had been brought thither, in the great migration of the American nations from the north-west to the south-east. The Maypures execute, with the greatest skill, ornaments formed by straight lines. Among the Maypures, the making of pottery is an occupation by women. The colours used are oxides of iron and yellow and red ochres. Not only the Maypures, but the Caribs and Ottomies, and even the Guayanes are distinguished on the Orinoco, as makers of painted pottery; and the manufacture extended formerly towards the banks of the Amazon."

Again, "In the forests of South America which extend from the Equator as far as the 8th degree of N. Lat., from the foot of the Andes to the Atlantic, this painted pottery is discovered in the most desert places, but it is found accompanied by hatchets of jade and other hard stones, skilfully perforated. No metallic tools or ornaments have ever been discovered; though in the mountains,—on the shores and at the back of the Cordilleras, the art of melting gold and copper —of mixing the latter metal with tin, to make cutting instruments, was known."

"The Incas of Peru had pushed their conquests and their religious wars as far as the banks of the Napo and the Amazon, where their language extended over a small space of land; but the civilization of the Peruvians,— of the inhabitants of Quito and of the Muyscas of New Granada, never appears to have had any sensible influence on the moral state of the natives of Guiana."

It cannot escape notice, that in the last chapter, there is frequent reference to death and the dead. "Minos is Judge of the dead, sitting in the middle of the shades." This remarkable feature in the myth of Minos adapts itself curiously to Peru and the institutions of the land. Among the practices which were noticed by the Spaniards, there were none more remarkable, than those which related to the funereal customs of the people. There appears to have been a sort of superstition, in regarding deceased ancestors as a sort of family Gods. Instead of burial, a parent was preserved in a state of mummification, or as a skeleton; or the bones were preserved in vases. Hence it is said that "mummies were found by millions; Egypt could not have had more."

In the accounts given by early travellers, these mummies and skeletons or household gods, have the name of Mallquis or Manaos. The institution appears to have excited the ire of the zealous priests and monks of the Roman Catholic Church, and when reported to the heads of the Church in Spain, Father Arriga was selected and sent to New Spain, with express instructions to destroy every thing of this sort, and they are reported to have demolished 617 of these Manaos.

This curious superstition, carrying as it does, the native Peruvian word of Manaos, naturally recalls the reference made to the same sort of superstition in other lands. When the Manaos of the Peruvians are put into comparison with the Manes of the dead, it is sufficient to excite some astonishment to find, that this peculiar practice had in Peru, the same word or name as in Asia and Europe. It is going too far to suppose, that a country so long unknown to the outside world as that on the upper waters of the Amazon, should have designated this superstition by the same name as other nations, by mere accident, or without intercourse and consanguinity. Under these circumstances, it is necessary to look a little into this subject of the Manes of the dead.

The tradition of the Manes is as follows: "A name generally applied by the ancients, to the souls when separated from the body. They were reckoned among the infernal deities,

2 N

generally supposed to preside over the burying places and
the monuments of the dead.   They were worshipped with
great solemnity, particularly by the Romans.   Their augurs
always invoked them, when they proceeded to exercise the
sacerdotal office.   Virgil introduces his hero as sacrificing to
the infernal deities and to the Manes, a victim whose blood
was received in a ditch.   The word Manes is supposed to be
derived from Mania, who was by some reckoned the mother
of these tremendous deities."

The myth of Mania is short, but useful.   "Mania, a goddess,
supposed to be the mother of the Lares and Manes."

To this may be added some observations from Rees' Cyclopœdia.   "Manes, a poetical term signifying the shades or souls
of the deceased.   The original may be referred to a prevailing
opinion, that the world was full of Genii, some of whom
attended on the living and others on the dead : that some
were good and others bad, and that the former were called
"familiar lares, and the latter lemures or larvæ."   "Apuleius,
in his explication of the Lemures and Larvæ, says that the
lares and larvæ are denominated "Dii manes," and that the
designation of Gods is added to them, by way of honour.   The
evocation of the Manes of the dead, seems to have been very
frequent among the Thessalians, but it was expressly prohibited by the Romans."

To this it must be added that Apuleius makes "Isis to
have been the sole divinity of the universe,—origin of all
things,—queen of the Manes,—most ancient inhabitant of
heaven."—Dupuis.

There can be no doubt at all, that the Lemures are correctly
located, when they are placed on the west coast of South
America, from the following circumstances.   It is said that
"the Romans had the superstition to celebrate festivals in their
honour, called Lemuria or Lemuralia, in the month of May.
They were first instituted by Romulus to appease the Manes
of his brother Remus, from whom they were called Remuria,
or by corruption Lemuria.   These solemnities continued three
nights, during which the temples of the gods were shut and
marriages prohibited.   It was usual for the people then, to
throw black beans on the graves of the deceased, or to burn

them, as the smell was supposed to be insupportable to them. They also muttered magical words, and by beating kettles and drums, they believed that the ghosts would depart, and no longer come to terrify their relations upon earth."

This has to be compared with an extract from Dr. Rees' Cyclopœdia. "Lima, a famous city of the audience of Lima, and capital of the vice-royalty of Peru. This city, called "Cividad de los Reyes" or the city of the kings, from its having been founded by Don Francisco Pizarro, on the feast of the Epiphany, A.D. 1535, is situated in the spacious and delightful valley of Rimac, whence by corruption the name Lima is derived: Rimac being the appellation of an idol to which the native Indians used to offer sacrifices, as the Yncas did after they had extended their empire hither, and as it was supposed to return an answer to the prayers addressed to it, they called it by way of distinction, Rimac, or he who speaks."

The Lemuria or Remuria of Italy have to be compared with the feast of Raymi, in Peru. "The Peruvians had four festivals. The chief was that of Raymi. There was a high priest with offerings and sacrifices of Llamas. Four servants held the animal, and the priest cut out the heart. The feast lasted eight or nine days, with toasts and dancing. There was a dance similar to that of the Scotch. On the eve of the festival was the renewal of the sacred fire. They produced a light by a mirror and the rays of the sun, like Numa." In this comparison it has to be noticed, that the fire rites referred to were common to both the Peruvians and the Romans.

Few will deny, that there is a strong resemblance between the European superstition of the Manes of the dead and the Manaos of ancient Peru. The evidence is exceedingly strong, and the myths that belong to the subject, with the relationship of the several characters comprised in the group of traditions, form a series of links so complete, as to throw them out of the category of fable, into that of genuine history. But there are not so many, as will admit the conclusions deducible from the comparison. It is too much to expect, that the reading public will admit, that a country so distant as Peru, and so little known, can have created a superstition, or an Idolatry, so universal as that of the Manes of the dead.

Yet, it is very difficult to deny, that the early influence of South America must have created this wide-spread superstition. To deny it, wants more faith than to admit it. The subject must be judged by the rule which has been applied to many other cases of a like kind, in the course of this treatise. The natural is parent to the unnatural, and precedes it in history. In the present case, the Manaos of South America, form a simple funereal process, by which the semi-civilized races of the Amazon are accustomed to bury their dead. Indeed, the custom does not appear to be limited to the races over which the Incas of Peru exerted their benign influence. The Baron von Humboldt found it to prevail in the cave of Ataripe, and elsewhere on the Amazon.

On the other hand, the superstition and idolatry of the Dii Manii have nothing about them natural. The funereal vase is turned into a religion. The Manes are Gods. Every one who has visited the famous Museum of Florence called the Uffizi gallery, will call to mind the peculiar altars, ranged along the passages of that splendid building ascribed to these "Venerable Gods." Nor is the Idolatry of the Manes confined to Italy or Etruria. There is the same superstition in Asia. It is hard to come to any other conclusion than that the early inhabitants of South America must, by migrations into distant parts of the globe, have unintentionally given rise to a species of religion, which has haunted the imaginations, and disturbed the repose of the whole world.

These vases appear to have created among the ancient Peruvians, a species of Idolatry. It is said, that "at Sanacamorma, in the territory of Chanca, they occupied a cave, like the Idols already referred to as in a cave. There was a large jar, in the centre of eight painted or pictured jars, and two cups of clay, which the Indians pledged to the Huaca, or Idol. In the religious festivals, the Indians covered it with clothing like Pallas." The three central Vases are here given.

Mr. Hawkes says that "Under the collective name of Canopa, or Chanca, they meant all minor deities, worshipped by families or individuals. The word, itself, is a Quichna word—the native language of Peru. Every small stone or piece of wood was worshipped as a Canopa. They were buried with their owners;

or hung upon the neck of the corpse. Sometimes they had a human figure. Those most esteemed, were made of bezoar

VASES IN PERUVIAN CAVE.

stone, or quartz. The form of the Canopa was derived from events which had influenced their lives. Dolls, or puppets of corn, or roots, were used. Many were made of basalt, or clay, or silver. They were without feet, and had a cavity for the corn used in the sacrifices. One that was found, was a silver sheep."

These Canopas seem specially to have excited the indignation of the Spanish priests, or there must have been a prodigious number of them in the country; for it was reported, that Father Arriga destroyed no less than 3418 of them.

This word Canopa naturally attracts to itself more than usual attention; inasmuch, as it is not at all unknown in the old continent. On the contrary, it forms a very conspicuous object in the idolatry of the world. The Egyptians in particular used the word, to denominate a beneficial spirit or tutelary God, under the form of a bird, or human head. Now this use of the word is very nearly the same, as that of the ancient Peruvians.

Considered by itself, it certainly is a very remarkable circumstance, to find a word like this, used in a distant country, like Peru, with the same signification as that employed, at very remote periods of time, in the valley of the Nile. Supposing South America to have been unknown to the ancients, or to have had no historical or ethnological connection with the old continent, it creates the inevitable conviction, that there must be something essentially wrong in modern notions of the old world and its histories.

The following is the description of the Egyptian Canopus, from Montfaucon, accompanied with a picture from the Coptic Zodiac.

GENIUS OF AMENTI.	CANOPUS.	CANOPUS ON A CENTAUR.

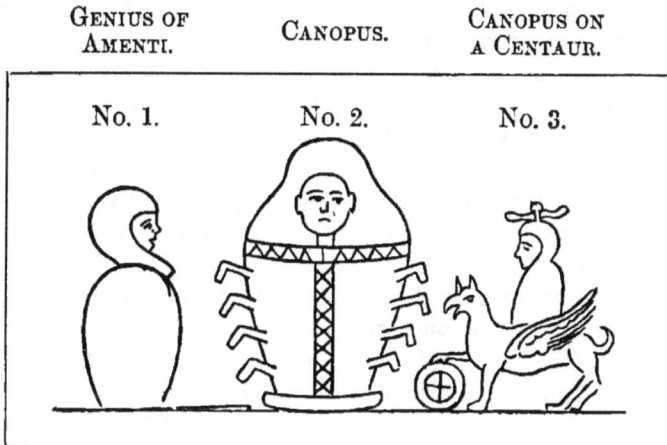

No. 1.   No. 2.   No. 3.

"Canopus, a famous God. It is nearly the figure of a pot, or vase, with the head of a man or woman. It was the God of water. They say, that "the Chaldeans formerly carried their God (fire) into all countries, to shew the superiority of their God over all others. The priest of Canopus advised a stratagem. He filled the vase with water, having waxed the holes. On this melting, the water extinguished the fire. The Canopus is marked with figures of Isis, Osiris, Anubis, Crocodiles, Hawks, Monkeys, and Scorpions."

To this must be added from Dupuis that "Canopus was the pilot of the ship of Osiris or Menalaus. The Egyptians thought that the souls of the chiefs were in it."

To this must be superadded from Lempriere, "Canopus, a city of Egypt, twelve miles from Alexandria. It is celebrated for the temple of Serapis. It received its name from Canopus, the pilot of the vessel of Menalaus, who was buried in this place."

The description of Serapis has been given before. " By the Egyptians, Serapis is Pluto. Serapis answers to Osiris, after he had changed his nature. Pluto is called the Sun,—the great Serapis. Some thought him to be Esculapius,—others Jupiter. Serapis is a modified form of Osiris. Is not Egyptian."— Wilkinson.

With these materials for the formation of opinions, it is not impossible to understand this obscure subject, and to deduce from the study a number of interesting conclusions respecting the origin and spread of idolatry, as well as the relative position of Egypt and South America, in times of high antiquity. It now turns out, that not only is the word Canopa common to Egypt and Peru, but that the use of it is the same in both countries; but with such differences as serve to detect the course of history by which two countries so far removed from one another, have been linked together in consanguinity.

The rule which has been used all through this treatise, must be brought in once more to decide the question—did Egypt give the Canopa to Peru, or did Peru give it to Egypt? But there cannot be two opinions about the decision. It is too plain for dispute. The Canopa of Peru is a simple funereal object, by which the people of the land exhibit their filial regard for deceased ancestors. On the other hand, the Egyptians have turned the Canopa into a Captain of a ship,—or they have made of it a God,—or they have constructed out of it, a contrivance for extinguishing the fires of the Chaldean fire rites. It must be put down in the category of what may be called—the mistaken remembrances of ancient people. Change of country, maritime travel and lapse of time, have wiped out the real and original use of the Canopa; but the remembrance has been kept alive by vases, temples and festivals, in which the original idea has been well nigh extinguished.

In the picture given of the Canopus, at page 294, are two

additional specimens of Egyptian Canopes,—Nos. 1 and 3.
They both serve to teach that the Egyptian Canopus hangs on
historically to South America. The first of them, No. 1, may
be pronounced not a bad specimen of the Peruvian Canopa,
as seen in the Peruvian caves. But what is it? It is one
of the four Genii of Amenti. The four Genii of Amenti, ought,
therefore, to have had an existence in ancient Peru. The other
No. 3 is an Egyptian Canope carried on the back of a Centaur,
exhibiting to the eye, the way in which the Canope went into
Egypt. It was brought by the Centaurs. It will be observed,
that the nondescript forms a link between the Zodiacal Centaur
and an Egyptian sphinx.

ANOTHER EGYPTIAN CANOPE.

The present vase is an Egyptian Canope, and it is selected because of the peculiar figures painted on its surface. It will be noticed, that it is covered with the figures of Osiris, Isis, Anubis, Crocodiles, and Scorpions. All these figures belong to South America. The crocodiles and scorpions are the Coptic Zodiacal delineation of the country. Osiris, Isis, Anubis, are all characters which belong to the mythology of the Wolf, the Libra, and the Centaur.

The historical inferences deducible from the present subject are manifest. The history of Egypt must, to some extent, hang on to the west coast of South America. There must have been migrations from that land into the valley of the Nile, sufficient in extent and influence to have created a religion and given Egypt—a God. Nor is it difficult to see the way in which it happened. The tradition of the Canopus contains in it an explanation of the navigation by which the two countries were connected. The Canopus was the pilot of the ship Menelaus. He must, therefore, have been the navigator of the ship Argo, which, in the Ptolemaic Zodiac, lies in the route between the two lands.

CHINESE GOD VITEK OR NINIFO, WITH DEMONS.

This curious subject of the Peruvian Vase, as giving birth to Idolatry in some of the greatest nations of the ancient world, must be carried further. The Canopa has been deified in China,—on the opposite banks of the Pacific Ocean.

In the Hierarchy of the Chinese Gods, there is a God called Vitek or Ninifo. In the great work of Picard, there is a grand picture of a Chinese temple. The picture is taken from Dapper. It represents one of the grandest temples appertaining to the religion of China. The God sits in great state upon a pedestal supported by a couple of demons.

When the picture is examined with a little care, by one familiar with such things, it is found to be an exact representation of a Peruvian Canopa. It squats down in a very significant manner, and is easily detected as the same object as one of the images in the Peruvian Cave, see page 262, given in a former chapter. This identity of the two figures is fully confirmed, when it is noticed that the God himself carries the name of Canopa. There is no difference between the two words Canopa and Ninifo, except the spelling. It is quite manifest, that the Chinese have signified their recognition of advantages derived from South America, by the deification of a Canopa. The following is the description given of this Idol.

"Chang-Ko is the God which the Bachelors of the sect of letters revere particularly, as the Greeks and Romans do Minerva. There is seen also here the Idol, or the divinity, which presides over pleasure. The Idol, which they also call Ninifo, is regarded as a Xin, notwithstanding he is the Genius which directs illicit pleasures; worthy minister for a being qualified for the name of Xin, which may be translated by that of Saint. There is seen in the same picture the Genius which presides over immorality, the grand tutelary divinity of China, which, perhaps, is no other than the God of war, or Kito, which the Chinese men of war honour as their patron."

This deification of the Peruvian Canopa is traceable, likewise, into the great valley of the Euphrates. It has had the same history in Babylon and Assyria. This is seen in the description given of Ninip in the Babylonian mythology. In that system, Ninip is the God whose emblem is the man-bull, that occupies a position so imposing in the sculptures of Assyria. This teaching is so strange that at first sight it can hardly be believed. Yet, upon careful examination, it has to be admitted. Let the legend of Ninip be read.

"Ninip is the fish God, dwelling in the deep,—opener of aqueducts, chief of the Spirits, Light of the Gods. His emblem is the Man-bull."

This legend justifies to the full the interpretation now put upon the myth of Ninip, as having its origin in Peru and the Peruvian Canopa. Ninip is not native to Babylon and Assyria. He must have been a foreign God; for he dwells far off in the deep. He is a Spirit, an inhabitant of the unseen hemisphere and land of spirits. This language can apply to none other than ancient Peru. Then he is the opener of Aqueducts, just the very thing for which the Peruvians were celebrated. In the deluge tablet, Ninip is called Lord of Hades, see page 93.

It now becomes quite manifest, that the grand compound figure which stood at the gates of the labyrinthine palaces of Assyria, is a visible memento of certain national migrations, between the shores of South America and the valley of the Euphrates. It is a grand exhibition of a combined sidereal Heraldry, by which the Centaur, that delineates the country of the Inca of Peru, is joined to the Bull which pourtrays Assyria; and the combined heraldry carries the name of the Canopa of Peru. It is not easy to estimate the histories which must underlie a coat of arms so imposing; nor to conceive aright of the maritime movements that must have produced it. All that can be done, is modestly to admit that the histories of the vast past are hidden beneath the mistakes and forgetfulness of time and change.

How vast the difference between the God of the Christian and the God of the Heathen world! The Christian's God is the infinite and immaterial spirit, in whom we live, move, and have our being. The God of China, Assyria, and Egypt is a threepenny jug, not quite good enough for Molly to fetch the beer!

CHAPTER XXXI.

THE INFLUENCE OF ANCIENT PERU UPON CHINA, ASSYRIA, AND EGYPT.

Among the numerous constellated figures which pourtray the country of Peru is that of the building tools. The Zodiacal figures all over the world have some appropriateness to the countries. There ought, therefore, to have been some reason for the selection of building tools for Peru and the surrounding lands. The accounts given by the Spaniards, in their numerous works concerning New Spain, supply a natural and sufficient cause for the selection. The Spaniards appear to have been struck with surprise and admiration at the numerous buildings and vast works of the land.

The following extract from Mr. Prescott's Conquest of Peru bears upon this subject. "The edifices of the better sort were of stone or faced with stone. The walls were sometimes stained or painted with gaudy tints, and the gates were sometimes of coloured marble. In the delicacy of the stone work, the natives far excelled the Spaniards, though the roofs of the dwellings were only of thatch. The most important building was the fortress, planted on a solid rock. It was built of hewn stones, so firmly wrought, that it was impossible to detect the line of junction between the blocks, and the approaches to it were defended by three semi-circular parapets, composed of such heavy masses of rock, that it bore resemblance to the kind of work known to architects as the Cyclopean. The streets were long and narrow, and from the great square diverged four principal streets. Through the heart of the capital ran a river of pure water,—if it ought not to be rather termed a canal, the banks of which, for the distance of 20 leagues, were faced with stone. Across the stream were bridges constructed of similar broad flags. The most sumptuous building was the great temple, dedicated to the sun, which, studded with gold plates, was surrounded by convents and dormitories for the priests, with their gardens and parterres sparkling with gold."

A people in possession of great building capacity, such as

that now described, could not have been without influence
on the old continent. It has been ·already shown that the
Chinese God Vitek or Ninifo, drew his name and his being
from Peru. This God stands at the head of one of the
native dynasties of China, as Vitey; so that the influence of
ancient Peru upon China can be easily studied. The national
pedigrees of China, so far as relates to their commencement,
were transcribed at the beginning of the 28th chapter. It will
be noticed, that Vitey stands at the outbreak of the mythic
histories of China. It is true, that chronology cannot safely
be deduced from mythic pedigrees; but those documents do
give the comparative antiquity of the races that comprise
the pedigrees. In the present case, the giant race of Vitey
is placed above Anchosau, presumably the Anchises of the
classic mythology, and he is of a different race to Vitey.
"He is the root of a new race," whereby it is seen, that the
giant race of America, gives way to some other people, native
or otherwise. If so, all the histories connected with the mythic
Æneas in the underground hemisphere, must have been subsequent to the times of Vitey and his progeny, in the
Empire of China, This puts the departure of the Peruvian
Giants from South America before the Inca.

Now, let the particulars concerning Vitey and his descendants be considered. He reigns 100 years and is famous for
architecture. He has 25 sons, whose offspring reign 2257
years in 116 kings. Then Tzintzom, the last of Vitey's offspring,
reigns 40 years and he builds the wall of China.

These details are certainly very remarkable in themselves.
When taken into consideration, in an estimate of the comparative civilization of Asia and America, they form a very
important feature in the argumentation. If they are to be
depended upon, they teach that the Chinese art of building
must have been attributable, in whole or in part, to the
inhabitants of the country now called Peru: for not only
is Vitey the giant famous for architecture, but a long race
of kings follows, 116 in number, who must be supposed to
have been in possession of the same building arts and
practices, for Tzintzom, who is said to have been the last
of the race, is credited with having built the wall of China,

a stupendous erection which competes advantageously with all the celebrated great works of antiquity for massiveness and extent. In view of this plain and conclusive teaching, it is not difficult to understand and not hard to believe, that the earliest map makers in the construction of their pictorial maps, have put the building tools as descriptive of the country which was entitled to them, as being the first or the most prominent of the nations that by means of forced labour erected great public works.

Still, one is hardly prepared to admit conclusions so extraordinary. They require confirmation. It is natural, in accordance with ordinary literature, not based on the tracings of mythology, to look to the great nations of Asia for their own enlightenment, and civilization. Before admitting America to have been first in architecture and the use of tools, one looks into works on China in its earliest forms to find if there is any thing said, that can be considered as a corroboration of the theory. The best work on the earliest history of China is that of M. Pouthier on China before the Chouking.

In that work, there are extracts from Father Premaire, which bear upon the subject, and which shew that the learned Chinese themselves attribute their civilization to mythic characters, which, on comparison and research must be treated as American. " There were three Hoangs, Fien hoang, Gin hoang, and Fi hoang. These Hoangs are called Serpents. They are authors of letters, and discoverers of gold and precious stones. These Hoangs reigned Sovereign, in the midst of the earth, and are called dragon kings. They had the head of a dragon and the feet of a horse." A note says, that these Hoangs (emperors of men) "are the civilizers of China. They divided the country into nine parts and chose the middle for their own abode." It would seem as if that gave rise to the idea of the middle kingdom.

The influence of Peru upon Assyria, in the mythic period, is traceable in the tradition of the Minotaur, a figure which must be considered as a modification of the Centaur. But before the myth is introduced, it is necessary to make some preliminary observations, in consequence of the confessed confusion in the myth of Minos. Minos is one of the most important characters in the antiquities of mankind, when put in his proper place in history; but when confounded with his grandson and put in Crete, some of the most important events of history are cast under the veil of obscurity.

Minos is Judge of the infernal regions, and must therefore be localized at the antipodes of Crete. This is confirmed by his parentage of Hecate. "She is the same as Proserpine or Diana." Minos has two wives. The first is Ithona. By her he has Lycastes, father of Minos the second—king of Crete. There must, therefore, have been migrations from South America across the Atlantic and up the Mediterranean Sea to Crete carrying the code of laws which the Judge had constructed.

Minos has a daughter, one Euryale: she has been mentioned before. She is one of the three Gorgons. She is the mother of Orion by Neptune. This is a most extraordinary piece of history. Orion is the grand constellated Giant, who girdled by brilliant stars, mounts the heavens in great state. He is portraiture for Iran. He spans the deserts of Arabia and the country of Babylon. This is consistent with the myth of Orion, which gives him a triple parentage. Jupiter, Neptune, and Mercury are his fathers. By this marriage, Minos becomes the ancestor of some portion of the population of the Orient— of the native Iran,—of the historical Babylon and Assyria. This enrichment of population must have come by ship, because the fatherhood is referred to Neptune.

Minos has a second wife, one Pasiphae: and it is this marriage which links ancient Peru to Assyria, and shews that the people of South America must have migrated into ancient Persia. This is seen in the myth of Æetes, who is "king of Colchis, son of Sol and Perseis, daughter of Oceanus. Æetes was father of Medea, Absyrtus, and Chalcione, by Idya, one of the Oceanides." Pasiphae has the same parents as Æetes: so that this family must represent great histories and migrations by which the two hemispheres must have been joined in consanguinity and history. With these observations the myth of Pasiphae may be understood.

"Pasiphae, a daughter of the Sun and Perseis, who married Minos, king of Crete. She disgraced herself by her unnatural passion for a bull, which, according to some authors, she was

enabled to gratify by means of the artist Dœdalus.   This
celebrated bull had been given to Minos by Neptune, to be
offered on his altars.   But as the monarch refused to sacrifice
the animal, on account of his beauty, the god revenged his
disobedience by inspiring Pasiphae with an unnatural love
for this favorite bull.   Minos had four sons by Pasiphae,
Castreus, Deucalion, Glaucus, and Androgeus, and three
daughters, Hecate, Ariadne, and Phædra."

Of course, any one who reads stories of this sort without
thought, or as poetry or natural phenomena, reads this
"cunningly devised fable" or rather myth,—laughs or blushes,
and goes on to the next page.   But to any one who sees
in them the great histories of the human race,—concealed,
misunderstood, and made ridiculous, this tradition is full of
historical significance.

In this myth, Pasiphae takes a fancy for the Bull.   Nobody
in his senses can suppose it to be a natural bull.   All the
myths in the Greek Lexicon are to be interpreted by the
pictorial map that belongs to them.   In this case, the bull
is portraiture for Assyria.   It is Taurus Major.   In the Ptolemaic sphere, only the head and shoulders are drawn; but
in the Coptic sphere, there is the entire animal.   When Pasiphae
takes a fancy for the bull, she takes a fancy for Assyria,
and she and her husband's people forsake their Oceanic
home and link their fortunes with the great nationalities of
the Orient.

In this fancy for the bull, Pasiphae is assisted by one
Dœdalus an artist.   Artist! what could an artist have to do
with such a piece of business?   Surely ladies do not commonly
employ artists in their love adventures.   The following is the
myth of Dœdalus.   "He was the most ingenious artist of his
age.   He made the statues which moved of themselves.
Dœdalus made a famous Labyrinth for Minos, who ordered
him to be confined in the Labyrinth which he had constructed.
Here he made himself wings, with feathers and wax, and
carefully fitted them to his body and that of his son Icarus,
who was the companion of his confinement.   They took their
flight in the air from Crete, but the heat of the sun melted
the wax on the wings of Icarus, whose flight was too high,

and he fell into that part of the Ocean which, from him, has been called the Icarian Sea."

The fruit of the marriage of Pasiphae and the Bull, was the Minotaur, the myth of which may be shortened, as it is not nice reading. "Minotaur a celebrated monster half a man and half a bull. It was the fruit of Pasiphae's amour with a bull. Minos confined in the Labyrinth a monster which convinced the world of his wife's lasciviousness. The Minotaur usually devoured the chosen young men and maidens, which the tyranny of Minos yearly exacted from the Athenians. Theseus delivered his country from this horrible tribute, when it had fallen to his lot to be sacrificed to the voracity of the Minotaur, and by the help of Ariadne, the king's daughter, he destroyed the monster and made his escape from the windings of the Labyrinth." It is afterwards said, that "Pasiphae sometime after brought twins into the world, one of whom greatly resembled Minos and the other Taurus."

With these myths and localizations, it is not at all difficult to understand what the Greeks mean by the Minotaur. It is the grand colossal piece of sculpture, which the pickaxe has brought to light within the memory of the present generation, in the Labyrinthine palaces of the great monarchs of Assyria. It is the man-bull of the museums. An ocular inspection of the figure reveals at a glance the meaning of the myth. In front it is a man, the resemblance of Minos. In the rear, it is a bull. The two together are the twins of Pasiphae. The part which Dœdalus took in the assistance afforded to the queen, is the construction of the colossal image. Down deep in the forsaken and earth-covered passages of the long lost cities of Nineveh, the Minotaur has for ages been confined.

The colossal Man-bull of Assyria is a magnificent piece of national heraldry, disclosing to the eye of the beholder, the constituent parts of those great historical movements and migrations by which the mighty Empires of Babylon and Assyria were formed. The Bull is the ancient emblematical animal, which gave a Zoomorphic crest to the Oriental Tzour. The man stands for the mighty kings, whose ancestors came from the ends of the earth. The wings are the heraldic enrichment supplied by the winged men. Together, they form a grand coat of arms of combined nationalities.

2 P

Let not this teaching be thought inconsistent with Assyrian-ology. The Chaldean legend appertaining to the Colossal man-bull has already been given. It is the emblem of Ninip, the Chaldean fish god, dwelling far off in the deep, opener of aqueducts. Let it not be considered inconsistent with the native mythology of the Orient. It would seem as if the Greeks were in possession of the native Iranian traditional histories, for the Minotaur has its name in one of the greatest monarchs of the East.—Minoutcher. This Minoutcher has two sons, who are "likened to angels of fire," an expression that recalls the myths of the winged men. Then the story of two young men being cast to the monster, has its counterpart in the Shahnameh. They are given as food for the Serpents. Let it not be considered inconsistent with the Zodiac. Both the Minotaur and Minoutcher appear in the sign of Monoceros—the Unicorn.

The details of the group of classic myths that have been brought together for the understanding of the tradition of the Minotaur, lead to the inference that the ancient Peruvians and the Inca's court must have been a migratory and aggressive people. They must not only have conquered many of the countries that lie along the coast of the Pacific Ocean : they must have sent out colonies into Asia. The territory of the Inca must have contributed very early in history, to the forma-tion of the very important Empires of Irania. Those Empires must owe some of their greatness to South America. To acquire, therefore, a just conception of the remote histories which laid the basis of Assyrian, and Babylonian, and Median greatness, America must be brought within the scope of events which led to the birth, and subsequently to the histories of the five Great Monarchies.

The myth of the Minotaur is not the only tradition which exhibits historical alliance between Peru and Assyria. There is another which at once corroborates and elucidates it : but it goes further than Assyria, it carries the bull into Egypt, and gives birth to that peculiar form of the Centaur, which is so great an object of astonishment to travellers in the valley of the Nile. The myth is as follows :—

"Io, a daughter of Inachus, or Jasus, or Pirene, a priestess of Juno, at Argos. Jupiter became enamoured of her, but Juno, jealous of his intrigues, discovered the object of his affection and surprised him in the company of Io. Jupiter changed. his mistress into a beautiful heifer, and the Goddess, who well knew the fraud, obtained from her husband the animal whose beauty she had condescended to commend. Juno commanded the hundred eyed Argus to watch the heifer. But Jupiter, anxious for the situation of Io, sent Mercury to destroy Argus, and to restore her to liberty. Io, freed from the vigilance of Argus, was now persecuted by Juno, who sent one of the Furies, or rather a malicious insect, to torment her. She wandered over the greatest part of the earth, and crossed over the sea, till, at last, she stopped on the banks of the Nile, still exposed to the unceasing torments of Juno's insect. Here she intreated Jupiter to restore her to her ancient form; and when the God had changed her from a heifer to a woman, she brought forth Epaphas. Afterwards she married Telegonus, king of Egypt, or Osiris, according to others, and she treated her subjects with such mildness and humanity, that after death, she received divine honours, and was worshipped under the name of Isis. She is sometimes called Phoronis, from her brother Phoroneus."

It will readily be admitted that this myth, as it is commonly read, is quite unintelligible. The least said about it the better. But under the system of localization practised in this work, it becomes not only quite easy to understand, but of signal importance, for the elucidation of the great histories of the uncertain past. Let it be studied.

Io is the daughter of Inachus, and brother to Phoroneus. These two characters made their appearance in the chapter on Oceanus, page 44. Inachus, being a son of Oceanus and Tethys, must have been an American. In the chapter referred to, his localization was treated as uncertain, but now that Io comes into the story, as a daughter of Inachus, the localization of Inachus himself gets fixed. Io, in this myth, is only another name for Isis. Isis is identical with Puzza, the Chinese Goddess. In America, as granddaughter of Oceanus and Tethys, she is American. In that position, she is queen of the Manes, who, in the last chapter, were located in Peru.

From this it is quite manifest, that Inachus is the Inca of Peru. It is the word exactly, and the story of Io shews that Inachus must have been the Greek and European conception of the Inca. This is confirmed, when it is observed that Phoroneus is the son of Inachus. Without adopting the theory, that the name of Phoroneus is descriptive of the Peruvians themselves, it is sufficient to notice, that Phoroneus, in Greece, is exactly the same character as Minos. He is the teacher of laws and religion.

Then Io, who now ought to be a representative of the Inca's court, travels. She goes all round the world, and passes into maritime countries. Where she went to, is plain enough from the story. The hundred eyed Argus is set to watch her. The Ptolemaic Zodiac fixes that location. The ship Argos is in the Erythrean Sea and at the entrance to the Persian gulf. There Io is changed into a heifer. This transformation takes her into Assyria, the land of the Bull. It is the story of the Minotaur in a new form. Instead of marrying the Bull, she is transformed into it. Her race enters into the constitution of the Assyrian people.

But Io travels further, she goes into the valley of the Nile, where she recovers her human form, as Egypt is not represented by any animal in the symbolism of Poetical Astronomy. Restored to her human form, she brings forth Epaphas. Then she marries a king, and rules her people with the mild humane laws with which the Incas of Peru are credited. This brings out to view the probability that the Peruvian race must have formed a constituent part of the population of Egypt as well as Assyria.

But it may fairly be said, that this teaching needs confirmation. It is only an interpretation of myths, which may or may not be correct. That is true, but as the ancients have transmitted all their histories in this allegorical form, the historian must interpret them, or remain in ignorance. But there is ocular demonstration of the presence of the Centaur race in Egypt. Its existence in former ages in the valley of the Nile is attested by symbolic images, wrought in solid marble — of a colossal stature, and imperishable as the men-bulls in the palaces of Assyria. The Sphinx is a Centaur. It is a human being, coupled with some nondescript animal. That constitutes a Centaur in all its essential features.

SPHINX OF PHRE.

The monument now presented for study is the Sphinx of Phre. It has about it all the marks required to identify it with the Zodiacal Centaur which the Poetical Astronomers have employed to represent the lands and people of the Inca of Peru. The image crouches upon the heavens, which are bespangled with stars; so that it must be Zodiacal. At page 92 has been exhibited another specimen of the Egyptian heavens of a like kind. In that specimen, the name is given as Tiphe. Later studies have shown that Tiphe is the proper name by which to designate the northern parts of South America, as they are peopled by the race of Tupy and the

Tupy Indians. Then the Sphinx of Phre carries on its head the Sun, of which Orb the Inca was supposed to be a son, and the sun has the asp emblem, which ties it to the Serpent land.

At page 92 is a picture of the boat of Phre. It is there given as indicative of an ancient maritime Asiatic emigration to the shores of America. The boat carries the company of the Amenti Gods down to the lower world. The imagination must be called in to fill up the long ages of the Amenti life. These Gods appear chiefly to have entered Egypt by the western route. The myth of Io exhibits an Eastern passage likewise. The Sphinx of Phre is an imperishable memento of ancestral residence in the land of the building tools—of the superintendent of forced labour and of the Centaur.

In the former parts of this work several attempts have been made to test the correctness of the conclusions arising from the tracing of mythic writings, by putting them into comparison with the Ethnology, Topography and Gods of the several countries which were the subject of research. It is now possible to do the same with South America.

Typhon is found	in	the Tupy Indians
Lupus the Wolf	„	the Lupacas
Centaur	„	the Condor
The Latin Æneas	„	the Inca
The Greek Inachus	„	the Inca
Serapis	„	the Caribs
Pluto	„	La Plata
The Hindoo Yama	„	the Province of Yamea
The Japanese Jemma	„	the Province of Yamea
Remus	„	the Idol Rimac
The Lemures and Lamies	„	Lima
Manes of the dead	„	the Manaos of Peru
Canopus of Egypt	„	the Canopa of Peru
Ninifo of China	„	the Canopa of Peru
Ninip of Chaldea	„	the Canopa of Peru
Aelo of the Greeks	„	Oello the Peruvian civilizer
Themis	„	Thomas the Peruvian civilizer

CHAPTER XXXII.

THE ISLANDS OF THE PACIFIC OCEAN AND AUSTRALIA, IN THEIR TRADITIONS AND STRUCTURAL REMAINS, ATTEST THE MOVEMENTS OF THE AMERICAN RACES BY SEA IN A WESTERLY DIRECTION.

THE SIGN OF THE IBIS AND ITS MYTHOLOGY.

The extraordinary historical inferences which have been deduced from mythology in the two last chapters, cannot but meet with some amount of incredulity. It is difficult to bring oneself to believe that a land so remote as South America could ever have participated in the formation of the great Empires of Asia. It is necessary, therefore, to search into the writings of travellers who have visited the South Sea Islands, to find out if there exist traditions or structural remains which can bear upon the early histories of Polynesia.

In the Ptolemaic Zodiac there is a small constellation in the form of a bird, and called Apus. In the Coptic Zodiac this sign has the name of Ibis. The position of the sign in both instances is dubious. As the ancients took no notice of Oceans in the formation of their maps, the sign may belong to one of the Islands of the South Seas; whether it does or not can only be determined by research. As the Ibis is found in the Egyptian mythology, as an emblem of the God Thoth, it can be studied easily.

"The Ibis was sacred both to the first and second Thoth or Taut; but it is the latter God that carries the bird instead of the human head. The first Thoth is mentioned by Manetho as the preceptor of Isis. The second Thoth is called the god of letters. As scribe of the lower regions, he noted the actions of the dead and read them to Osiris the Judge of Amenti. To him the Egyptians owe social institutions. He passed for a son of Agathademon. He invented writing, astronomy, and music. He was institutor of the sacerdotal class. Champollion has a picture of him where he is described as counsellor to Pooh, the moon. He presided over the agitated air (eight regions) just above the four regions of the earth.

The zone depended on the moon, which comprehended another zone of sixteen regions of pure air."

This description of Thoth and his domicile is as equivocal as the sign of Ibis. What is meant by " presided over agitated air," one is left to conjecture. But there is an Island in the South Seas which bears the name of Thoth, to this day. It is Tahiti, and its position in relation to South America would admit of the supposition that the sign of the Ibis must be intended for Tahiti. There is in the British Museum a pectoral of Tahiti exactly like that of Thoth. Under these circumstances it is proper to search into the description given of Tahiti, when first discovered, to ascertain if there were anything about the Island that would connect it with the Ibis-headed God.

The work that answers this purpose, is the " Missionary Voyage in the Ship Duff." This ship was sent out by the London Missionary Society, with the first missionaries to the South Seas. In that work the Island is called Tahiti Noe. This is material to the present enquiry, as the Agathademon bears the name of Now, and as the word equally belongs to the Nahoas or Toltec race of Mexico and Central America.

There is a very well engraved picture of what is called the Morai of Oberea. This erection is a sort of Pyramid of solid masonry, not cyclopean, but built of wrought stones. Its dimensions seem quite marvellous. It is 270 ft. long, 94 ft. wide, and 51 ft. high. This is not a great deal less than the Post Office in St. Martins-le-grand, London. It is quite plain, that this erection could not have been built by savages. As Pyramidal buildings all over the world are " imitations of the fabled Meru, which was the worldly temple of the Supreme Being, and considered by the followers of Buddha, as the tomb of the son of the spirit of heaven, whose bones and limbs were scattered over the face of the Earth" *(Asiatic Researches)*, the Island of Tahiti may have been an out-station of the same Asiatic settlements that have been found in America.

This makes it necessary to transcribe an account of the inhabitants of Tahiti, before the arrival of the Europeans, from a work by Grasset de St. Sauveur, entitled Encyclopedie des Voyages. " The people had priests in a religion of nature,

immolating infants to divinities. They had arts, commerce, and navigation. Their manner of dressing had a curious agreement with that of the ancient Romans. They had houses, 300 ft. long. They dressed for table with the punctuality and respect of Europe. With them, marriage was a religious ceremony. They had canoes,—vessels constructed differently from other South Sea Islanders, with a mast and triangular sails. In war, they united many vessels, forming a war stage. They were astronomers, and had names for all the stars. They knew the movements of their rise and setting, and they directed their navigation by the situation of the sun and moon. Their day was composed of 12 equal parts. Their year had 13 months, commencing and closing with the moon. They measured by feet, and calculated by dozens. They believed in the immortality of the soul. They had temples, but no idols. Their name for peasant was Touton, and they had a God called Toaheite.

Putting these facts together, it is now manifest, that the Island of Tahiti must once have been in a state of civilization much more advanced than when first visited by the modern missionary. The great Morai must have been the work of some American race or races, as substantial buildings of that kind are not common in Eastern Asia. The name of the Island as Tahiti Noe, links it on to the Nahoas race of Mexico, while the pyramidal character of the Morai corresponds to the pyramid of Cholula.

Under these circumstances, it is reasonable to infer, that the Island has been visited and colonized by the Oceanides of America, and that it has been a sort of stepping stone between the two hemispheres. The character of the shipping mentioned, and the knowledge of maritime movements, create the supposition, that it was by such means that the passage of the Pacific Ocean was in early times performed. In that case, the Island must have been a part of that mystic bridge, which the Oriental writings call Tchinavar, and on which they place Mihr and Sorush.

Tahiti is not the only Island which bears testimony to the former presence of people in a state of civilization higher than that which is now characteristic of the Island. In the Island now called Easter Island, there have been found specimens of rude sculpture. These are now deposited in the British Museum. On inspection, the observer will not fail to notice that the unique symbol of Egypt, called the Egyptian tau, is chiselled or more properly cut upon them. In the Ethnological room of the same institution there are now deposited a row of images which exhibit marks of some advance in art.

In the Island of Fiji, there is ocular evidence of the former residence of the Aztec race. Travellers in the Island discovered an erection, which from its form, can be detected as a teecallis. If this identification be correct, it can excite no surprise that the people of Fiji should be the most barbarous and savage of the inhabitants of the coral islands. The horrible practice of human sacrifice must to a great extent be credited with the savagery and cruelty observable in all lands where it has prevailed.

In the work already referred to at page 312, there is a description of Tongataboo, one of the Islands, where it is said that Captain Cook visited the Island in 1777: "In one place was observed a curious causeway built of coral stone, across a morass, with a kind of circus in its centre, apparently of very ancient construction." Such a causeway must belong to a state of society much in advance of that which prevails in the Islands at the present time.

In another work of travels, the visitor says that "he was shown a native map or chart, which described the route of navigation between the groups of Islands."

The vast insular continent of Australia is one of the great terræ incognitæ of ancient maps. Like America itself, it is a blank, as if the inhabitants of the old world were totally unaware of its existence. Yet there is some slight reason to suspect, that it once formed a part of the known world. Its geographical position is such, as that it could scarcely have been unvisited, if there were any common maritime intercourse between the two hemispheres. The modern settlements in Australia, Tasmania, and New Zealand have not disclosed great remains of ancient towns. Yet there are not wanting traditions among the degraded aborigines, which, to say the least of them, hint at a former association with the outside world. In particular, there is a tradition which betrays an acquaintance with Mexico in an indirect form. In works published on Australia, there is a native tradition which bears a close resemblance to the myth of Prometheus. Some one ascended to heaven and brought down fire. It will be remembered, that this tradition, in the Greek myth, hangs on to Mexico.

There is a very curious and interesting tradition published in the work of William Howitt, entitled " A Boy's adventures in Australia," which deserves transcription. " They speak of a great flood, that rose above the high trees and hills. Some were drowned, and some caught up by a whirlwind to another similar country above them. After the flood, two kangaroos and opossums appeared. The race rose and the antediluvians became stars. Amongst them was Pungil, their principal deity, Karackock, their female Prometheus, Teer and Teerer, sons of Pungil, Betwood and Bobinger, son and daughter of Pungil, the first pair who dwelt on the earth after the flood, from whom the present race of mortals are sprung. Wang, the Crow, became a star. Pungil was often upon the earth. Pungil was put into darkness. The white people became our ruin then."

This tradition would escape notice, except to one who is familiar with the Ptolemaic Zodiac, and who regards it as a terrestrial map. The constellation of the Crow corresponds with the position of Australia. It is one of two, which stand upon the tail of the Hydra. The curious thing about the tradition is, that the aborigines of the land are in possession of the same ideas as those of the old Poetical Astronomers of Europe. The tradition says, that "the Antediluvians became Stars." That is in curious accord with the principle on which the present work is written. All the old nations of the Earth are set in the Stars; so that they become a geography, by which the traditionary histories of all nations can be traced and localized. It is certainly very remarkable to find such a notion among the degraded aborigines of Australia; but it shews that they have retained the old principle, which the civilized inhabitants of other lands have forgotten. But it shews also, that Australia must have been a known part of the ancient world, and that its inhabitants must have been acquainted with America.

PANTOMIMIC FIGURES.

COPIED (BY PERMISSION) FROM MESSRS. DEAN & SON'S *Pantomimic Toy Books.*

CHAPTER XXXIII.

On Anthropology.

In the theatres it is usual for the actors to make their appearance in a body, at the close of the performance, to make their *congé*. In accordance with this custom, the *dramatis personæ* in this long and eventful story now present themselves. The great mother of the Gods, of whom the reader has read so much as Ceres, Pandora, Tonacacique, and Cybele, stands erect in the middle of the company,—as Columbine. The great chief of the Red Indians has descended from his sacred mountain, in the Earthworks,—dressed in all the habiliments of his barbaric grandeur, with scalp knot and paint—as Clown. Pan has left Tabasc, and squats upon the ground, his tagrag and bobbery metamorphosed into vandyks and buttons—as Pantaloon. The noble figure who has been seen in company with Minerva, as Saca, Quetzalcoatl, and Mercury,—all in one, with his domino of concealment and his magic wand or caduceus, completes the company—as Harlequin.

There can be no doubt at all, that the figures now before the reader, represent the Oceanides mentioned by Plato, as making great warlike eruptions from beyond the Pillars of Hercules, 9,000 years before his time, on the fair plains of Western Europe. Their picturesque costume is the last dying remains of the fantastic and barbaric attire of the races who had forsaken the mound cities of North America and the now ruined cities of Central America, in quest of new homes and fortunes. It is within the recollection of living men, that the people of Ireland and Wales dressed in this way, and in the mountains of Scotland it can be seen to this day, in forms of colour and fancy which even Lairds delight to exhibit.

There is reason to believe that the Pantomimic company had, in Western Europe, a religious character. Cybele is commonly put in Phrygia; but M. Martin, in his Work on the Religion of the Gauls, has shown that Cybele was the Cimmerian goddess. He says, that "there were several monuments of Cybele, with the tower on her head, in France." M. Martin quotes Saint Symphorien, in the second century, and says that "they carried her through the streets in a car drawn by bulls. Gregory of Tours confirms it. People of affluence preceded it, singing and dancing; she was covered with a white veil." If this were so, the performance which is now laughed at as a farce, must once have been reverenced as a religion. The Pantomimic figures are so firmly fixed in the memory of Western Europe, that neither time nor change of religion can efface it. They constitute a living memento of the Oceanides, who, fantastically painted and dressed in barbaric finery, re-created the old continent.

The passage from the Pantomime to Anthropology is easy and short. The Pantomime is not a bad illustration of the history of mankind. The characters begin as Gods and end as Actors in a two-penny booth. The intervening grades of descent from the sublime to the ridiculous constitute the long continuity of chapters which compose the shifting history of migratory races.

It is refreshing to hear of Anthropological societies for the collection of "*finds*" and structural remains which may serve to throw light upon the mysteries of a buried and fossilized world. The word is new, but it is well chosen and expressive. It seems to lift mankind into a science or a philosophy. It is quite time that that lever were applied to man, for he has too long lain prostrate on the low level of insignificance. It is not that man has been neglected. The structure of his frame has gained for him a school of scientists. His ailments have reared for him palatial hospitals. His mental culture has created for him the Academy and the University. His social necessities have called into being the Hall of legislation, and his moral and religious nature has filled the world with sacred edifices and teachers.

It is in the matter of history and the antiquities of the human race that man has been neglected. The learned and the religious alike have contented themselves with the most cursory and ill digested conceptions of remote time. If at the creation, the Divine Governor of all things gave express injunctions to man "to replenish the earth and subdue it," it cannot be supposed that the high mandate was unfulfilled. A world in which that behest was regarded must have had histories extending over the great arena of the earth's surface, and dating from periods too high even for the imagination. Yet the learned, without thought or question, content themselves with histories that make mankind the outcome of some two or three hundred generations. On the most unsatisfactory evidence, they allow one-third of the human family to be blotted out of being altogether. Laughing at the great Empires of the East, which claim for themselves the moderate antiquity of three or four hundred thousand years, they deliberately content themselves with the belief or the fancy, that man is but the creature of a day.

Some part of this work was written in the vicinity of a slate quarry, in a mountainous region. There was an inclined plane for the trucks from the valley below to a platform. Thence arose a second incline, which led up to a second platform. Thence a third incline led to a higher platform. Others, in like manner, reached upwards, till at length, the highest was lost to view in the cloudy mist that enshrouded the summit of the mountain. Such is history. The passing world is visible and its current annals can be written with distinctness. An earlier period precedes the present, and carries time to a higher platform of antiquity, on which were enacted historical events less distinctly traceable. Then there is another and another platform, till at length, the earliest period is lost in the misty uncertainty of a vast antiquity, out of the reach of research.

Moses recognizes this gradual ascent and renewed basis of being, in his epitome of human antiquities. The historic period of his age is written in lines intelligible to the understanding of a child. Above the historic period is the stage of semi-history, the great dispersion and the scattering of new races over the length and breadth of the earth. Thence a higher period of human existence reveals those mysterious histories faintly traced in the foregoing pages, till at length, Adam himself is reached. Then higher still, the Sacred Chronicler places six great periods of human being, each ascending higher and higher, till at last he reaches the darkness which casts its murky veil over the outburst of history. Then as if emerging from the overshadowing mist, he reaches the sublime conception of a creation and a Creator, far beyond the reach of the human understanding.

It is common to conceive of man as having his origin in a condition of babyhood. Owing to the concealed language of the early writers of history, the forefathers of the present noble occupants of the globe are supposed to be small people— Lilliputians in stature and infantile in attainments. These poor little things learned to speak by listening to the chirping of birds, the prattle of monkeys, and the grunting of pigs. They lived before the discovery of tailors' shops, and wore, for their comfort and adornment, a narrow loin cloth composed of feathers. They lived in gardens and constructed their abodes in the entangled vegetation of nature, till at length, some little genius, in advance of his generation, discovered the art of eating fruit from trees. Another struck out quite a new idea and actually went so far as to catch some wild animal and make of his skin a leather garment. In process of time they found out a thing or two, especially the art of striking and to make a light. This grand discovery was followed by others, more or less ingenious, till at last one of the poor little things actually discovered the art of making huts from sticks and leaves.

It is strangely out of harmony with the babyhood theory, that the oldest structural remains found in the earth, are the biggest—most durable and most cleverly constructed. Witness the vast Morai of Tahiti, a picture of which has been given at page 312, of which it is said, that the joints of the superincumbent stones are so accurately made, as to be out of sight. Witness further the Pyramid of Cheops in Egypt, and especially the vaster Pyramid of Cholula in Mexico. Witness also the tombs of Egypt, the caves of India, and the subterranean palaces of Assyria. The same thing is noticeable in the images erected by the ancients, in many lands. The oldest are of colossal dimensions. Witness the statues of Jainadewa in Canary, in India, 75 feet high. Witness also the well-known statue of the Olympic Jupiter in Greece—of the same elevation, 75 feet high. Witness again the Colossal images of Shamana and Salsala, posted at the gateway of the vast temple at Bamiyan, the metropolis of Buddhism, also of the same height, 75 feet high.

They teach in the Schools, that "man's chief end is

to glorify God and to enjoy him for ever." It was in the spirit of this teaching that the Bridgewater Treatises were written. Poor glory does God have from history! A world, of which one third has no history at all, except that it stuck in the mud in the West Indies, gives little glory to its Divine Creator. It rather detracts from his glory than adds to his high renown. Another third, comprising the vast insular continent of Africa, with its countless millions of swarthy inhabitants, bearing upon their visage the marks of great antiquity, has found no historian, and gives no glory to God at all. Another third, composed of the white and tawny races of Europe and Asia, has the most meagre and ill-arranged histories, and gives but scant glory to the Great Superintendent of human affairs.

It is quite possible that God may have been glorified by the history of the small people, supposed to have been the inhabitants of the new created world, if it could be known, for God is glorified in the small as much as in the great,— in the tiniest fly that settles upon the summer flower, as in the great elephant that roams the forests of Central Africa. But the existence of the Pyramids, buried cities, and colossal Gods, affords ocular demonstration that the Infinite One has presided over a world the inhabitants of which have been a very different order of people to the babies, and who must have had histories of a very different kind.

By any philosophical and painstaking student, it will not be denied, that ancient history is unsatisfactory in the highest degree. There is nothing at all that can be depended upon earlier than the time of Julius Cæsar, except what belongs to the Holy Land. The early histories of Italy and Greece can hardly be called ancient, and they present so many difficulties as to baffle all attempts at arrangement. In the writings of Homer, Herodotus, and Diodorus, the real is so intermixed with the mythical, as to be beyond separation.

It may be said, that however desirable it is to enlarge the histories of the world and to correct them, there are no materials for the purpose. But that is a mistake. The literature of the Greek, Roman, and Sanscrit period, is exceedingly voluminous. The writers of the hermitages and

2 R

the cloisters were the inheritors of the traditions and the songs and the pedigrees of earlier times. The Muses and the Bards made use of the newly invented alphabet, to commit to leather and parchment and papyrus, the historical facts which they had been trained by their fathers to recite in the highways and cross roads, on festivals and holydays. They seem to have spared no pains to preserve the treasured knowledge. Every scrap of ancient story has been kept with religious care. In process of time, the accumulated manuscripts of the Muses were collected and transferred to the pages of enormous folios, richly ornamented and bound.

In those early days, the pen was not the only instrument by which the treasured traditions were handed down to posterity. The philosophic barbarians had brought with them the custom of committing historical events and the lives of heroes to the artist. Hence were accumulated countless thousands of historical pictures. Every book was ornamented with pictorial scenes of great traditionary value. Every vase was made the medium of the preservation of some world-wide history. The cherished amulets and gems were transferred to parchments and enlarged into pictures, which, in time, gave form to Church altar pieces and the adornment of Church windows.

One might say that if the histories of high antiquity were transmitted only in traditions and pictures, it were better to leave them alone. But this is not the time to shrink from a literary research, because it is difficult. There is hardly anything that has baffled the ingenuity and keen wittedness of man. The laboratory has been forced to disclose the elements of nature. The sun has been made to perform the task of the artist. Space has been annihilated and East joined to West. The planets have been weighed and their movements calculated to a nicety. Hieroglyphics and languages have been read off without a dictionary.

Shall the historian be the only man that has allowed himself to be outwitted in the performance of the impossible? Shall the students of Germany, France, America, and England, all be put down in the category of incompetents? Shall the Universities of all nations be compelled to admit, that they have not among them a man capable to interpret the riddles and dark sayings, handed down to posterity by their little baby ancestors? There is nothing in the Mythological Lexicon more obscure, intricate, and puzzling than has appeared in many of the *causes célèbres* of the courts of law, and shall it be said that the Professor of history has allowed himself to be out-paced by a policeman?

Some may think that it is unnecessary to raise the question of the accuracy of history. The common notions of the past world, as handed down by the monks of the cloister, may be thought good enough for the purposes of education. If this were so, it would be a pity to unsettle old theories. "If ignorance were bliss, 'tis folly to be wise." But this is not the age of ignorance. That age is past and gone. The Board schools are built and the free library is open. Collegiate examinations have become a part of common school tuition. University lectures have come into the town lecture rooms and church schools. The admission to government offices and official life is closed to the man that will not think. Raw Irish lads can be found learning Homeric Greek behind the counter of a second-hand boot shop, and a situation of £50 a year is open only to the youth that can tell off in a moment the exact age when Asshur idanni pal ascended the throne.

It is not the want of materials that impedes the researches of the Anthropologist. It is the mystical form in which the materials are cast. The moderns love light—the ancients loved obscurity. At the present day, the school door is wide open, and an officer is sent round the streets with authority to compel attendance. In ancient times, the philosopher shut himself and his disciples in an academic grove. He restricted knowledge to the initiated, and kept all the rest of the world in ignorance. His teaching was duplex. He had the Esoteric for the inside of the grove, and the Exoteric outside. For everybody except the favoured few, he taught history in riddles and conundrums, and the cleverest thing he could do was to hide his meaning, on the principle that the Gods loved secrecy. The mythological lexicon is the embodiment of histories so obscured and mystified. The apostle Peter admirably describes this sort of history as "cunningly devised fables"—not fables in the sense of untruths, but truths so cunningly concealed, as to throw the cleverest man off his guard when he read them.

Fashions in literature and education have changed wonderfully since those days. At the present time, the teacher hates the mythology which was the glory of the Greek and Sanscrit school. He will neither study it himself, nor teach it to his pupils. He prefers no history at all, to history muddled and misty; so he shuts up the book, and in that act obliterates the great and illimitable past of human existence. As nothing has come down from the Bards and Muses in any other form than that of concealment, by that course of action he closes the door against the enquirer who would wish to find out something concerning the vast past.

If the Anthropologist of the future is to meet with any success in his laudable enquiries into the obscure histories that belong to the ruined cities of the world, he will have to throw away his prejudices against mythology. He will have to admit that it constitutes the lost histories of the world. He will have to study it—classify and arrange the myths that form its details—localize the heroes of which it treats—and learn to interpret the dark sayings, geographical riddles and ethnological puzzles that belong to it. It is not in the power of old stones, unknown hieroglyphics and ancient idols with numerous arms and heads, to tell their own tale. They require traditions of some kind to reveal their historic origin. By attaching the tradition to the structural remains, and deducing the natural conclusions concerning them, the mysterious histories of the past world will be discovered.

In this view, the subject of mythic history assumes great importance— an importance which it has not been supposed to possess,—and second to nothing in the realm of letters. Mythic history is the gazetteer in which can be found the names of the countries and kingdoms of the old world. It is the dictionary of the heroes that have played a part in the rise and fall of the great Empires of the Earth. It is the map by which can be located the Kings and Gods that have distinguished themselves in the wars by which the Earth has been redistributed. It is the mysterious heirloom, which contains the pedigrees and contracts of marriage by which the territories of the great have changed hands. It is the escutcheon which emblazons the crests and symbolic animals, which appertain to nations and which mark their histories. It is the log-book in which can be discovered the maritime migrations which have connected distant races of men in one great confraternity.

Yet there are many that will dispute this theory. While it is the result of long research by some, it is not the accepted opinion of the many. The muses of history have been badly treated. When they composed their cunningly devised myths, · they little thought that in a later world their heroes would be metamorphosed into poetry and natural phenomena. It may have served them right. They metamorphosed their gods and heroes into trees and animals, so that they could not complain that a later world should metamorphose the gods and heroes into natural phenomena and ideal conceptions, But, if they could rise from the dead, they would certainly be astonished to find that the great king of the gods, to whom they had assigned a wife and countless children, had got turned into thunder and lightning !

The natural phenomenon theory has gained the approval of the philosopher, but it will not stand the test of scrutinizing research. There is a passage in the history of the Atlantis, given at p. 102, which proves it unreliable. The writer, speaking of Helio and Selene (the sun and moon) on their disappearance from the Island, says, "The people hereupon, admiring the prodigy, began to transfer the name of Helio and Selene to the sun and moon in the heavens." In this passage, the orbs of heaven are only epithets. The history precedes the symbolism. The gods acquire the honourable emblems, in consequence of their distinguished excellence.

Diodorus Siculus appears to have entertained conceptions concerning the mythic histories of his time, which are intelligible and credible. There is a passage in his excellent histories, which reveals the true nature of symbolic emblems and compound figures. "They say, that there were some of the Athenian generals that came out of Egypt. For they affirm, that Peteos, the father of Menestheus, who was a captain in the Trojan war, was an Egyptian and afterwards king of Athens. That the Athenians had not wit enough to find out the true reason why two natures were ascribed to him, for every man knows, that he was called half-a-man and half-a-beast, and the true ground was because he was a member of two several common-wealths—a Grecian and a Barbarian."

In this extract it appears that, in later ages of the Grecian state, the Athenians had lost the significance of their own highly mythic writings. The writer attributes to them want of wit. This word wit is aptly employed. In the extract it also appears, that in Sicily the true nature of mythic history was understood. It will be remembered that Faunus, the first king of Italy, was called half-a-man and half-a-goat. He, therefore, must have been half Italian and half barbarian. He or his ancestors must have come from Central America, where Pan was God.

The nature of mythic history is lucidly described in the Phœnician Cosmogony. Eusebius says, " All these things, the son of Thabion, the first Hierophant of all among the Phœni-cians, allegorized and mixed up with the occurrences and accidents of nature and the world, and delivered to the priests and prophets, the superintendents of the mysteries, and they perceiving the rage for these allegories increase, delivered them to their successors and to foreigners." See page 104. Here the practice of allegory is ascribed to the Phœnicians, who, in earlier chapters, have been traced to the Atlantic Isle ; so that mythic history must have been introduced into Europe by the Oceanides. It may be observed that in that extract, Eusebius supplies an excellent illustration of concealment. He calls the first Hierophant the son of Thabion. It requires little pene-tration to see that he means a priest of Thebes, in Egypt: he teaches Isiris, the inventor of three letters, of course, that is Assyria. Then Chna—the Hebrew Canaan, is called the brother of Isiris. Here the Egyptians, Assyrians, and Phœnicians are all credited with Hierophantism.

It is certainly very unfortunate that the histories of antiquity should have been committed to men who loved concealment, and to satisfy the rage for allegory " mixed up the occurrences " with the accidents of nature. It is just that jumbling of fact with nature, that creates mythic history. It might have tickled the fancy of people who were carefully excluded from the Academic grove, but it has spoiled history and made it very difficult to understand. The Anthropologist of the modern world is put at a great disadvantage in his research. He has to separate "the fact" from "the nature" before he can arrive at safe conclusions. However, one thing is gained by the confession of Eusebius. They say that "to be forewarned is to be forearmed." The complex elements of mythic history must be severed. The real underlying history must be extracted from the Allegory. The myth must be interpreted.

But the interpretation is not so difficult as it looks. Like all riddles, when it is read off, it is as simple as possible. The "device" is so "cunning," that when discovered it is provocative of laughter and a slight shudder of mortification at being made a fool of. Turn the name from a person to a country, and the riddle is read. Perseus is Persia. Orion is Iran. Medea is Media. Taurus is Assyria. Ursa is Russia.

Perhaps the best illustration of this subject is found in the Bible, especially as the identity of profane and sacred mythology is there discovered. At Rev. xiii. 18, the apostle John says, "Here is wisdom. Let him that hath understanding count the number of the beast: for it is the number of a man; and his number is six hundred three score and six." This myth is very simple. The Greek letters had numerical powers assigned them. In this case, six hundred is the numerical force of Chi; sixty is that of Xi: and six is that of Sigma. Put together they form the word Kakus. See page 140, where Cacus is shown to be the Great Dragon.

They say that nature is full of compensations. The mythic histories are puzzling, but the ancients had some advantages over the moderns, in their construction of history. The "cunning device" enabled them to retain a thousand facts, national alliances and maritime movements, in a short sententious myth, which would have been lost altogether without the concealment. The Anthropologist will find, on research, that the mythic writings of Greece, India, and Scandinavia are exceedingly complete. They constitute an epitomized history of the world's great being. The myths of each of those countries embrace the wide world, and stretch back to periods of the highest antiquity. Except for the mysticism which obscures their application, it would be seen that in former ages men must have had a large and comprehensive acquaintance with foreign nations—the rise and fall of distant Empires and the origin of nations.

It will readily be admitted, that the mythic systems of the ancient world are of themselves insufficient to produce a reliable universal history. But it was a part of the mystic system, to accompany the myths with a pictorial map. The Zodiacs form a constituent part of the system. Having upon their face the same nomenclature as the myths, they serve satisfactorily to locate the histories comprised in the tradition. Without a map in position it would be impossible to utilize the mythological Lexicon, but with its assistance, any intelligent and painstaking student could trace out the real histories of the human race.

If the Anthropologist of the future will use the mythic histories of the ancients in conjunction with the pickaxe and the exploration of travel, much may be done to expand history and rectify its mistakes. It will hardly be denied that such enlargement and rectification would serve the purposes both of the teacher and the divine. To content oneself with the imperfect histories extant, spoils the instruction of the one and frustrates the labours of the other.

The mythological lexicon and the ten thousand pictures which belong to it might be used as fuel for the bonfire, or, more in the spirit of the present sordid age, sold to the chandlers' shops as waste paper to tie up tobacco and sweets, were it not for the Bible. It so happens that the sacred writers have prefixed to their history of the Israelitish people a mythological document. It is the eleven first chapters of Genesis which create a demand for the study of mythic history. This invaluable document is the text book of Anthropology, but it is written in the style of concealment common to the mythic ages, and its contents can only be developed and understood by comparison with the profane mythology of Asia and Europe. Hence it follows, that the divine who would explain the sacred writings must make himself acquainted with common mythic history.

To form an estimate of the present work, it should be kept in mind, that it is a book of research and not the enunciation of a theory. There is a marked difference between the two kinds of writing. Theory admits only the materials that sustain it. Research gives unbounded liberty to the admission of matter, even to the verge of doubt. The writer has used his liberty; it is for the reader to exercise his judgment.

But now that the work has come to a conclusion, it is possible to deduce from the materials of research a fair and natural hypothesis, concerning the mysterious questions at issue. That may now be done. One thing is quite plain: America has had histories—histories of the highest possible importance, and its people have played a great rôle in the histories of the other three quarters of the globe. It is a part of the theory deducible from this work, that America, in ancient times, has been the residence of a great race of men, frequently mentioned in the literature of Europe as Oceanides—that is to say, living in the Ocean, a word used for the vast accumulation of waters that stretches from Britain to Japan. In the spirit of poetry and myth, it has been deified as a God. The inhabitants of the land were not isolated and alone, but in frequent intercourse with the rest of the world. In this magnificent conception, America was the domicile of Europe's Gods, Three thousand rivers, some the largest in the world, form the river system of the land. In this point of view the names of the ancient inhabitants of the whole hemisphere have been preserved in the Chronicles of the Grecian Muses, with great care.

In times less remote, when myth gave way to natural writing, America stands forth in European literature as the Atlantic Isle. It is divided into the three divisions which it is now found to have,—North, South, and Central. Its general histories are given by Diodorus Siculus and Plato, which last celebrated author, instructed by an Egyptian priest from the famed repository of ancient knowledge, shews how the inhabitants of the Island, headed by kings, have migrated into Europe, and seizing the western countries have mingled their

2 s

blood with the people of the Old Continent. It is a part of the theory deducible from this work, that the Ptolemaic and Coptic Zodiacs are old pictorial maps of the world—in position. In these maps America appears, so that the figures can be used to discover the ancient Geography and Ethnology of the lands. These figures adapt themselves, not badly, to the history of the Atlantic Isle. The Crown, on the North West, introduces Uranus, the first king of the Atlantic Isle. The Serpent, which lies along the west coast and Mexico, answers well to Hyperion, the tyrant King, as he himself is drawn as a dragon, with nine heads. The Sagitarius, delineation of Central America, is associated with Chiron, a son of Saturn, one of the most renowned kings of the Atlantic Isle. Hercules and Ophiuchus or Serpentarius give portraiture to the great region of the Red Indians, and they answer to the Titan-Giants, who are specially the inhabitants of the Atlantic Isle. Cerberus the three-headed dog, is posted in the Caribean Sea, the entrance to the Atlantic Isle. It is a part of this theory, that the races of men found in more modern times to be the occupants of America, correspond with great exactness to the races that European authors have put in the Atlantic Isle. Those races are termed Titan or Titanides. In the Greek system of mythic ethnology, Titan is the head of this famous race. Titan is found in the Totonacques, "the most ancient inhabitants of Anahuac"—another name for Mexico. Japetus the son of Titan is found in the Zapotecs, who are identified with the Toltecs, the civilizers of Mexico. Pro-metheus and Epi-metheus are found in Lower and Upper Mexico. Deucalion is found in Calua, a name of the Mexicans, in the time of Cortez. Atlas, another son of Japetus, is found in the Aztlans, both of them astronomers, and Maia, the son or daughter of Atlas is found in the Mayas of Yucatan. This close identification is observable in the region of the Mound Cities. Hercules is found in the Iroquois,—Saturn is found in the Shawnees, called by the Iroquois Satanas,—the Faunii are found in the Pawnees—the Aloids in the Alli, said to be the builders of the Earthworks,—the Eumenides in the Oman or Missourian Indian,—the Atlantides are found in the race of Atalan or Cutan, the native race of Central America and

Yucatan. Lastly, in South America, Typhœus is found in the Tupy Indians. It is likewise part of the theory deducible from the foregoing work, that the area of the United States has been covered with towns,—occupied by inhabitants in possession of the arts of life, agriculture and astronomy. It must have been a vast Empire, with Saturn, "one of the most renowned kings of the Atlantic Isle," for Emperor. Central America must have been even more civilized, and in later ages, there must have been a league of kings, who issued from Quiche and Yucatan—crossed the Atlantic Ocean, and conquered the western parts of the Old Continent.

The present volume must be considered only as a clue for further studies. It gathers up a few scattered rays of light, and concentrates them upon the mysterious histories and ruins of America. It does little more than point to the numerous media of research, by which this great and dark subject may be studied. But if it should, happily, lead some large minded men to follow it up, it will not have been written in vain.

The work is also incomplete, from another point of view. The American question cannot thoroughly be understood, till the Oceanides, after their arrival in Western Europe and Africa, shall have been tracked into all parts of the Old Continent. Diodorus Siculus, in his description of India, says, that "the strangers that dwelt there are Oceanides of the western parts," and he says that Jupiter Triphilius brought the Indian priests from Crete. If so, the American races must have gone into Hindoostan, and they must have crossed Europe in their route.

It would seem to call for an apology for troubling the reading public with a work like the present, of a character so abstruse and difficult. Yet an apology can hardly be required, while learned men continue to hold biennial Congresses to study the question. One thing is certain; it will add another star to the banner of the Stars and Stripes, when the literati of the United States shall produce a record of the world's past existence, in which America and the American people shall be put into their proper place in History.

THE END.

INDEX.

www.ingramcontent.com/pod-product-compliance
Lightning Source LLC
Chambersburg PA
CBHW021115270326
41929CB00009B/887